Southern Living

40 Years of Our Best Recipes

our best
40 years
recipes

Hardcover ISBN-13: 978-0-8487-3119-9
Hardcover ISBN-10: 0-8487-3119-0
Library of Congress Control Number: 2006908794
Printed in the United States of America
First Printing 2007

Editor in Chief: Nancy Fitzpatrick Wyatt
Executive Editor: Susan Carlisle Payne
Copy Chief: Allison Long Lowery

Southern Living®

40 Years of Our Best Recipes

Foods Editor: Jane Elizabeth Lorberau
Nutrition Editors: Anne Cain, M.S., R.D.;
  Rachel Quinlivan, R.D.
Senior Copy Editor: L. Amanda Owens
Assistant Editor: Julie Boston
Photography Director: Jim Bathie
Senior Photographers: Ralph Anderson, Van Chaplin,
  Joseph De Sciose, Art Meripol, John O'Hagan,
  Mark Sandlin, Charles Walton IV
Photographers: Jean Allsopp, Mary Margaret Chambliss,
  Gary Clark, Tina Cornett, William Dickey, Beth Dreiling,
  Laurie W. Glenn, Meg McKinney, Becky Luigart-Stayner
Senior Photo Stylists: Kay E. Clarke, Buffy Hargett
Associate Photo Stylist: Alan Henderson
Photo Stylists: Lisa Powell Bailey, Cindy Manning Barr,
  Katherine Eckert, Sarah Jernigan, Rose Nguyen,
  Mindi Shapiro, Cari South
Director, Test Kitchens: Elizabeth Tyler Austin
Assistant Director, Test Kitchens: Julie Christopher
Food Stylists: Vanessa McNeil Rocchio, Angela Sellers,
  Kelley Self Wilton
Test Kitchens Professionals: Kathleen Royal Phillips,
  Catherine Crowell Steele, Ashley T. Strickland
Director of Production: Laura Lockhart
Senior Production Manager: Greg A. Amason
Production Manager: Terri Beste
Production Assistant: Faye Porter Bonner

Contributors
Designer: Nancy Johnson
Indexer: Mary Ann Laurens
Editorial Assistant: Laura K. Womble
Interns: Jill Baughman, Amy Edgerton, Amelia Heying,
  Ashley Leath, Mary Katherine Pappas,
  Vanessa Rusch Thomas, Lucas Whittington

Cover: Key Lime Pie, page 382
Back Cover (clockwise):
1.) Sour Cream Pound Cake, page 125
2.) Light King Ranch Chicken Casserole, page 308
3.) Tomato-Basil-Asparagus Pasta Salad, page 218
4.) Our Best Southern Fried Chicken, page 104

To order additional publications, call 1-800-765-6400.

For more books to enrich your life, visit
oxmoorhouse.com.

Southern Living

40 Years of Our Best Recipes

Compiled and Edited by
Jane Elizabeth Lorberau

Oxmoor House

Contents

Welcome

This unique cookbook represents the top recipes and Test Kitchen secrets from the beginning of *Southern Living* magazine in 1966 to present, but it's so much more. Over the years you've invited us into your homes and made us a part of your family, letting us showcase your best recipes on our pages. So, 40 Years of Our Best Recipes is a four-decade snapshot of what's been going on in home kitchens all over the South.

Our fast-paced lives have redefined the way we cook and shaped our choice of recipes for the magazine. We've streamlined ingredient lists and methods as well as broadened our use of convenience products. And the slow cooker has become a fixture in our pages because you love it so. That said, there will always be room for a Hummingbird Cake, knockout homemade rolls, top-notch fried catfish, and other regional favorites. Some dishes are just worth a little extra effort.

We still believe—as you do—that magic is created when loving hands prepare a meal for friends and family to share around the supper table. This joy is beautifully expressed in "Lots of Love," one of our favorite Southern Journals that we share on the opposite page. We encourage you to make that emotional and physical connection through food. Let this cookbook be your guide.

Happy cooking!

Scott Jones
Executive Foods Editor

Lots of love

the real secret ingredient in my mother's cooking

As I thumbed through my mother's *Auburn Cookbook,* I found more than a good cookie recipe. There was a note stuck to a page with a straight pin. It read, "I used this Standard Cookie recipe for Christmas cookies in 1982. Adam helped."

Adam, my 23-year-old son, is in graduate school. The note was written when he was 4. Mama didn't leave behind a diary, but as I took a closer look at the cookbook, I found a scrapbook of memories of her life, illustrated in notes, recipes, and stains on the pages.

The inscription reads, "To Pearl, from Mrs. Britton 1957." This book was a gift to my mother from her mother-in-law—and a timely present, too. I would have been 4 years old myself at the time and in constant need of food in mass quantities. I was in good hands.

"Everything in moderation," Mama said, when it came to food. But Daddy and I both urged excess when it came to the pies, cookies, and cakes she conjured. I found her recipe for piecrust on one dog-eared page, and her pastry really did flake with a fork, just like they used to show on TV.

On the front cover she taped a recipe for chocolate chip cookies—the ones Daddy and I clamored for often. Inside the cookbook cover is a yellowed clipping from *The Birmingham News* with a recipe for Red Velvet Cake, my birthday favorite when I was a teenager.

Buttermilk Pie, Pineapple Pride Cake, Baked Chicken Casserole—these recipes were taken from magazines and stuck inside the book. Favorites, like Fudge Cake and Betty Crocker One Bowl Cake, got a "good" written beside them. Mama didn't use a lot of words. She used her hands.

Mama had dinner on the table every night at the exact moment Daddy pulled into the garage at 5:30. I remember him opening the kitchen door, announcing, "I smell fried chicken."

A puzzling index card listed the ingredients for "Punch for 50." Mama did not like crowds much. Our family was small, and her compact kitchen was the center of her tiny kingdom. Mama had dinner on the table every night at the exact moment Daddy pulled into the garage at 5:30. I remember him opening the kitchen door, announcing, "I smell fried chicken," his face as alight as the brightest Christmas tree.

Her favorite newspaper column, "Hints From Heloise," was well represented, too, with a recipe for pralines. She'd say we had to have a dry day for candy making. Mama always made fudge, divinity, and pralines for Christmas, a once-a-year extravagance.

Her practical side shows throughout the pages. A handwritten note inside the back cover explains how to prevent weeping meringue. On the back of the cookbook, a household hint from Heloise tells how to repair curtains. Mama made do. She knew how to stretch a pound of hamburger seven different ways and could cut up a chicken to make three meals from it. As a young woman working in a South Alabama bank during the Depression, she saw people lose their homes. Home meant everything, and food fueled the home.

Lots of love was the real secret ingredient in mother's cooking. She found comfort showing her feelings in this way. I used to think her kitchen wizardry was an inborn gift. But in her book of happy memories, I can see by the splatters, the notes, and the well-worn pages that she had a guide to help show her the way.

Thankfully and gratefully, so did I.

—Wanda Butler McKinney

the 1970s

Congealed salads, avocado-colored appliances, and recipe-card boxes graced kitchens during the first decade of *Southern Living*. Take a step back with us to recall how things used to be.

1 **"In" Ingredients** Minute rice, cottage cheese, canned shrimp, canned crabmeat, deviled ham, smoked oysters, envelopes of onion soup mix, canned mushrooms, rock Cornish game hens, and cured boneless ham were but a few ingredients that created convenient cooking in this first decade. In fact, canned mushrooms were a luxury ingredient—they dressed up simple dishes, topped veal, stuffed tomatoes, and filled quiche. Flounder and mullet were the catch of the day. Cabbage, cauliflower, and broccoli filled grocery bags. And we were fearless of oysters—fried, scalloped, skewered, and even on the half shell.

2 **Slow 'n' Easy** The slow cooker, also called the Crock-Pot®, debuted in the 1970s kitchen.

3 **Seasonings Go Fresh** Ubiquitous seasonings consisted of onion and garlic powder, pie spice, and poultry seasoning. But we also began to venture into new flavor territory with fresh herbs. Parsley and mint began the rage as mainstream grocery items.

4 **Simpler Times** We stored our recipe cards, usually handwritten, in little boxes. But cookbooks, fueled by Julia Child's popularity as an author and television chef, were published at an ever-increasing rate. In 1979, *Southern Living* Annual Recipes

was launched. To date, 21 million copies of this annual volume have been sold.

5 **Canning Was King** A keen interest in home canning helped preserve fresh produce and save on food costs. Most folks even owned a pressure canner.

6 **No Fear** We weren't intimidated by soufflés in the '70s.

7 **Colors of the Times** Kitchen colors were avocado, harvest gold, paprika, and coppertone. We even made food colorful by stuffing zucchini, yellow squash, eggplant, potatoes, peppers, and mushrooms with a rainbow of vegetables, breading, and cheeses.

8 **"Frank"ly Speaking** Franks were in. We served Oriental Franks, Batter-Fried Franks, Creole Franks, and Sweet-and-Sour Franks.

9 **Molded, Congealed, and Inverted** We're talking salads, folks. We clamored for these shapely salads, varying in color and flavor from carrot to avocado to strawberry.

the 1980s

W ith the dawn of big hair came "cooking en papillote" and Tex-Mex flavor that had the South exclaiming "Ole!" And if it grew in the garden, we pickled it: cucumbers, okra, squash, and watermelon.

1 **"In" Ingredients** Cream cheese, pork sausage, fresh spinach, Cheddar cheese, refrigerated crescent dinner rolls, fresh button mushrooms, egg noodles, macaroni, diced pimiento, grated Parmesan cheese, Italian dressing, and sherry were top ingredient choices.

And we did say "fresh" button mushrooms. We stuffed 'em, marinated 'em, and sherried 'em. Tuna stretched the budget with Tuna Mousse, Tuna Ring, and Tuna-Egg Croquettes.

Stuffing was popular, but not just the bread variety. Cantaloupe halves were scalloped and stuffed with melon balls. We baked Sweet Potato-Stuffed Orange Cups. We ate chicken salad in scooped-out avocados. And, of course, we stuffed celery sticks.

2 **Groovy Garnishes** Recipes weren't ready until we finagled a fancy garnish. We carved radishes and tomato roses, frosted grapes, and curled our butter.

3 **Egg Taboo** We enjoyed Caesar Salad with coddled (partially cooked) egg!

4 **Time for What?** We found time to make mayonnaise and pizza from scratch.

5 **From Our Kitchen** The "From Our Kitchen To Yours" column was introduced, answering reader questions and offering Test Kitchens secrets about cooking.

6 **Cooking Light** We saw the birth of our monthly column *Cooking Light* in 1982. Today, *Cooking Light* has been named the best new magazine launch in the past 20 years and has over 11 million readers.

7 **Southern Cooking Defined** The first edition of The *Southern Living* Cookbook was published in 1987, defining the New South cuisine for cooks everywhere. Now in its third edition, there are over 2,682,000 copies in print.

8 **Fried Food, Fancy That!** There was fried cheese, fried pickles, French-fried mushrooms, fish fries, and even crispy frog legs.

9 **The Unbelievable Microwave** Casseroles came from the microwave and so did everything else: microwave meat loaf in a ring, potatoes, manicotti, and lasagna—even a layer cake!

the
1990s

Pansies garnished cakes, berries adorned sandwiches, and "al dente" entered our vocabulary as we moved into the '90s. Take a peek at this era's essentials that we still embrace today.

1 "In" Ingredients Olive oil, balsamic vinegar, fresh garlic, roasted red pepper, goat cheese, and couscous were the craze. Goat cheese was a top choice for appetizers. We snubbed salt and fat in favor of fresh herbs and other seasonings. Fresh ingredients and refreshing flavors decked updated recipes and even infused such desserts as Jalapeño-Mint Sherbet, Fennel Ice Cream, and Roasted Garlic Crème Brûlée. Olive oil was used in everything thanks to the Mediterranean diet buzz. With fragrant green thumbs, we became bold and expanded our herb gardens with cilantro, basil, rosemary, and oregano.

2 Egg Advice For food safety, the USDA convinced us to cook eggs completely.

3 Mix and Match We mixed and matched china and flatware for fresh new entertainment settings.

4 No-Rules Wine Fine wine with good food reigned. And there were no rules anymore as we sipped Pinot Noir with swordfish and salmon and slurped oaky Chardonnay with steak.

5 Gulp, Gulp. Bottled water was our favorite drink.

6 Farmhouse Breakfast Grits weren't the only thing for breakfast anymore. Baked polenta with cheese entered the picture. And for a fancy supper, we served Spoonbread Grits with Savory Mushroom Sauce.

7 Fusion Confusion Cooking crossed all borders as ethnic flavors blended with regional favorites.

8 What Was Brewing? Coffee, of course! Gourmet coffee became a luxurious dessert as well as a recipe ingredient in Java Cream Puffs, Coffee Crème Brûlée, and Coffee Tart.

9 Quick & Easy Craze The appeal of less time in the kitchen and more time with family spawned a quick and easy cooking frenzy. From easy weeknight solutions to one-dish meals and 15-minutes-or-less recipes, moms across the South were transformed into superwomen who, in addition to working outside the home and driving car pools, also liked to set the table with their homecooked meals.

10 The Holiday Table As always, the holidays wouldn't be complete without a to-die-for coconut cake for Christmas.

the 2000s

The 2000s make their presence known with bright colors and the revisiting of slow cooking. As some things change and some stay the same, take a glimpse of where we are today.

1 "In" Ingredients Quail and venison, fresh fruits, pomegranate juice, kumquats, and sunflower oil are in high demand. Goat cheese continues its popularity and moves from a pleasing appetizer to a flavorful role in main dishes. Strawberries still adorn shortcake, and the shortcake has returned to the biscuit. Fresh herbs grow all over the South and find favor with virtually every type of recipe.

2 Slow Is Back Slow cooking is back and better than ever. The fever spans all ages as readers learn that anything from lasagna to breads to desserts can be made using a "dump and go" method of cooking. Fancy new slow cookers

simmer a little faster than yesteryear's models and have timers that turn the cookers to "warm" when cooking is complete.

3 Vibrant Color Returns Brick red, canary yellow, and vivid blues bathe kitchens of this decade as white trim and cabinetry keep the atmosphere light and airy.

4 The New Recipe Box Recipes once stored in tiny metal boxes have upgraded to a fancier box—a computer. **Southernliving.com** is the definitive source for recipes at your fingertips by ingredient, course, cuisine, and more. And *Southern Living* cooks chat, share tips, and contribute home-tested recipes.

5 Fine Wine. Wine is still fine—with any type of meal.

6 Salads Go Bright Chicken salad gets a makeover with bright summer fruits.

7 Slathered with Sauce. As outdoor kitchens become the rage, more grills and smokers than ever are fired up across the South. Recipes for slow-smoked brisket and succulent barbecue ribs entice even timid cooks to become backyard chefs.

8 Cooking Pays. In 2002 we inaugurated the *Southern Living Cook-Off* that offers a $100,000 grand prize for the winning recipe. Sifting 40,000 entries down to the winning Pecan Pie Cheesecake wasn't an easy assignment, but it sure was a tasty one.

9 Mother of Invention Southerners love comfort foods, and they love them even more with a new twist. Pound Cake Banana Pudding, Chicken Cobbler Casserole, and Barbecue Pot Pie with Grits Cheese Crust are a trio of recipes heralding new renditions of old favorites.

Company's coming

Guests are always welcome in the South. Whether you have a month to plan a gathering or only a few hours, turn to one of these menus to save the day in style.

BLACKBERRY PUDDING TARTS, PAGE 55

Beef Fillets
with Cognac-Onion Sauce
Roasted potato wedges
Baby Blue Salad
Black-Bottom Pie

Romantic
dinner serves **2**

southern classic

Beef Fillets with Cognac-Onion Sauce

MAKES 2 SERVINGS
Prep: 30 min., Cook: 56 min., Other: 10 min.

*Three kinds of onion plus shallots and garlic are caramelized before being cloaked in cognac.
What's not to love about this sauce atop tender fillets?*

2 (6- to 8-oz.) beef fillets
½ tsp. salt
¼ tsp. pepper
1 Tbsp. canola oil

1 Tbsp. butter or margarine
1 small yellow onion, sliced
    and separated into rings
1 small red onion, sliced
    and separated into rings

1 bunch green onions,
    chopped
6 shallots, chopped
2 garlic cloves, minced
¼ cup cognac*
¼ cup beef broth

Salt and pepper to taste
Garnish: fresh parsley sprigs

1. Sprinkle beef evenly with ½ tsp. salt and ¼ tsp. pepper. Brown fillets in hot oil in an ovenproof or cast-iron skillet over medium-high heat 3 minutes on each side. Remove fillets, reserving drippings in skillet.

2. Melt butter in drippings over medium-high heat. Add yellow and red onion rings, and sauté 5 minutes.

3. Add green onions, shallot, and garlic, and sauté 10 to 15 minutes or until lightly browned. Stir in cognac and broth; cook over medium-high heat, stirring constantly, until liquid evaporates (about 5 minutes). Place fillets on top of onion mixture in skillet. Cover with aluminum foil.

4. Bake at 400° for 15 to 20 minutes or until a meat thermometer inserted into thickest portion of meat registers 140° (let stand until temperature rises to 145°).

5. Remove fillets from skillet, reserving onion mixture in skillet; cover fillets loosely, and let stand at room temperature 10 minutes.

6. Cook onion mixture over medium heat, stirring constantly, 5 minutes or until liquid evaporates. Add salt and pepper to taste. Serve with fillets. Garnish, if desired.

*Substitute ¼ cup red wine or beef broth for cognac, if desired.

Baby Blue Salad

MAKES 2 SERVINGS
Prep: 10 min.

Piquant blue cheese, sweet strawberries, and crunchy pecans are a combination likely to evoke culinary bliss. Balsamic Vinaigrette wraps the package in puckering satisfaction.

1 (5-oz.) bag mixed spring
   salad greens
2 oz. crumbled blue cheese
1 orange, peeled and
   sectioned
½ pt. fresh strawberries,
   quartered
½ cup Sweet-and-Spicy
   Pecans

Balsamic Vinaigrette

1. Toss together first 5 ingredients in a large bowl.
2. Drizzle salad with desired amount of Balsamic Vinaigrette, gently tossing to coat.

Taste of the South

Chef Franklin Biggs, of Homewood, Alabama, has a way with salads, and we're eternally grateful that he shared Baby Blue Salad with us in our April 2000 issue. Our staff makes this in their homes all the time. You'll have a little dressing left over, which is a real bonus because it's great as a marinade for chicken, fish, or steamed veggies. And the spiced pecans used as croutons? You might want to double the recipe because it's hard to stop nibbling once you taste them. For ease, make the Sweet-and-Spicy Pecans and Balsamic Vinaigrette ahead of time.

Sweet-and-Spicy Pecans

MAKES 1 CUP
Prep: 5 min., Cook: 10 min., Other: 10 min.

¼ cup sugar
1 cup warm water
1 cup pecan halves

2 Tbsp. sugar
1 Tbsp. chili powder
⅛ tsp. ground red pepper

1. Stir together ¼ cup sugar and warm water until sugar dissolves. Add pecans; soak 10 minutes. Drain, discarding syrup.
2. Combine 2 Tbsp. sugar, chili powder, and red pepper. Add pecans, tossing to coat. Place pecans on a lightly greased baking sheet.
3. Bake at 350° for 10 minutes, stirring once.

Balsamic Vinaigrette

MAKES 1⅔ CUPS
Prep: 5 min.

½ cup balsamic vinegar
3 Tbsp. Dijon mustard
3 Tbsp. honey
2 garlic cloves, minced
2 small shallots, minced
¼ tsp. salt
¼ tsp. pepper

1 cup olive oil

1. Whisk together first 7 ingredients until blended.
2. Gradually whisk in olive oil.

Black-Bottom Pie

MAKES 8 SERVINGS
Prep: 20 min.; Cook: 5 min.; Other: 2 hrs., 30 min.

2 Tbsp. water
2 Tbsp. rum
1 envelope unflavored
    gelatin

⅔ cup sugar
1 Tbsp. cornstarch
2 cups milk
4 egg yolks

1 cup semisweet chocolate
    morsels
Gingersnap Crust

2 cups whipping cream
3 Tbsp. powdered sugar

Garnish: chocolate curls

1. Stir together 2 Tbsp. water and rum in a small bowl. Sprinkle gelatin over mixture. Stir mixture.

2. Combine ⅔ cup sugar and cornstarch in a heavy saucepan; gradually whisk in milk and egg yolks. Bring to a boil over medium heat, whisking constantly; boil 1 minute. Stir in gelatin mixture until dissolved.

3. Stir together 1 cup custard mixture and chocolate morsels until smooth. Pour into Gingersnap Crust; cover with wax paper, gently pressing paper directly onto custard. Chill 30 minutes or until set. Set aside remaining custard mixture.

4. Beat whipping cream at high speed with an electric mixer until foamy; gradually add powdered sugar, beating until soft peaks form.

5. Fold 1 cup whipped cream into remaining custard mixture. Spoon over chocolate mixture. Chill pie and remaining whipped cream 2 hours or until pie is set. Spread remaining whipped cream over pie. Garnish, if desired.

Gingersnap Crust

MAKES 1 (9-INCH) CRUST
Prep: 10 min., Cook: 10 min.

1½ cups gingersnap
    cookies (about
    26 cookies)
2 Tbsp. sugar
⅓ cup butter or margarine,
    melted

1. Stir together all ingredients. Press into bottom and up sides of a 9-inch deep-dish pieplate.
2. Bake at 350° for 8 to 10 minutes. Cool on a wire rack.

From Our Kitchen

We place wax paper on the surface of hot custard fillings before placing them in refrigerator to chill. The paper prevents a film from forming on top of the custard.

quick & easy

Chicken Cakes with Rémoulade Sauce

MAKES 4 SERVINGS
Prep: 15 min., Cook: 12 min.

2 Tbsp. butter or margarine

½ medium-size red bell
    pepper, diced
4 green onions, thinly sliced
1 garlic clove, pressed

3 cups chopped cooked
    chicken
1 cup soft breadcrumbs
1 large egg, lightly beaten
2 Tbsp. mayonnaise
1 Tbsp. Creole mustard
2 tsp. Creole seasoning

¼ cup vegetable oil

Rémoulade Sauce (following
    page)

1. Melt butter in a large skillet over medium heat.
2. Add bell pepper, green onions, and garlic; sauté 3 to 4 minutes or until vegetables are tender.
3. Stir together bell pepper mixture, chopped chicken, and next 5 ingredients in a bowl. Shape chicken mixture into 8 (3½-inch) patties.
4. Fry 4 patties in 2 Tbsp. hot oil in a large skillet over medium heat 3 minutes on each side or until golden brown. Drain on paper towels.
5. Repeat procedure with remaining 2 Tbsp. oil and patties. Serve immediately with Rémoulade Sauce.

From Our Kitchen

Speed up prep time by having chopped cooked chicken on hand. Whether you start with a rotisserie chicken from the deli or you start from scratch by cooking a whole chicken at home, follow these easy tips:
• Pulling the meat from a deli-roasted or home-cooked chicken yields about 3 cups chopped chicken.
• Remove the meat from the bones while the chicken is still warm, and then chop, shred, or cube the meat.
• Refrigerate chopped cooked chicken up to three days or freeze up to one month in a zip-top freezer bag.

Rémoulade Sauce

MAKES ABOUT 1¼ CUPS
Prep: 5 min.

1 cup mayonnaise
3 green onions, sliced
2 Tbsp. Creole mustard
2 garlic cloves, pressed
1 Tbsp. chopped fresh
    parsley
¼ tsp. ground red pepper

Garnish: sliced green onions

1. Stir together first 6 ingredients until sauce is blended.
2. Cover and chill sauce until ready to serve. Garnish, if desired.

weeknight wonder

Cheesy Mashed Potatoes

MAKES 4 TO 6 SERVINGS
Prep: 35 min., Cook: 15 min.

*Gournay cheese embellishes the creamy texture of Yukon gold potatoes.
The addition of half-and-half and butter propels these 'taters over the top.*

2 lb. Yukon gold potatoes,
    peeled and cubed

2 (4-oz.) packages spiced
    Gournay cheese product
⅔ cup half-and-half
¼ cup butter or margarine
¼ tsp. salt
¼ tsp. pepper

1. Bring potato and water to cover to a boil in a large saucepan; reduce heat, and cook 15 to 20 minutes or until tender. Drain and return to saucepan. Cook over medium heat 30 seconds. Remove from heat.
2. Add cheese and remaining 4 ingredients; beat at medium speed with an electric mixer until smooth. Spoon into a 2½-qt. baking dish.
3. Bake at 350° for 15 minutes.

Garlic Green Beans

MAKES 4 SERVINGS
Prep: 10 min., Cook: 37 min.

A buttery lemon-pepper and garlic sauce bathes simple green beans.

1 lb. fresh green beans,
 trimmed
½ cup boiling water
½ tsp. salt

2 Tbsp. butter or margarine
2 garlic cloves, pressed
⅛ tsp. lemon pepper
2 Tbsp. chopped fresh
 parsley

1. Place first 3 ingredients in a Dutch oven; cover and cook over medium heat 30 minutes. Drain.
2. Melt butter in Dutch oven; add garlic and lemon pepper, and sauté mixture over medium heat 1 to 2 minutes. Add green beans, and sauté 5 minutes. Sprinkle with chopped parsley.

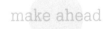

Marinated Tomatoes

MAKES 6 SERVINGS
Prep: 15 min., Other: 2 hrs.

Summer tomatoes are ideal for swimming in this herb-infused marinade. If you prepare this dish during another season, plum tomatoes are a flavorful alternative.

3 large tomatoes

⅓ cup olive oil
¼ cup red wine vinegar
1 tsp. salt
¼ tsp. pepper
½ garlic clove, crushed
1 Tbsp. chopped parsley
1 Tbsp. chopped fresh basil
 or 1 tsp. dried whole
 basil
2 Tbsp. chopped onion

1. Cut tomatoes into ½-inch-thick slices, and arrange in a large shallow dish.
2. Combine oil and remaining 7 ingredients in a jar; cover tightly, and shake vigorously. Pour over tomato slices. Cover and marinate in refrigerator 2 to 24 hours.

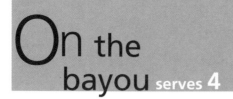
southern classic

Catfish Lafitte

MAKES 4 SERVINGS
Prep: 12 min., Cook: 30 min.

2 large eggs
1 cup milk

2 cups all-purpose flour
1¼ tsp. salt, divided
1½ to 2½ tsp. ground red
    pepper, divided
4 catfish fillets (about
    1½ lb.)

Vegetable oil

12 unpeeled, large fresh
    shrimp

1 Tbsp. butter or margarine
2 tsp. minced garlic

¼ cup vermouth
2 cups whipping cream
¼ cup chopped green
    onions, divided
2 tsp. lemon juice

3 very thin cooked ham
    slices, cut into strips
Garnish: lemon wedges

1. Combine eggs and milk, stirring until well blended.
2. Combine flour, 1 tsp. salt, and ½ tsp. ground red pepper in a shallow dish. Dredge fillets in flour mixture; dip in milk mixture, and dredge again in flour mixture.
3. Pour oil to a depth of 3 inches into a Dutch oven; heat to 360°. Fry fillets 6 minutes or until golden; drain on paper towels. Keep warm.
4. Peel shrimp, and devein, if desired.
5. Melt butter in a large skillet over medium heat; add shrimp and garlic, and cook, stirring often, until shrimp turn pink. Remove shrimp, reserving drippings in skillet.
6. Stir vermouth into reserved drippings; bring to a boil, and cook 1 minute. Add whipping cream, 2 Tbsp. green onions, lemon juice, remaining ¼ tsp. salt, and remaining 1 to 2 tsp. ground red pepper; cook, stirring often, 12 to 15 minutes or until sauce is thickened.
7. Place catfish on a serving plate; drizzle with sauce. Top with shrimp and ham; sprinkle with remaining 2 Tbsp. green onions. Garnish, if desired.

Taste of the South

"I've been eating catfish all my life," says the best-selling author John Grisham. "Although I enjoy it cooked in a variety of ways, pan-fried catfish in a Cajun cream sauce is my favorite." In fact, Catfish Lafitte, an uptown version of fried catfish from the Downtown Grill in Oxford, Mississippi, is the novelist's favorite catfish recipe.

Citrus Vinaigrette

MAKES ABOUT 1 CUP
Prep: 15 min., Other: 1 hr.

*Spoonfuls of sugar, sea salt, and pepper perfectly balance
the flavors from tart juices and zest.*

2 tsp. orange zest
1 tsp. lime zest
1 tsp. lemon zest
5 Tbsp. orange juice
3 Tbsp. lime juice
2 Tbsp. lemon juice
½ cup extra-virgin olive oil

1 Tbsp. minced chives
1 tsp. sugar
½ tsp. sea salt
¼ tsp. pepper

1. Stir together first 6 ingredients in a medium bowl. Whisk in olive oil until incorporated.
2. Stir in chives and sugar; add sea salt and pepper. Let stand at room temperature 1 hour before serving.

Easy Pan Biscuits

MAKES 20 BISCUITS
Prep: 15 min., Cook: 15 min.

The carbonation of lemon-lime soft drink gives these biscuits a little extra lift.

2 cups all-purpose baking mix
(we tested with Bisquick)
½ cup sour cream
6 Tbsp. lemon-lime soft drink
(we tested with Sprite; do
not use diet Sprite)

3 Tbsp. butter, divided

1. Stir together first 3 ingredients; lightly flour hands, and divide dough into 20 equal portions. Shape each portion into a ball, and place in a lightly greased 8-inch square baking pan. (Dough portions will touch.)
2. Melt butter; brush evenly with half of butter.
3. Bake at 425° for 15 minutes or until golden brown. Brush evenly with remaining half of butter. Serve immediately.

Vidalia Onion Soufflé, page 30

party pleaser

Peppered Bacon-Wrapped Pork Tenderloin

MAKES 8 SERVINGS
Prep: 20 min., Cook: 30 min.

A savory mushroom-onion filling is rolled jelly-roll fashion into flattened pork tenderloins; thick-sliced bacon wraps the package securely and bastes it while it bakes.

¼ cup butter or margarine
¾ lb. mushrooms, sliced
1 small onion, chopped
¼ cup chopped pecans, toasted

2 (12-oz.) pork tenderloins, trimmed
1 tsp. salt
1 tsp. ground black pepper

8 thick bacon slices
¼ cup firmly packed brown sugar
1 tsp. cracked black pepper

1. Melt butter in a large skillet over medium-high heat; add mushrooms and onion, and sauté 8 minutes or until tender. Stir in pecans, and set aside.

2. Place pork between 2 sheets of heavy-duty plastic wrap; flatten to ¼-inch thickness, using a meat mallet or rolling pin. Sprinkle with salt and ground pepper.

3. Spread mushroom mixture evenly on 1 side of each tenderloin, leaving a ¼-inch border. Roll up jelly-roll fashion, starting with 1 long end. Wrap 4 bacon slices around each tenderloin, and secure with wooden picks. Place, seam sides down, on a lightly greased rack in a roasting pan. Rub evenly with sugar and cracked pepper.

4. Bake, uncovered, at 450° for 15 minutes. Reduce temperature to 400°.

5. Bake at 400° for 15 more minutes or until a meat thermometer registers 160°. Slice each tenderloin into 4 medallions.

Vidalia Onion Soufflé

MAKES 8 SERVINGS
Prep: 30 min., Cook: 45 min.
(pictured on page 28)

2 Tbsp. butter or margarine
5 medium Vidalia or sweet
    onions, chopped (about
    4 cups)

10 white bread slices, crusts
    removed and cubed (we
    tested with Pepperidge
    Farm)
1 (15-oz.) can fat-free
    evaporated milk
3 large eggs, lightly beaten
1¾ cups (8 oz.) shredded
    Parmesan cheese,
    divided
1 tsp. salt

1. Melt butter in a large skillet over medium heat; add onion, and sauté 10 to 15 minutes or until tender.
2. Place onion and bread cubes in a large bowl. Stir in milk, eggs, 1 cup cheese, and salt. Pour into a lightly greased 1½-qt. soufflé or baking dish. Sprinkle with remaining ¾ cup cheese.
3. Bake at 350° for 45 minutes or until golden and set.

Garlic-Tarragon Green Beans

MAKES 12 SERVINGS
Prep: 15 min., Cook: 11 min.

2 qt. water
2 Tbsp. salt
2 lb. thin fresh green beans

2 garlic cloves, minced
½ tsp. dried tarragon leaves
2 Tbsp. olive oil
½ tsp. salt
½ tsp. pepper

1. Bring 2 qt. water and 2 Tbsp. salt to a boil in a Dutch oven; add beans. Cook 6 minutes or until crisp-tender; drain. Plunge into ice water to stop the cooking process; drain.
2. Sauté garlic and tarragon in hot oil in Dutch oven over medium heat 2 to 3 minutes or until garlic is tender. (Do not brown garlic.) Add beans, salt, and pepper; cook, stirring constantly, 2 minutes or until thoroughly heated.

Turtle Cheesecake

MAKES 10 SERVINGS
Prep: 30 min.; Cook: 1 hr., 15 min.; Other: 9 hrs., 50 min.

For those who love turtle candies, here's the cheesecake version.

40 chocolate wafers (9-oz. package), crushed
¼ cup sugar
⅓ cup butter, melted

3 (8-oz.) packages cream cheese, softened
1¼ cups sugar
4 large eggs
1 (8-oz.) container sour cream
1 Tbsp. vanilla extract

¼ cup butter
1 cup semisweet chocolate morsels

1 (12-oz.) jar caramel topping (we tested with Smucker's)
1 cup chopped pecans

1. Combine first 3 ingredients; stir well. Firmly press mixture in bottom and 1 inch up sides of a lightly greased 9-inch springform pan. Bake at 325° for 10 minutes. Cool in pan on a wire rack.

2. Beat cream cheese at medium speed with an electric mixer until creamy; gradually add 1¼ cups sugar, beating well. Add eggs, 1 at a time, beating after each addition and scraping sides and bottom as needed. Stir in sour cream and vanilla. Pour batter into prepared crust.

3. Bake at 325° for 1 hour and 5 minutes. (Center will not be completely set.) Turn oven off, and partially open oven door; leave cake in oven 1 hour. Cool completely on a wire rack; cover and chill at least 8 hours. Carefully remove sides of pan; transfer cheesecake to a serving plate.

4. Melt ¼ cup butter in a small heavy saucepan; add chocolate morsels. Stir over low heat just until chocolate melts and mixture blends. Spread warm chocolate mixture over cheesecake; chill 15 minutes.

5. Combine caramel topping and pecans in a small saucepan. Bring to a boil, stirring constantly, over medium heat; boil 2 minutes. Remove from heat, and cool 5 minutes. Spread over chocolate; cool completely. Serve immediately, or cover and chill. Let stand at room temperature at least 30 minutes before serving.

From Our Kitchen

Making a cheesecake is a piece of cake when you heed these tips:
• Let cream cheese soften at room temperature before you begin.
• Don't overbeat the batter when adding eggs. Beat only until blended.
• To prevent cracks, run a knife or a small metal spatula around edge of cheesecake immediately after removing it from the oven. This allows the loosened sides to contract freely.
• You can freeze cheesecake up to one month. Remove pan, place cheesecake on a cardboard circle, if desired, and wrap tightly in heavy-duty aluminum foil. Thaw in the refrigerator the day before serving.

Weekend
delight serves **4**

Turkey Tenderloin Scaloppine
Special Scalloped Potatoes or cheese grits
Steamed broccoli
Mascarpone Cream Pie with Berry Glaze

quick & easy

Turkey Tenderloin Scaloppine

MAKES 4 SERVINGS
Prep: 15 min., Cook: 15 min.

This impressive entrée is special enough to serve to guests, and its quick cooking time and relatively low cost allow it to double as a great weeknight dish.

1½ lb. turkey breast
   tenderloins

⅓ cup all-purpose flour
½ tsp. salt
½ tsp. pepper

3 Tbsp. butter, divided
1 Tbsp. olive oil

½ cup dry white wine
3 Tbsp. lemon juice

2 Tbsp. chopped fresh
   Italian parsley
2 garlic cloves, minced
2 Tbsp. capers
Garnishes: lemon wedges,
   fresh Italian parsley

1. Cut turkey into ½-inch-thick slices. Place between 2 sheets of heavy-duty plastic wrap; flatten to ⅛-inch thickness, using a meat mallet or a rolling pin.

2. Combine flour, salt, and pepper; dredge turkey slices in mixture.

3. Melt 2 Tbsp. butter with oil in a large skillet over medium-high heat. Add turkey; cook, in batches, 1½ minutes on each side or until golden. Remove from skillet, and keep warm.

4. Add remaining 1 Tbsp. butter, wine, and juice to skillet, stirring to loosen bits from bottom of skillet. Cook 2 minutes or just until thoroughly heated.

5. Stir in parsley, garlic, and capers; spoon over turkey. Garnish, if desired. Serve immediately.

From Our Kitchen

Much like pork, turkey tenderloins are versatile because of their mild flavor and ease of preparation. Cut into strips for a quick stir-fry or into cubes for kabobs. For a fabulous weeknight entrée, try Turkey Tenderloin Scaloppine. It calls for medallions that are flattened with a mallet for superfast cooking.

Special Scalloped Potatoes,
following page

Special Scalloped Potatoes

MAKES 8 SERVINGS
Prep: 14 min., Cook: 54 min., Other: 15 min.
(pictured on previous page)

Garlic and Gruyére cheese make classic comfort food out of plain potatoes.

1 large garlic clove, minced
1 shallot, chopped
½ tsp. dried crushed red
    pepper
3 Tbsp. butter, melted

1¼ cups milk
1½ cups whipping cream
½ tsp. salt
¼ tsp. freshly ground black
    pepper

2½ lb. red potatoes,
    unpeeled and cut into
    ⅛-inch slices
1 cup (4 oz.) shredded
    Gruyère cheese or Swiss
    cheese
¼ cup grated Parmesan
    cheese

1. Sauté garlic, shallot, and crushed red pepper in butter over medium heat in a Dutch oven 2 minutes.

2. Add milk and next 3 ingredients, stirring well.

3. Add potatoes. Bring to a boil over medium heat, stirring occasionally. Spoon into a lightly greased 13- x 9-inch baking dish. Sprinkle with cheeses.

4. Bake at 350° for 45 minutes or until bubbly and golden brown. Let stand 15 minutes before serving.

Mascarpone Cream Pie with Berry Glaze

MAKES 6 TO 8 SERVINGS
Prep: 35 min., Cook: 15 min., Other: 8 hrs.

6 Tbsp. butter or margarine
1 (6.75-oz.) package
    Bordeaux cookies,
    crushed (we tested with
    Pepperidge Farm)
½ cup chopped pecans

¼ cup cornstarch
2 Tbsp. sugar
1½ cups whipping cream
2 egg yolks, lightly beaten

1 (8-oz.) package
    mascarpone cheese,
    softened
2 tsp. orange liqueur or
    fresh orange juice
1 tsp. vanilla extract

Berry Glaze
Garnish: orange rind strips

1. Melt butter in a medium saucepan over medium-high heat. Cook 3 minutes or until golden brown. Stir in cookie crumbs and pecans. Press mixture into bottom and up sides of a lightly greased 9-inch tart pan. Bake at 350° for 15 minutes or until golden brown; cool.

2. Combine cornstarch and sugar in a medium saucepan; stir in cream. Cook over medium heat, stirring constantly, until thickened and bubbly. Stir about ¼ cup hot mixture into egg yolks; add to remaining hot mixture, and cook, stirring constantly, 1 minute. Remove mixture from heat.

3. Stir in mascarpone cheese, liqueur, and vanilla until smooth. Pour into prepared crust.

4. Spread ⅔ cup Berry Glaze over filling; chill 8 hours. Serve with remaining Berry Glaze. Garnish, if desired.

Berry Glaze

MAKES ABOUT 1½ CUPS
Prep: 10 min., Cook: 7 min.

1 cup whole-berry cranberry
    sauce
⅓ cup seedless blackberry
    jam
1½ Tbsp. orange liqueur or
    fresh orange juice
1½ tsp. grated orange rind

1. Cook all ingredients in a small saucepan over medium heat 5 to 7 minutes, stirring until cranberry sauce and jam melt. Strain mixture, discarding solids.

Crab Cakes with Lemon Rémoulade
Green beans with grape tomatoes
Mixed baby greens
Vanilla Soufflés with Vanilla Crème Sauce

editor's choice

Crab Cakes with Lemon Rémoulade

MAKES 4 SERVINGS
Prep: 20 min., Cook: 30 min., Other: 1 hr.

Just before serving, toss mixed baby greens with olive oil, salt, and pepper to taste, and place crab cakes on top, as many restaurants do.

3 Tbsp. butter, divided
1 large red bell pepper, finely chopped
½ medium onion, finely chopped

1 cup finely crushed saltine cracker crumbs
½ cup mayonnaise
1 large egg, lightly beaten
2 tsp. Old Bay seasoning
2 tsp. Worcestershire sauce
¾ tsp. dry mustard
¼ tsp. hot sauce
1 lb. fresh lump crabmeat, drained and picked

1 Tbsp. vegetable oil
Lemon Rémoulade (page 38)
Garnishes: lemon wedges, fresh parsley sprigs

1. Melt 2 Tbsp. butter in a large nonstick skillet over medium heat; add bell pepper and onion, and sauté 10 minutes or until tender. Remove from heat.

2. Stir in cracker crumbs and next 6 ingredients. Gently stir in crabmeat. Shape mixture into 8 patties; cover and chill at least 1 hour or up to 24 hours.

3. Melt ½ Tbsp. butter with ½ Tbsp. oil in a large skillet over medium-high heat. Cook 4 crab cakes 4 to 5 minutes on each side or until golden. Drain on paper towels. Repeat procedure with remaining ½ Tbsp. butter, remaining ½ Tbsp. oil, and remaining crab cakes. Serve with Lemon Rémoulade; garnish, if desired.

Tip: Handle the crabmeat as little as possible in order to keep the succulent lumps intact.

Lemon Rémoulade

MAKES ABOUT 2¼ CUPS
Prep: 10 min., Other: 30 min.

*In addition to accompanying the crab cakes on the previous page,
this sauce can also be used as a dip for boiled shrimp or steamed asparagus;
or add a little milk to make a tangy salad dressing.*

2 cups mayonnaise
¼ cup Creole mustard
2 garlic cloves, pressed
2 Tbsp. chopped fresh
    parsley
1 Tbsp. fresh lemon juice
2 tsp. paprika
¾ tsp. ground red pepper

1. Whisk together all ingredients until blended. Cover and chill 30 minutes or up to 3 days.

From Our Kitchen

Planning an intimate dinner for four with little time to spare is a cinch with these make-ahead tips.

The Day Before:
1. Shape crab cakes.
2. Blanch green beans in boiling water for about 8 minutes; shock in ice water to stop the cooking process. Cover and chill.
3. Prepare Lemon Rémoulade.
4. Prepare Vanilla Crème Sauce.

The Day of:
1. Sauté crab cakes as directed.
2. To reheat green beans, toss with halved grape tomatoes and melted butter in a warm skillet; season with fresh thyme, salt, and pepper.
3. Toss mixed baby greens in olive oil, salt, and pepper.
4. Stir up the soufflés just before dinner, and bake them while you're eating so you can enjoy them warm from the oven.

Vanilla Soufflés with Vanilla Crème Sauce

MAKES 4 SERVINGS
Prep: 30 min., Cook: 25 min., Other: 20 min.

Granulated sugar

3 Tbsp. butter or margarine
3 Tbsp. all-purpose flour

¾ cup half-and-half
6 Tbsp. granulated sugar, divided

4 large eggs, separated
2 Tbsp. vanilla extract

Sifted powdered sugar
Vanilla Crème Sauce

1. Coat the bottom and sides of 4 (6-oz.) baking dishes with vegetable cooking spray; sprinkle with granulated sugar. Set aside.

2. Melt butter in a small saucepan over medium heat; add flour, stirring until smooth. Cook flour mixture, stirring constantly, 1 minute.

3. Add half-and-half, stirring constantly; stir in 4 Tbsp. sugar. Cook over medium heat, stirring constantly, until thickened. Remove from heat.

4. Beat egg yolks until thick and pale. Gradually stir half of hot half-and-half mixture into egg yolks; add to remaining hot mixture, stirring constantly. Cook over medium heat 2 minutes; stir in vanilla. Cool 15 to 20 minutes.

5. Beat egg whites at high speed with an electric mixer until foamy. Gradually add remaining 2 Tbsp. sugar, beating until soft peaks form. Gradually fold egg whites into egg yolk mixture. Spoon into prepared baking dishes.

6. Bake at 350° for 25 minutes or until puffed and set. Sprinkle with powdered sugar, and serve immediately with Vanilla Crème Sauce.

Vanilla Crème Sauce

MAKES 3 CUPS
Prep: 5 min., Cook: 10 min.

1 tsp. vanilla extract
1 cup sugar
2 tsp. cornstarch
2 cups whipping cream

8 egg yolks

1. Combine first 3 ingredients in a heavy saucepan; gradually stir in whipping cream. Cook, stirring constantly, over low heat until sugar dissolves.

2. Beat egg yolks until thick and pale; gradually stir about half of hot whipping cream mixture into yolks. Add to remaining hot mixture, stirring constantly.

3. Cook, stirring constantly, over medium heat until thickened. Pour through a wire-mesh strainer into a small bowl, discarding lumps. Cover and refrigerate up to 3 days. Serve sauce with Vanilla Soufflés, fresh fruit, or pound cake.

The holidays are here serves 8

Cream Cheese and Olive Biscuits with
Olive-Parsley Spread (page 198)
Baked Ham with Bourbon Glaze
Roasted Vegetables
Brussels Sprouts Medley
Chocolate Pound Cake

southern classic

Baked Ham with Bourbon Glaze

MAKES 12 TO 14 SERVINGS
Prep: 10 min.; Cook: 2 hrs., 30 min.

1 cup honey
½ cup molasses
½ cup bourbon or orange
    juice
¼ cup orange juice
2 Tbsp. Dijon mustard

1 (6- to 8-lb.) smoked ham
    half

1. Microwave honey and molasses in a 1-qt. glass dish at HIGH 1 minute. Whisk to blend. Whisk in bourbon, juice, and mustard.

2. Remove skin and fat from ham; place ham in a lightly greased 13- x 9-inch pan. Make ¼-inch-deep cuts in ham in a diamond pattern. Pour glaze over ham.

3. Bake on lower oven rack at 350° for 2 to 2½ hours or until a meat thermometer inserted into thickest portion registers 140°, basting every 15 minutes with glaze.

4. Remove from pan, reserving drippings. Cover ham, and chill, if desired. Chill reserved drippings.

5. Remove and discard fat from drippings. Bring drippings to a boil in a small saucepan. Serve warm with ham.

Taste of the South

According to legend, a Baptist preacher named Elijah Craig is credited as the originator of bourbon whiskey in what was then Bourbon County of the Kentucky territory. However, Craig's 1789 corn liquor was most certainly not the first distillery, as property inventories show that there were about 2,000 stills in the state by 1811. During pre-Prohibition, the South lead the nation in bourbon manufacturing, and even today some of our region's famous whiskeys are legally manufactured in counties where their sale is prohibited by law.

Roasted Vegetables

MAKES 6 TO 8 SERVINGS
Prep: 10 min., Cook: 30 min.

*Roasting emphasizes the natural sweetness in vegetables. High heat creates
a caramelized or crisp surface, sealing in flavor. It makes these veggies extra yummy.*

1½ lb. sweet potatoes,
   peeled and cut into
   1½-inch pieces
   (2 medium)
¾ lb. turnips, peeled and
   cut into 1½-inch pieces
   (3 small)
1 large onion, peeled and
   cut into 1½-inch
   wedges
6 garlic cloves, peeled
3 Tbsp. olive oil

1 Tbsp. chopped fresh
   rosemary
1 Tbsp. chopped fresh
   oregano or marjoram
1 tsp. salt

1. Combine first 5 ingredients in a large bowl; toss well.
Arrange vegetables in a single layer in a large roasting pan
or broiler pan.
2. Roast at 450° for 25 to 30 minutes or until well
browned, stirring gently every 10 minutes. Stir in herbs
and salt just before serving.

Brussels Sprouts Medley

MAKES 8 SERVINGS
Prep: 20 min., Cook: 20 min.

1½ lb. fresh Brussels
    sprouts*

3 cups water
2 chicken bouillon cubes
1½ cups thinly sliced carrot
1½ cups sliced celery

⅓ cup butter or margarine
¾ cup dry-roasted cashews
¼ tsp. salt
¼ tsp. dried thyme
⅛ tsp. pepper

1. Wash Brussels sprouts thoroughly, and remove discolored leaves. Cut off stem ends, and slash bottom of each sprout with a shallow X.

2. Place water and bouillon cubes in a medium saucepan; bring to a boil. Add Brussels sprouts, carrot, and celery; return to a boil. Cover, reduce heat, and simmer 12 to 15 minutes or until vegetables are tender. Drain; place vegetables in a serving bowl.

3. Melt butter in a small skillet; add cashews and seasonings. Cook over low heat 3 to 4 minutes or until cashews are lightly toasted; pour over vegetables.

*Substitute 3 (10-oz.) packages frozen Brussels sprouts for fresh, if desired.

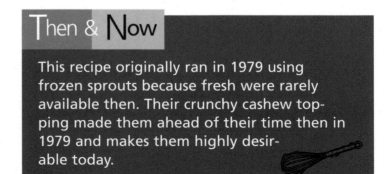

Then & Now

This recipe originally ran in 1979 using frozen sprouts because fresh were rarely available then. Their crunchy cashew topping made them ahead of their time then in 1979 and makes them highly desirable today.

Chocolate Pound Cake

MAKES 8 SERVINGS
Prep: 20 min.; Cook: 1 hr., 15 min.; Other: 15 min.

½ cup shortening

1 cup butter or margarine, softened

3 cups sugar

5 large eggs

2 cups all-purpose flour

½ tsp. baking powder

½ tsp. salt

½ cup unsweetened cocoa

1¼ cups milk

1 tsp. vanilla extract

Chocolate Glaze

Chopped pecans (optional)

1. Cream shortening and butter; gradually add sugar, beating well at medium speed with an electric mixer. Add eggs, 1 at a time, beating after each addition.

2. Sift flour, baking powder, salt, and cocoa together. Add to creamed mixture alternately with milk, beginning and ending with flour mixture. Mix just until blended after each addition. Stir in vanilla.

3. Pour batter into a greased and floured 10-inch tube pan. Bake at 350° for 1 hour and 15 minutes or until a wooden pick inserted in center comes out clean. Cool in pan 10 to 15 minutes; remove from pan, and cool completely on a wire rack.

4. Spoon Chocolate Glaze over top of cake, allowing it to drizzle down sides. Sprinkle top of cake with chopped pecans, if desired.

Chocolate Glaze

MAKES 1⅓ CUPS
Prep: 5 min.; Cook: 1 min., 30 sec.

3 (1-oz.) unsweetened chocolate baking squares

¾ cup sifted powdered sugar

2 Tbsp. hot water

1 large egg

1 egg yolk

5 Tbsp. butter or margarine, softened

1. Microwave chocolate in a large glass bowl at HIGH 1½ minutes or until melted, stirring twice. Add sugar and water, beating at medium speed with an electric mixer until blended. Add egg, and beat until blended. Add egg yolk, and beat until mixture cools. Add butter, 1 Tbsp. at a time, beating until blended.

Then & Now

With a pound each of flour, butter, sugar, and eggs, great-grandmother lovingly baked her family's favorite dessert: pound cake. Our recipe doesn't call for a pound of every ingredient, but this cake does capture the simplicity and goodness of the old-fashioned version (with the addition of chocolate).

Down-home fixin's serves 4

Chicken-Fried Steak
Sweet Corn Pudding
Simple Turnip Greens
Caramel-Applesauce Cobbler with
Bourbon-Pecan Ice Cream

party pleaser

Chicken-Fried Steak

MAKES 4 SERVINGS
Prep: 15 min., Cook: 30 min.

¼ cup all-purpose flour
½ tsp. salt
½ tsp. pepper
1 lb. cubed beef steaks

1 large egg, lightly beaten
2 Tbsp. milk
1 cup saltine cracker crumbs

Vegetable oil

3 Tbsp. all-purpose flour
1¼ cups chicken broth
½ cup milk
Dash of Worcestershire sauce
Dash of hot sauce

1. Combine first 3 ingredients; sprinkle on both sides of steaks.

2. Combine egg and 2 Tbsp. milk in a shallow dish. Dip steaks in egg mixture; dredge in cracker crumbs.

3. Pour oil to depth of ½ inch into a large, heavy skillet. Fry steaks in hot oil over medium heat until browned, turning once. Cover, reduce heat, and simmer, turning occasionally, 15 minutes or until tender.

4. Remove steaks, and drain on paper towels. Keep warm. Drain off drippings, reserving 3 Tbsp. in skillet.

5. Add 3 Tbsp. flour to drippings in skillet, stirring until smooth. Cook 1 minute, stirring constantly. Gradually add broth and ½ cup milk; cook over medium heat, stirring constantly until thickened and bubbly. Stir in a dash of Worcestershire sauce and hot sauce. Serve gravy with steaks.

Then & Now

Popular in the South and Midwest, this comfort food refers to a thin, inexpensive cut of steak that has been tenderized by pounding. It's dipped into a batter of milk, egg, and seasoned flour, then deep-fried like chicken until crisp and served with a rich and creamy seasoned country gravy. This dish is not quite suitable for a low-fat diet. "I don't see too many people worrying about it— they just don't eat it every day," says Eddie Wilson, owner of Threadgill's in Austin, Texas, the legendary mecca for restaurant-style chicken-fry fans. "Fifteen years ago we sold so much chicken-fried steak it was almost sinful. Now folks eat more of that chicken-fried chicken, which, to me, is a lot like drinking a bourbon and Diet Coke."

Sweet Corn Pudding

MAKES 6 SERVINGS
Prep: 10 min.; Cook: 1 hr., 5 min.; Other: 10 min.

1 cup fresh breadcrumbs
6 Tbsp. self-rising white
    cornmeal mix
1½ Tbsp. sugar
½ tsp. salt

3 large eggs
1¼ cups milk
½ cup half-and-half
2 Tbsp. butter, melted
1 (20-oz.) package frozen
    cream-style corn,
    thawed

Garnish: green onions

1. Combine breadcrumbs and next 3 ingredients in a large bowl.
2. Whisk eggs in a large bowl until pale and foamy; whisk in milk, half-and-half, and butter. Whisk egg mixture into breadcrumb mixture; stir in corn. Pour into a lightly greased 9-inch square baking dish.
3. Bake at 325° for 1 hour to 1 hour and 5 minutes or until set. Let stand 10 minutes before serving. Garnish, if desired.

Simple Turnip Greens

MAKES 4 TO 6 SERVINGS
Prep: 1 hr., 30 min.; Cook: 35 min.

1 bunch fresh turnip greens
    (about 4½ lb.)

1 lb. salt pork (streak of
    lean) or smoked pork
    shoulder

3 qt. water
¼ tsp. freshly ground
    pepper
2 tsp. sugar (optional)

1. Remove and discard stems and discolored spots from greens. Wash greens thoroughly; drain and tear greens into pieces. Set aside.
2. Slice salt pork at ¼-inch intervals, cutting to, but not through, the skin.
3. Combine salt pork, 3 qt. water, pepper, and, if desired, sugar in a Dutch oven; bring mixture to a boil. Cover, reduce heat, and simmer 1 hour.
4. Add greens, and cook, uncovered, 30 to 35 minutes or until tender. Serve with a slotted spoon.

Sweet Corn Pudding

Caramel-Applesauce Cobbler with Bourbon-Pecan Ice Cream

MAKES 8 SERVINGS
Prep: 45 min., Cook: 25 min.

This recipe was inspired by an applesauce pie with hard sauce that Test Kitchens staffer Mary Allen Perry enjoyed at her grandmother's house as a child. After devouring it, family members may drift away from the table to doze off.

½ cup butter or margarine
12 large Granny Smith
    apples, peeled and
    sliced
2 cups sugar
2 Tbsp. lemon juice

1 (15-oz.) package
    refrigerated piecrusts

Bourbon-Pecan Ice Cream

1. Melt butter in a large Dutch oven over medium-high heat. Add apple, sugar, and lemon juice; cook, stirring often, 20 to 25 minutes or until apple is caramel-colored. Spoon into a shallow, greased 2-qt. baking dish.

2. Cut each piecrust into ½-inch strips. Arrange strips in a lattice design over filling; fold edges under. Place remaining strips on a baking sheet.

3. Bake remaining strips at 425° for 8 to 10 minutes or until golden. Bake cobbler at 425° for 20 to 25 minutes or until crust is golden. Serve warm with pastry strips and Bourbon-Pecan Ice Cream.

Bourbon-Pecan Ice Cream

MAKES 2 PT.
Prep: 5 min., Other: 4 hrs.

2 pt. homemade-style
    vanilla ice cream,
    softened (we tested
    with Blue Bell
    Homemade Vanilla)
1 cup chopped toasted
    pecans
¼ cup bourbon

1. Stir together all ingredients; freeze at least 4 hours.

Kids'
choice serves 4

Buttermilk Baked Chicken
Steamed broccoli with cheese sauce
Lemon-Basil Potato Salad
Chocolate chip or oatmeal cookies

kid friendly

Buttermilk Baked Chicken

MAKES 4 SERVINGS
Prep: 20 min., Cook: 35 min.

¼ cup butter or margarine

4 skinned and boned
chicken breasts
½ tsp. salt
½ tsp. pepper
1½ cups buttermilk, divided
¾ cup all-purpose flour

1 (10¾-oz.) can cream of
mushroom soup
Garnish: chopped fresh
parsley

1. Melt butter in a lightly greased 13- x 9-inch baking dish in a 425° oven.

2. Sprinkle chicken with salt and pepper. Dip chicken in ½ cup buttermilk, and dredge in flour.

3. Arrange chicken, breast sides down, in baking dish.

4. Bake at 425° for 15 minutes. Turn chicken, and bake 10 more minutes.

5. Stir together remaining 1 cup buttermilk and cream of mushroom soup; pour over chicken, and bake 10 more minutes, shielding chicken with aluminum foil to prevent excessive browning, if necessary. Drizzle gravy over chicken. Garnish, if desired.

Then & Now

Buttermilk upholds not only a long, special status as a homestead beverage, but also as a key ingredient in breading chicken for frying and in traditional Southern baked goods, such as buttermilk biscuits, pancakes, and crumb and layer cakes. Folklore proclaims that buttermilk immunizes against such toxins as poison oak and ivy. And many a pioneer woman used a buttermilk facial wash to create a flawless, creamy, butterlike complexion.

Lemon-Basil Potato Salad

MAKES 6 SERVINGS
Prep: 25 min., Cook: 25 min.

*Crisp, roasted potato wedges combine with a
lively vinaigrette in Lemon-Basil Potato Salad.*

2½ lb. small Yukon gold
   potatoes, cut into
   wedges

¼ cup lemon juice
4 garlic cloves, minced
1 (1-oz.) package chopped
   fresh basil (about
   ⅓ cup)
1 Tbsp. Dijon mustard
1 tsp. salt
½ tsp. freshly ground
   pepper
⅔ cup olive oil
½ medium-size red onion,
   sliced

1 (10-oz.) package fresh
   spinach, cut into thin
   strips
10 thick bacon slices,
   cooked and crumbled

1. Arrange potato wedges in an even layer on a lightly
greased broiler pan; coat wedges with vegetable cooking
spray.

2. Bake at 475° for 20 to 25 minutes or until tender and
golden.

3. Whisk together lemon juice and next 5 ingredients;
whisk in oil in a slow, steady stream. Gently toss potatoes,
onion, and ½ cup lemon mixture.

4. Wash spinach thoroughly; pat dry with paper towels.
Arrange spinach evenly on a platter or in 6 bowls. Drizzle
with remaining lemon juice mixture. Top with potato mixture, and sprinkle with bacon.

kids love it

Three-Cheese Baked Pasta

MAKES 8 TO 10 SERVINGS
Prep: 20 min., Cook: 30 min.

Tossed with creamy Alfredo sauce and a trio of Italian cheese,
Three-Cheese Baked Pasta heats up for a speedy, make-ahead side dish.

1 (16-oz.) package ziti
    pasta*

2 (10-oz.) jars Alfredo sauce
1 (8-oz.) container sour
    cream

1 (15-oz.) container ricotta
    cheese
2 large eggs, lightly beaten
¼ cup grated Parmesan
    cheese
¼ cup chopped fresh
    parsley
1½ cups mozzarella cheese

1. Cook ziti according to package directions; drain and return to pot.

2. Stir together Alfredo sauce and sour cream; toss with ziti until evenly coated. Spoon half of ziti mixture into a lightly greased 13- x 9-inch baking dish.

3. Stir together ricotta cheese and next 3 ingredients; spread evenly over pasta mixture. Spoon remaining pasta mixture evenly over ricotta cheese layer; sprinkle with mozzarella cheese.

4. Bake at 350° for 30 minutes or until bubbly.

*Ziti pasta is shaped in long, thin tubes. Substitute penne or rigatoni pasta, if desired.

From Our Kitchen

Want a head start? Prepare this up to one day ahead; cover and refrigerate. Let stand at room temperature 30 minutes, and bake as directed.

Broccoli with Orange Sauce

MAKES 6 TO 8 SERVINGS
Prep: 20 min., Cook: 11 min.

Looking for an alternative to the everyday broccoli-and-cheese combo?
Add a little sweet to your broccoli with orange sections and flavored yogurt.

2 oranges

1½ lb. fresh broccoli florets

1 tsp. butter or margarine
1 small onion, chopped
2 tsp. finely chopped
    crystallized ginger

1 (8-oz.) container low-fat
    lemon yogurt

1. Grate 1 orange to equal 1 tsp. grated rind; set aside. Peel and section oranges, removing seeds; set aside.

2. Place broccoli florets in a steamer basket over boiling water, and cook 3 to 4 minutes or until crisp-tender.

3. Melt butter in a nonstick skillet over medium-high heat; add onion and ginger, and sauté until tender. Remove from heat.

4. Toss together broccoli florets, onion mixture, 1 tsp. orange rind, and orange sections in a large bowl. Stir in yogurt. Serve immediately.

Blackberry Pudding Tarts

MAKES 10 (4½-INCH) TARTS
Prep: 29 min., Cook: 43 min., Other: 30 min.
(pictured on page 17)

If you live in the South, you probably love blackberry cobbler but might not love the seeds. This pastry treat, which is, intense both in color and flavor, gives you pure blackberry pleasure without the seeds.

1 (15-oz.) package
   refrigerated piecrusts

8 cups fresh or frozen
   blackberries, thawed
1 cup water

1½ cups sugar
½ cup all-purpose flour
¼ cup butter, cut into
   pieces
2 tsp. vanilla extract

Sweetened whipped cream

1. Unfold 1 piecrust, and roll into a 15-inch circle; cut into 5 (5½-inch) circles. Fit each circle into a 4½-inch round tart pan with removable bottom, and place pans on a baking sheet. Prick bottom and sides with a fork. Bake at 450° for 7 minutes or until lightly browned. Cool in tart pans on a wire rack; remove shells from tart pans.

2. Meanwhile, repeat procedure with remaining piecrust.

3. Combine blackberries and water in a Dutch oven; bring to a boil. Reduce heat, and simmer, uncovered, 5 minutes or until blackberries are soft, stirring occasionally. Mash berries with a fork or potato masher; pour through a large wire-mesh strainer into a 4-cup liquid measuring cup, discarding pulp and seeds. Bring blackberry liquid to a boil in same pan over medium-high heat, and boil 10 minutes or until mixture reduces to 2 cups.

4. Combine sugar and flour in a medium saucepan; gradually add blackberry liquid, stirring constantly until smooth. Bring to a boil, stirring constantly, over medium heat. Reduce heat, and simmer, stirring constantly, uncovered, 3 minutes or until slightly thickened. Remove from heat; stir in butter and vanilla.

5. Spoon about ¼ cup filling into each tart shell. Cool 30 minutes; cover and chill. Serve with whipped cream.

Taste of the South

Blackberries are sometimes called bramble berries because they grow wild on bramble vines along rural Southern roadsides from May through August. Blackberries can be eaten out-of-hand, in pies, or topped with sweetened whipped cream. The only drawback to the blackberry is its fairly large, crunchy seeds. We've solved this by pureeing the blackberries and pressing them through a sieve to remove the seeds and pulp.

Everyday dinners

Please hearty Southern appetites any day of the week with these meals that require minimal hands-on time in the kitchen. Pair them with items from your local deli, and you've got a menu that's ready in no time.

our best
40 years
recipes

BAKED MACARONI AND CHEESE, PAGE 76

Tomato-Beef-Wild Rice Soup

MAKES 6 CUPS
Prep: 20 min.; Cook: 1 hr., 10 min.

Swedish Rye Bread, on page 8, pairs well with this soup for a rustic winter meal.

1 lb. beef tips
2 Tbsp. olive oil
4 celery ribs, chopped
    (about 1 cup)
2 large onions, sliced
    (about 2½ cups)
2 garlic cloves, minced
1 Tbsp. dried Italian
    seasoning

3 (14-oz.) cans beef broth
1 (6-oz.) package wild rice
1 (14½-oz.) can diced
    tomatoes
1 cup sliced fresh mushrooms
¼ tsp. hot sauce
½ to 1 tsp. salt
1 tsp. pepper
1 bay leaf

1. Sauté beef, in batches, in hot oil in a Dutch oven over medium-high heat until brown. Add chopped celery and next 3 ingredients; sauté 5 minutes or until vegetables are tender.

2. Stir in beef broth and remaining ingredients; bring to a boil. Reduce heat, and simmer 30 minutes. Cover and simmer 30 more minutes or until rice is tender. Remove and discard bay leaf before serving.

kids love it

Meatball Lasagna

MAKES 8 SERVINGS
Prep: 15 min., Cook: 1 hr., Other: 15 min.

1 (15-oz.) container ricotta
  cheese
1 (8-oz.) container chive-
  and-onion cream
  cheese, softened
¼ cup chopped fresh basil
½ tsp. garlic salt
½ tsp. seasoned pepper
1 large egg, lightly beaten

2 cups (8 oz.) shredded
  mozzarella cheese,
  divided
1 (3-oz.) package shredded
  Parmesan cheese,
  divided

2 (26-oz.) jars tomato-basil
  pasta sauce (we tested
  with Classico Tomato
  and Basil)

1 (16-oz.) package egg roll
  wrappers
60 to 64 frozen cooked
  Italian-style meatballs

1. Stir together first 6 ingredients until blended.
2. Stir in ½ cup mozzarella cheese and ½ cup Parmesan cheese; set aside.
3. Spread 1 cup pasta sauce in a lightly greased 13- x 9-inch baking dish.
4. Cut egg roll wrappers in half lengthwise; arrange 10 egg roll wrapper halves over pasta sauce. (Wrappers will overlap.) Top with meatballs.
5. Spoon 3 cups pasta sauce over meatballs; sprinkle with ¾ cup mozzarella cheese.
6. Arrange 10 wrapper halves evenly over mozzarella. Spread ricotta cheese mixture over wrappers; top with remaining wrapper halves and pasta sauce.
7. Bake at 350° for 50 minutes. Top with remaining ¾ cup mozzarella cheese and remaining ¼ cup Parmesan cheese.
8. Bake 10 more minutes. Let stand 15 minutes. Serve with fresh salad greens and Italian vinaigrette.

From Our Kitchen

We especially like this lasagna because it goes into the oven in record time—no beef to brown and no noodles to boil.

Spicy-Sweet Ribs and Beans

MAKES 8 SERVINGS
Prep: 50 min., Cook: 6 hrs. or 10 hrs.

There may be no better or easier way to make dinner than using this, our favorite slow-cooker recipe. Bottled hickory-flavored barbecue sauce and hot jalapeño jelly make preparation a breeze—and the long, slow cooking makes the meaty ribs extra tender.

2 (16-oz.) cans pinto beans, drained

4 lb. country-style pork ribs, trimmed
1 tsp. garlic powder
½ tsp. salt
½ tsp. pepper

1 medium onion, chopped

1 (10.5-oz.) jar red jalapeño jelly
1 (18-oz.) bottle hickory-flavored barbecue sauce (we tested with Kraft Thick 'n Spicy Hickory Smoke Barbecue Sauce)
1 tsp. green hot sauce (we tested with Tabasco)

1. Place beans in a 5-qt. slow cooker; set aside.
2. Cut ribs apart; sprinkle with garlic powder, salt, and pepper. Place ribs on a broiler pan.
3. Broil 5½ inches from heat 18 to 20 minutes or until browned, turning once. Add ribs to slow cooker, and sprinkle with onion.
4. Combine jelly, barbecue sauce, and hot sauce in a saucepan; cook over low heat until jelly melts. Pour over ribs, and stir gently.
5. Cover and cook on HIGH 5 to 6 hours or on LOW 9 to 10 hours. Remove ribs. Drain bean mixture, reserving sauce. Skim fat from sauce. Arrange ribs over bean mixture; serve with sauce.

From Our Kitchen

Pick up French bread and deli potato salad on your way home—the rest of dinner will be ready when you walk in the door.

Italian Burgers

MAKES 4 SERVINGS
Prep: 15 min., Cook: 18 min.

Fennel seeds, a common ingredient in Italian sausage,
add a hint of sweetness to this recipe.

1 lb. lean ground beef
1 small onion, minced
¾ cup grated Parmesan
    cheese
¼ cup minced fresh parsley
1 large egg, lightly beaten
2 Tbsp. dried Italian
    seasoning
¾ tsp. pepper
½ tsp. garlic salt
¼ tsp. fennel seeds

4 (1-oz.) provolone cheese
    slices

4 English muffins, split

½ cup tomato pasta sauce
Garnish: fresh basil leaves

1. Combine first 9 ingredients; shape into 4 patties.

2. Grill, covered with grill lid, over medium-high heat (350° to 400°) 7 to 8 minutes on each side or until beef is no longer pink. Top patties with cheese, and grill 1 more minute or until cheese melts.

3. Place muffins, cut sides down, on grill. Grill 1 minute or until lightly toasted.

4. Top each muffin bottom with 2 Tbsp. pasta sauce and a cheese-covered patty. Garnish, if desired, and cover with muffin top. Serve with chips of your choice and sliced plum tomatoes.

Chicken-and-Sausage Gumbo

MAKES 10 CUPS
Prep: 55 min.; Cook: 2 hrs., 18 min.

1 lb. andouille sausage, cut into ¼-inch-thick slices

4 skinned bone-in chicken breasts

Vegetable oil
¾ cup all-purpose flour

1 medium onion, chopped
½ green bell pepper, chopped
2 celery ribs, sliced
2 qt. hot water
3 garlic cloves, minced
2 bay leaves
1 Tbsp. Worcestershire sauce
2 tsp. Creole seasoning
½ tsp. dried thyme
½ to 1 tsp. hot sauce

4 green onions, sliced

Filé powder (optional)
Hot cooked rice
Garnish: chopped green onions

1. Cook sausage in a Dutch oven over medium heat, stirring constantly, 5 minutes or until browned. Drain on paper towels, reserving drippings in Dutch oven. Set sausage aside.

2. Cook chicken breasts in reserved drippings in Dutch oven over medium heat 5 minutes or until browned. Remove to paper towels, reserving drippings in Dutch oven. Set chicken aside.

3. Add enough oil to drippings in Dutch oven to measure ½ cup. Add flour, and cook over medium heat, stirring constantly, 20 to 30 minutes, or until roux is chocolate-colored.

4. Stir in onion, bell pepper, and celery; cook, stirring often, 8 minutes or until tender. Gradually add 2 qt. hot water, and bring mixture to a boil; add chicken, garlic, and next 5 ingredients. Reduce heat to low, and simmer, stirring occasionally, 1 hour. Remove chicken; cool.

5. Add sausage to gumbo; cook 30 minutes. Stir in green onions; cook for 30 more minutes.

6. Bone chicken, and cut meat into strips; return chicken to gumbo, and simmer 5 minutes. Remove and discard bay leaves.

7. Remove gumbo from heat. Sprinkle with filé powder, if desired. Serve over hot cooked rice. Garnish, if desired.

From Our Kitchen

We give a tearful but heartfelt salute to former Foods Editor Dana Adkins Campbell, who passed away in 2003, for this gumbo recipe she shared in November 1990. Hailing from the Bayou State, Dana knew her gumbo and called it Cajun chicken soup. The trick to great gumbo is the roux. "It's an easy process, but not to be interrupted," Dana warned in her story that accompanied this recipe. "As long as you stir over medium heat for a half hour or so without stopping, you can get a rich, deep brown roux without any burned mishaps."

Peanut-Roasted Chicken

MAKES 4 SERVINGS
Prep: 15 min., Cook: 45 min., Other: 30 min.

4 chicken leg-thigh
    combinations (about
    2 lb.), separated

½ cup creamy peanut
    butter
2 Tbsp. soy sauce
2 Tbsp. honey
1 Tbsp. grated lemon rind
1 Tbsp. fresh lemon juice

1 (3-oz.) package honey-
    roasted peanuts
½ cup fine, dry
    breadcrumbs
2 garlic cloves, minced
1 tsp. salt
¼ tsp. ground red pepper

1. Place chicken pieces in a shallow dish or large zip-top freezer bag.

2. Stir together peanut butter and next 4 ingredients. Pour mixture over chicken; cover or seal, and chill 30 minutes, turning occasionally. Remove chicken from marinade, discarding marinade.

3. Process peanuts and remaining 4 ingredients in a blender until mixture is crumbly. Place crumbs in a zip-top freezer bag; add chicken, and seal. Shake to coat. Place chicken in a lightly greased 13- x 9-inch baking dish.

4. Bake, uncovered, at 375° for 45 minutes or until done.

From Our Kitchen

If you're looking for a bargain on chicken, let this recipe's leg-thigh combinations lead the way. Whether you buy a whole chicken and cut it up or just pick up a package of your favorite pieces, bone-in chicken is typically less expensive than the boneless, skinless variety.

Chicken Breasts Lombardy

MAKES 6 SERVINGS
Prep: 22 min., Cook: 40 min.

2 cups sliced fresh
  mushrooms
2 Tbsp. butter or margarine,
  melted

6 skinned, boned chicken
  breasts
½ cup all-purpose flour
4 Tbsp. butter or margarine,
  melted and divided

¾ cup Marsala
½ cup chicken broth
½ tsp. salt
⅛ tsp. pepper

½ cup (2 oz.) shredded
  mozzarella cheese
½ cup refrigerated
  shredded Parmesan
  cheese
2 green onions, thinly sliced

1. Cook mushrooms in 2 Tbsp. butter in a large skillet, stirring constantly, just until tender. Remove from heat; set aside.

2. Cut each chicken breast half in half lengthwise. Place chicken between 2 sheets of heavy-duty plastic wrap; flatten to ¼-inch thickness, using a meat mallet or rolling pin. Dredge chicken pieces in flour. Place 6 pieces of chicken in 2 Tbsp. butter in a large skillet; cook over medium heat 4 to 5 minutes on each side or until golden. Place chicken in a lightly greased 13- x 9-inch baking dish or other large casserole, overlapping edges. Repeat procedure with remaining chicken and butter. Reserve pan drippings in skillet. Sprinkle reserved mushrooms over chicken.

3. Add wine and broth to skillet. Stir in salt and pepper. Bring to a boil; reduce heat, and simmer, uncovered, 10 minutes, stirring occasionally. Pour sauce over chicken.

4. Combine cheeses and green onions; sprinkle over chicken.

5. Bake, uncovered, at 450° for 12 to 14 minutes.

Note: Instead of ¾ cup Marsala, you can use ⅔ cup dry white wine plus 2 Tbsp. Brandy.

Wine-Glazed Chicken

MAKES 4 SERVINGS
Prep: 10 min., Cook: 35 min.

For such a simple dish, this recipe adds grand colors of green, red, and golden brown to the dinner table. Feel free to substitute chicken thighs or wings, if you prefer.

1 tsp. salt
½ tsp. ground nutmeg
8 chicken legs

¼ cup butter or margarine

1⅓ cups dry white wine*
1 cup sliced fresh
    mushrooms
1 red bell pepper, thinly
    sliced
3 green onions, chopped

2 Tbsp. chicken broth
4 tsp. cornstarch
Hot cooked rice
Garnish: chopped flat-leaf
    parsley

1. Sprinkle salt and nutmeg over chicken.

2. Melt butter in a medium skillet over medium heat; add chicken. Cook, turning frequently, 10 minutes or until golden.

3. Stir in wine, mushrooms, bell pepper, and green onions; bring to a boil over medium heat. Reduce heat to medium-low; cover and simmer 20 minutes or until chicken is done. Remove chicken from skillet; keep warm.

4. Whisk together broth and cornstarch until smooth; add to drippings in skillet. Cook over medium heat, stirring constantly, 1 minute or until thickened. Serve drumsticks over hot cooked rice; spoon glaze over chicken. Garnish, if desired.

*Substitute sparkling white grape juice for white wine, if desired.

Honey-Chicken Salad

MAKES 4 SERVINGS
Prep: 20 min.

The mayonnaise-and-honey dressing on this salad is reminiscent of poppy seed dressing.
If you prefer a less-sweet dressing, reduce the amount of honey.

½ (10-oz.) package frozen
    tart shells (we tested
    with Dutch Ann)

4 cups chopped cooked
    chicken
3 celery ribs, diced
1 cup sweetened dried
    cranberries
½ cup chopped pecans,
    toasted

1½ cups mayonnaise
⅓ cup honey
¼ tsp. salt
¼ tsp. pepper

Garnish: chopped toasted
    pecans

1. Bake tart shells according to manufacturer's instructions. Set aside.

2. Combine chicken and next 3 ingredients.

3. Whisk together mayonnaise and next 3 ingredients. Add to chicken mixture, stirring gently until combined.

4. Spoon chicken salad evenly into baked tart shells. Garnish, if desired.

Shrimp Salad: Stir together 4 cups chopped cooked shrimp, ¾ cup mayonnaise, 4 thinly sliced green onions, 2 diced celery ribs, 2 tsp. grated lemon rind, ½ tsp. ground red pepper, and salt and black pepper to taste.

From Our Kitchen

Honey-Chicken Salad served in pretty tart shells accents a triple salad luncheon plate. Stir together a simple Shrimp Salad (recipe above) and toss a colorful mixture of sliced tomatoes, bell pepper strips, red onion slices, cucumber chunks, and mixed greens with your favorite vinaigrette to serve alongside.

Hearty Tex-Mex Squash-Chicken Casserole

MAKES 8 SERVINGS
Prep: 35 min., Cook: 35 min.

We adore the robust flavors of Tex-Mex foods, and we applaud the healthy addition of spinach and squash to this family-pleasing casserole. It even works just as well with reduced-fat soup, light sour cream, and reduced-fat cheese.

1 (10-oz.) package frozen chopped spinach, thawed

3 medium-size yellow squash, thinly sliced
1 large red bell pepper, cut into ½-inch pieces
1 small onion, thinly sliced
2 Tbsp. peanut oil

3 cups shredded cooked chicken or turkey
12 (6-inch) corn tortillas, cut into 1-inch pieces
1 (10¾-oz.) can cream of celery soup
1 (8-oz.) container sour cream
1 (8-oz.) jar salsa
1 (4.5-oz.) can chopped green chiles, undrained
1 (1.4-oz.) envelope fajita seasoning
2 cups (8 oz.) shredded sharp Cheddar cheese, divided

1. Drain chopped spinach well, pressing between paper towels; set aside.
2. Sauté squash, bell pepper, and onion in hot oil in a large skillet over medium-high heat 6 minutes or until tender. Remove from heat.
3. Stir in spinach, chicken, next 6 ingredients, and 1½ cups cheese. Spoon into a lightly greased 13- x 9-inch baking dish.
4. Bake at 350° for 30 minutes. Sprinkle evenly with remaining ½ cup cheese, and bake 5 more minutes.

Gorditas with Turkey Mole

MAKES 12 SERVINGS
Prep: 40 min., Cook: 12 min., Other: 30 min.

A gordita is a thick pancake made of masa harina (a special flour made from dried corn kernels); the edges are pinched together to hold a meat or bean filling.

2 cups masa harina
1¼ cups chicken broth
¼ cup shortening
9 Tbsp. all-purpose flour
½ tsp. salt
1 tsp. baking powder

Vegetable oil

1 cup refried beans
Turkey Mole
Toppings: 1 (15-oz.) can
    black beans, rinsed and
    drained; shredded
    lettuce; chopped
    tomato; sour cream

1. Stir together masa harina and broth in a large mixing bowl. Cover and let stand 30 minutes. Add shortening, flour, salt, and baking powder; beat at medium speed with an electric mixer until smooth.

2. Divide dough into 12 golf ball-size balls. Arrange on wax paper, and cover with damp towels. Pat each ball of dough into a 3-inch circle. (Lightly oil fingers to keep mixture from sticking.) Pinch edges of circles to form a ridge, and press a well into each center to hold toppings. Cover with a damp towel to prevent dough from drying.

3. Pour oil to a depth of ¼ inch into a large skillet; heat to 350°. Fry gorditas, in batches, 2 minutes on each side or until golden brown. Drain on paper towels.

4. Dollop each gordita with 2 Tbsp. refried beans; spoon 1 Tbsp. Turkey Mole over beans. (Reserve extra beans and mole for other uses.) Top with desired toppings.

Turkey Mole

MAKES 6½ CUPS
Prep: 10 min., Cook: 15 min.

1 (8.25-oz.) can mole
    sauce
1 (10-oz.) can enchilada
    sauce
4 cups chicken broth

1 Tbsp. creamy
    peanut butter
2 (1-oz.) unsweetened dark
    chocolate baking squares
1½ lb. cooked turkey,
    shredded (about 5 cups)
½ tsp. salt

1. Stir together mole and enchilada sauces in a medium saucepan, and add chicken broth. Bring mixture to a boil; reduce heat, and simmer 5 minutes.

2. Stir in peanut butter and chocolate until melted and smooth. Stir in turkey and salt; cook until thoroughly heated.

Note: *Mole* is a concoction of various chili peppers, onion, garlic, and chocolate cooked to a smooth, rich consistency and auburn color. Canned mole sauce can be found in the Mexican foods section of large supermarkets.

Southwestern Pizza

MAKES 4 SERVINGS
Prep: 10 min., Cook: 10 min.

*Two tortillas sandwiched with cheese make these
individual pizzas extra sturdy and extra tasty.*

8 (10-inch) flour tortillas
1 (8-oz.) package shredded
    Mexican four-cheese
    blend

1 cup chunky salsa
Black Bean Salsa
2 cups chopped cooked
    chicken
Garnishes: sour cream,
    chopped avocado

1. Place 4 flour tortillas on a lightly greased baking sheet. Top tortillas evenly with 1 cup cheese; cover with remaining flour tortillas.

2. Divide chunky salsa, Black Bean Salsa, chicken, and remaining 1 cup cheese over flour tortillas. Bake at 400° for 10 minutes or until cheese is bubbly. Garnish, if desired. Cut into wedges.

Black Bean Salsa

MAKES 3 CUPS
Prep: 10 min.

1 (15-oz.) can black beans,
    rinsed and drained
½ cup frozen whole kernel
    corn, thawed
2 plum tomatoes, seeded
    and chopped
1 green onion, chopped
2 Tbsp. fresh lime juice
1 Tbsp. chopped fresh
    cilantro
1 garlic clove, pressed
½ tsp. Creole seasoning

1. Stir together all ingredients. Cover and chill until ready to serve.

Pasta with Shrimp Scampi

MAKES 4 SERVINGS
Prep: 30 min., Cook: 10 min.

*Serve with a crisp green salad and crusty garlic bread
to round out this easy pasta meal.*

1½ lb. unpeeled,
   medium-size fresh
   shrimp

1 to 2 Tbsp. chopped
   chipotle peppers in
   adobo sauce
2 garlic cloves, minced
2 Tbsp. olive oil

¼ cup dry white wine or
   chicken broth
1 Tbsp. Dijon mustard
1 Tbsp. Worcestershire
   sauce

¾ cup butter, melted
½ tsp. salt
2 Tbsp. fresh lemon juice

1 lb. spaghetti or fettuccine,
   cooked
½ cup chopped fresh
   Italian parsley
½ cup shredded Parmesan
   cheese

1. Peel shrimp, and devein, if desired.

2. Sauté peppers and garlic in hot oil in a large skillet over medium-high heat until thoroughly heated.

3. Add shrimp, and cook, stirring constantly, 2 to 3 minutes or just until shrimp turn pink. Remove shrimp, and set aside.

4. Stir in wine, mustard, and Worcestershire sauce; cook over high heat 3 to 4 minutes.

5. Return shrimp to skillet. Stir in butter, salt, and lemon juice; cook 1 to 2 minutes or until combined and thoroughly heated.

6. Place pasta in a large serving dish; toss with shrimp mixture and parsley. Sprinkle with Parmesan cheese.

Shrimp Destin

MAKES 4 SERVINGS
Prep: 20 min., Cook: 12 min.

2 lb. unpeeled, large fresh
    shrimp

¼ cup chopped green
    onions
2 tsp. minced garlic
1 cup butter, melted
1 Tbsp. dry white wine
1 tsp. lemon juice
⅛ tsp. salt
⅛ tsp. coarsely ground
    pepper
1 tsp. dried dillweed
1 tsp. chopped fresh parsley

2 French rolls, split
    lengthwise and toasted

1. Peel shrimp, and devein, if desired.
2. Sauté green onions and garlic in butter until onions are tender. Add shrimp, wine, lemon juice, salt, and pepper; cook over medium heat about 5 minutes, stirring occasionally. Stir in dillweed and parsley.
3. Spoon shrimp mixture over toasted roll halves, and serve immediately.

Note: Shrimp Destin can be served over hot cooked rice instead of rolls, if desired.

From Our Kitchen

Shrimp Destin, from Frances Ponder of Destin, Florida, caught our eye when testing recipes for the February 1982 issue of *Southern Living*, and old-timers on our staff have made it in their homes ever since.

No time to peel shrimp? Purchase 1½ lb. shelled shrimp instead. Give shrimp a quick sauté in a garlic butter bath, and you'll be amazed how quickly you can make this memorable entrée.

Put crusty rolls on to toast as you start the sauté, and then drizzle the butter sauce along with the shrimp over the toast.

Baked Macaroni and Cheese

MAKES 8 TO 10 SERVINGS
Prep: 20 min., Cook: 50 min., Other: 10 min.

The eggs and milk form a custard base in this mac 'n' cheese. Crackers thicken it.

1 (8-oz.) package large
    elbow macaroni,
    cooked
16 saltine crackers, finely
    crushed
1 tsp. salt
1 tsp. seasoned pepper
1 (10-oz.) block sharp
    Cheddar cheese,
    shredded (we tested
    with Kraft Cracker
    Barrel)
1 (10-oz.) block extra-sharp
    Cheddar cheese,
    shredded (we tested
    with Kraft Cracker
    Barrel)

6 large eggs, lightly beaten
4 cups milk

1. Layer one-third each of macaroni, crackers, salt, pepper, and cheeses into a lightly greased 13- x 9-inch baking dish. Repeat layers twice.

2. Whisk together eggs and milk; pour over pasta mixture.

3. Bake at 350° for 50 minutes or until golden and set. Let stand 10 minutes before serving.

Taste of the South

There are rigorous standards for the perfect macaroni and cheese—just ask the *Southern Living* Foods staff. Whether the macaroni is bathed in cheesy sauce or layered with cheese, topped with eggs and milk, then baked (custard style), this dish's sturdy simplicity offers a happy reminder that no matter how rough the day has been, there is comfort to be found. The creamy vs. custard debate raged at our tasting table for days, with advocates on both sides advancing their causes.

In the end, your mac 'n' cheese preference bakes down to what you grew up eating. All the discussion and research in the world won't change the fact that your mama's recipe is the best—at least in your eyes. With that in mind, here is a stellar example of a custard-style version. (A creamier version follows.) Go ahead and serve it to your mama—she'll be impressed.

Skillet Macaroni and Cheese

MAKES 6 TO 8 SERVINGS
Prep: 10 min., Cook 20 min.

¼ cup butter
1 small onion, chopped
1 Tbsp. all-purpose flour
1½ tsp. salt
¼ tsp. dried oregano

1 (8-oz.) package elbow
   macaroni, uncooked
2 cups whipping cream
1½ cups milk
2 cups (8 oz.) shredded
   sharp Cheddar cheese

1. Melt butter in a large skillet over medium-high heat; add onion, and sauté until tender. Stir in flour, salt, and oregano. Cook 1 minute.

2. Stir macaroni, cream, and milk into skillet. Bring to a boil; cover, reduce heat, and simmer 15 minutes or until macaroni is tender, stirring occasionally. Add cheese, stirring until cheese melts (do not boil).

Then & Now

We applaud this simplified creamy macaroni and cheese that first appeared in *Southern Living* in 1970. It's all made in the skillet, and the noodles cook concurrently with the sauce. We made one minor change in the recipe, and that was substituting 2 cups whipping cream for part of the milk—just to make it extra-creamy. You can use 3½ cups milk instead of the milk and cream combo, if you'd like.

Maque Choux Pies

MAKES 1 DOZEN
Prep: 35 min., Cook: 12 min., Other: 30 min.

2 ears fresh corn

2 Tbsp. butter or margarine
½ cup chopped red bell
    pepper
½ cup chopped green bell
    pepper
⅓ cup diced onion

1 Tbsp. all-purpose flour
1 Tbsp. sugar
¼ tsp. salt
⅛ tsp. pepper
⅓ cup whipping cream

1 (17.3-oz.) package frozen
    puff pastry sheets,
    thawed

1 egg yolk
1 Tbsp. water
Tomato-Basil Sauce

1. Remove husks from corn cobs. Cut corn kernels from cobs, scraping to remove milk.

2. Melt butter in a large skillet over medium-high heat; add corn kernels, bell pepper, and onion; sauté 7 minutes or until corn is almost tender.

3. Stir in flour, sugar, salt, and pepper. Gradually add cream, and cook, stirring constantly, 3 minutes or until thickened. Cover and chill 30 minutes.

4. Roll puff pastry sheet into a 12- x 12-inch square on a lightly floured surface; cut each sheet into 6 circles with a 4¼-inch round cutter.

5. Spoon 2 slightly heaping Tbsp. corn mixture in center of each pastry circle; fold circles in half, and crimp edges with a fork to seal. Place on an ungreased baking sheet.

6. Stir together egg yolk and water; brush over pastry. Bake at 450° for 12 minutes or until pastry is golden. Serve pies with Tomato-Basil Sauce.

Tomato-Basil Sauce

MAKES 1⅓ CUPS
Prep: 10 min., Cook: 18 min., Other: 5 min.

1 shallot, minced
1 garlic clove, minced
1 Tbsp. olive oil
3 medium tomatoes,
    peeled, seeded, and
    chopped

2 Tbsp. minced fresh basil
¼ tsp. salt
¼ tsp. pepper

1. Sauté shallot and garlic in hot oil in a saucepan over medium-high heat 1 minute. Add tomato, and simmer 15 minutes.

2. Stir in remaining ingredients, and cook 2 minutes. Cool 5 minutes.

3. Process tomato mixture in a food processor until smooth, stopping to scrape down sides.

One dish
delish

Cleanup is easy when you make dinner in a single dish. Choose from hearty or spicy to saucy or cheesy for complete family meals any night of the week.

HAM, SAUSAGE, AND CHICKEN GUMBO, PAGE 86

Classic Lasagna

MAKES 8 TO 10 SERVINGS
Prep: 1 hr., 10 min.; Cook: 1 hr., 10 min.; Other: 10 min.

2 medium onions, chopped
2 Tbsp. olive oil, divided
4 garlic cloves, minced
1 lb. lean ground beef

1 (14½-oz.) can basil, garlic,
   and oregano diced
   tomatoes, undrained
2 (6-oz.) cans tomato paste
1 (8-oz.) can basil, garlic,
   and oregano tomato
   sauce
1 bay leaf
1 tsp. Italian seasoning
1¼ tsp. salt, divided
¾ tsp. pepper, divided

12 lasagna noodles,
   uncooked
8 cups boiling water

1 (16-oz.) container ricotta
   cheese
2 large eggs, lightly beaten
¼ cup grated Parmesan
   cheese

2 (6-oz.) packages part-skim
   mozzarella cheese slices

Garnish: chopped fresh
   parsley

1. Sauté onion in 1 Tbsp. hot oil in a large skillet over medium-high heat 5 minutes or until tender. Add garlic; sauté 1 minute. Add beef, and cook, stirring occasionally, 10 minutes or until beef crumbles and is no longer pink. Drain beef mixture; return to skillet.

2. Stir in diced tomatoes, next 4 ingredients, 1 tsp. salt, and ½ tsp. pepper; bring to a boil. Reduce heat, cover, and simmer, stirring occasionally, 30 minutes. Remove and discard bay leaf; set meat sauce aside.

3. While sauce simmers, place noodles in a 13- x 9-inch baking dish. Carefully pour 8 cups boiling water and remaining 1 Tbsp. olive oil over noodles. Let stand 15 minutes.

4. Stir together ricotta cheese, eggs, Parmesan cheese, remaining ¼ tsp. salt, and remaining ¼ tsp. pepper until blended.

5. Spoon half of the meat sauce mixture into a lightly greased 13- x 9-inch baking dish. Shake excess water from noodles, and arrange 6 noodles over meat sauce; top with half of ricotta mixture and 1 package mozzarella cheese slices. Repeat layers once.

6. Bake, covered, at 350° for 55 minutes. Uncover and bake lasagna 10 to 15 more minutes or until bubbly. Let stand 10 minutes before serving. Garnish, if desired.

From Our Kitchen

Make this ahead by lining a 13- x 9-inch baking dish with heavy-duty nonstick aluminum foil, allowing several inches to extend over the sides. Prepare recipe as directed in the foil-lined dish. Freeze the unbaked lasagna until firm. Remove from baking dish by holding the edges of the foil; fold foil over lasagna. Wrap in additional foil, sealing tightly. Freeze up to 1 month.

The day before serving, remove the lasagna from the freezer. Remove the foil; place the lasagna in a lightly greased 13- x 9-inch baking dish. Cover and thaw overnight in the refrigerator. Bake as directed. (Lasagna may also be baked frozen. Plan to double the baking time.)

Linguine with Meat Sauce Casserole

MAKES 8 SERVINGS
Prep: 40 min., Cook: 30 min., Other: 5 min.

Our Test Kitchens created this lightened version of an indulgent casserole that ran in Southern Living *in 2001. Low-fat mozzarella and fat-free sour cream and cream cheese keep the fat and calories at bay. You'll want to indulge, and the guilt's virtually gone.*

1 lb. extra-lean ground beef
1 tsp. bottled minced garlic

1 (28-oz.) can crushed
    tomatoes, undrained
1 (8-oz.) can tomato sauce
1 (6-oz.) can tomato paste
2 tsp. sugar
½ tsp. salt

8 oz. uncooked whole
    wheat linguine*

1 (16-oz.) container
    nonfat sour cream
1 (8-oz.) package fat-free
    cream cheese, softened
1 bunch green onions,
    chopped

1½ cups (6 oz.) shredded
    low-fat mozzarella
    cheese

1. Cook beef and garlic in a Dutch oven coated with cooking spray, stirring until beef crumbles and is no longer pink. Drain beef mixture; pat dry with paper towels. Return beef mixture to Dutch oven.
2. Stir in tomatoes and next 4 ingredients; simmer 30 minutes. Set meat sauce aside.
3. While sauce simmers, cook pasta according to package directions, omitting salt and oil; drain. Place pasta in a 13- x 9-inch baking dish coated with cooking spray.
4. Stir together sour cream, cream cheese, and green onions. Spread over linguine. Top with meat sauce.
5. Bake at 350° for 20 to 25 minutes or until thoroughly heated. Sprinkle with mozzarella cheese, and bake 5 more minutes or until cheese melts. Let stand 5 minutes.

*Substitute regular linguine for whole wheat, if desired.

Buster's Red Beans and Rice

MAKES 6 SERVINGS
Prep: 10 min.; Cook: 3 hrs., 40 min.

This legendary recipe originally ran in our The Southern Heritage Cookbook Collection *printed in 1985. The buttery concoction has simmered in many a pot since then.*

1 lb. dried red beans
2 qt. water
½ tsp. pepper

1 (1-lb.) ham hock
1 large onion, chopped
1 large green bell pepper,
    seeded and chopped
2 large garlic cloves, minced
¼ cup butter or margarine

1 to 1½ tsp. salt
Hot sauce
Hot cooked rice

1. Sort and wash beans. Combine beans, water, and pepper in a 6-qt. Dutch oven; cover and bring to a boil. Reduce heat to medium, and cook 40 minutes.

2. Add ham hock, onion, bell pepper, garlic, and butter; reduce heat. Cover; simmer 2 hours, stirring occasionally.

3. Remove ham hock. Remove fat and bone from meat; shred meat, and return to pot. Mash beans slightly with a potato masher. Cover and bring to a boil; reduce heat to medium-high. Cook, uncovered 45 minutes to 1 hour or until desired consistency, stirring frequently. Stir in salt. Serve beans with hot sauce over rice.

Then & Now

Chef Buster Holmes defined "red beans and rice," a New Orleans traditional dish, as we know it today. Most famous for this dish, he dedicated each Monday at Buster Holmes' Bar and Restaurant as red beans and rice day.

Chef Buster retired in the early 1980s and died in 1994—but his legacy lives on. Many New Orleans lunch counters still declare Mondays as red beans and rice day—and Buster Holmes' legendary recipe is as famous today as it was decades ago.

Ham, Sausage, and Chicken Gumbo

MAKES 8 TO 10 SERVINGS
Prep: 30 min.; Cook: 2 hrs., 35 min.
(pictured on page 81)

A savory roux enfolds tender meats and veggies
for a mouthwatering gumbo.

1½ lb. ham, cut into ½-inch
    cubes
1½ lb. smoked sausage, cut
    into ½-inch slices
6 skinned chicken thighs
6 Tbsp. vegetable oil

¼ cup all-purpose flour

1 large onion
4 garlic cloves, minced
½ green bell pepper,
    chopped
2 qt. water
½ tsp. dried crushed red
    pepper
½ tsp. dried whole thyme
¼ tsp. black pepper

½ cup chopped green
    onion tops
Hot cooked rice
Gumbo filé powder
    (optional)

1. Brown each meat, 1 at a time, in oil in a large Dutch oven, removing to drain on paper towels.
2. Add flour to oil remaining in Dutch oven; cook over medium heat, stirring constantly, until roux is caramel-colored (10 to 15 minutes).
3. Add onion, garlic, and bell pepper to roux; cook until vegetables are tender, stirring frequently. Gradually add water. Add ham, sausage, chicken, red pepper, thyme, and black pepper. Bring to a boil; reduce heat and simmer, uncovered, 1½ to 2 hours, stirring occasionally. Cool and skim fat from top. Remove bones from chicken; coarsely chop chicken, and return to pot.
4. Bring gumbo to a boil; add green onion tops. Cook 10 more minutes. Serve over hot cooked rice. Add filé, if desired.

From Our Kitchen

The longer and darker a roux is cooked, the less thickening power it has. When a roux is cooked to the dark or chocolate-colored stage, as is done in many gumbo recipes, filé powder—made from ground sassafras leaves—is often added for a little extra thickening. Filé powder is optional in this recipe because the roux is only cooked to a caramel color, which makes it naturally full textured. Add filé powder after the gumbo has completed cooking. If added while the gumbo cooks, it becomes stringy.

King Ranch Chicken Casserole

MAKES 6 TO 8 SERVINGS
Prep: 35 min., Cook: 45 min.

King Ranch Chicken, which we ran in February 1994, originated from the King Ranch in Kingsville, Texas. We liked it so much that we developed this quicker and easier version, which appeared in September 2002, to make for our families during the busy week. Instead of first boiling a chicken, this version starts with chopped cooked chicken that you might have left over or can buy in the freezer section; it also uses crushed tortilla chips instead of steamed and cut-up corn tortillas. You can even enjoy this recipe if you're watching your fat intake; just substitute low-fat soups for the full-fat versions, and use baked tortilla chips.

2 Tbsp. butter or margarine
1 medium onion, chopped
1 green bell pepper, chopped
1 red bell pepper, chopped

3 cups chopped cooked chicken
1 (10¾-oz.) can cream of chicken soup
1 (10¾-oz.) can cream of mushroom soup
1 (10-oz.) can diced tomatoes and green chiles, undrained
1 tsp. chili powder
1 tsp. ground cumin

2 cups crushed tortilla chips
2 cups (8 oz.) shredded Cheddar cheese

Garnish: chopped fresh cilantro

1. Melt butter in a medium skillet over medium-high heat. Add chopped onion and bell peppers; sauté 8 minutes or until tender.

2. Stir in chicken and next 5 ingredients; cook, stirring occasionally, 2 minutes.

3. Place 1 cup crushed tortilla chips in a 13- x 9-inch baking dish. Layer with half of chicken mixture and 1 cup shredded Cheddar cheese. Repeat layers, ending with cheese.

4. Bake, uncovered, at 325° for 45 minutes or until mixture is thoroughly heated. Garnish, if desired.

Note: Freeze casserole up to 1 month, if desired. Thaw in refrigerator overnight, and bake as directed.

Chicken Enchiladas

MAKES 6 SERVINGS
Prep: 33 min., Cook: 10 min., Other: 5 min.

1¼ lb. skinned and boned
    chicken breasts

1½ Tbsp. chopped onion
1½ Tbsp. chopped cilantro
1 jalapeño pepper, seeded
    and minced
3 (10-oz.) cans enchilada
    sauce, divided

12 (5½-inch) corn tortillas
1½ cups shredded sharp
    Cheddar cheese

Toppings: shredded lettuce,
    chopped tomatoes,
    sliced ripe olives, sour
    cream

1. Place chicken breasts in a medium saucepan; add just enough water to cover. Bring to a boil. Reduce heat, and simmer 15 minutes or until chicken is tender. Drain and cool slightly. Shred chicken, and set aside.

2. Coat a nonstick skillet with cooking spray; place over medium-high heat until hot. Add onion, cilantro, and jalapeño pepper; sauté until tender. Stir in 1 can enchilada sauce and shredded chicken. Cook 5 minutes or until heated through.

3. Layer tortillas in damp paper towels, and microwave on HIGH 10 seconds per tortilla or until soft. Fill each tortilla evenly with chicken mixture; roll up, and place, seam sides down, in a 13-x 9-inch baking dish. Heat remaining 2 cans enchilada sauce in a medium saucepan over medium heat; pour over enchiladas. Sprinkle cheese evenly over top.

4. Bake at 350° for 10 minutes or until cheese melts and enchiladas are thoroughly heated. Let enchiladas stand 5 minutes before serving. Serve with desired toppings.

Taste of the South

Peppers come in multiple colors and heat levels and can be substituted for each other in all sorts of recipes. Since some like it hot and some do not, here's a quick guide to identifying just the right pepper for your palate.

• **Anaheim or California green chile:** Slender green chile about 6 to 8 inches long with rounded tip; mild flavored. *Substitute:* Canned chopped green chiles.
• **Ancho chile:** Dried form of poblano chile. *Substitute:* ½ tsp. chili powder for each ancho chile.
• **Poblano chile:** Large dark green chile that resembles an elongated bell pepper; difficult to find outside of Texas and southwestern states. Ranges from mild to hot. *Substitute:* Sweet green pepper.
• **Jalapeño pepper:** Small green or red cigar-shaped chile about 2½ inches long; very hot. *Substitute:* Pickled jalapeño.
• **Serrano chile:** Dark green to red chile 1 to 1½ inches long; hot to very hot. *Substitute:* Jalapeño pepper.

Shrimp Creole

MAKES 8 TO 10 SERVINGS
Prep: 54 min.; Cook: 1 hr., 45 min.

*Dark, rich roux envelopes the piquant flavors of tomatoes, fresh vegetables, and spices.
Plump shrimp snuggle into the mix over a bed of saffron rice.*

¼ cup vegetable oil
¼ cup all-purpose flour

1½ cups chopped onion
1 cup sliced green onions
1 cup chopped celery
1 cup chopped green bell
  pepper
2 garlic cloves, minced

1 (14½-oz.) can diced
  tomatoes, undrained
1 (8-oz.) can tomato sauce
1 (6-oz.) can tomato paste
1 cup water
1½ tsp. salt
1 tsp. black pepper
½ tsp. ground red pepper
2 bay leaves
1 Tbsp. lemon juice
1 tsp. Worcestershire sauce
⅛ tsp. hot sauce

5 lb. unpeeled, medium-size
  fresh shrimp
2 (10-oz.) packages saffron
  rice mix, cooked
Garnish: finely chopped
  parsley

1. Heat oil in a large cast-iron skillet over medium heat; gradually whisk in flour, and cook, whisking constantly, until roux is chocolate-colored (about 15 minutes).

2. Remove from heat, and stir in chopped onion and next 4 ingredients; cook over medium heat, stirring occasionally, 15 minutes or until vegetables are tender.

3. Transfer mixture to a large Dutch oven; stir in tomatoes and next 10 ingredients. Bring to a boil; cover, reduce heat, and simmer 1 hour, stirring occasionally.

4. Peel and devein shrimp, if desired. Add to tomato mixture, and cook, stirring often, 15 minutes or just until shrimp turn pink. Remove and discard bay leaves. Serve over cooked saffron rice. Garnish, if desired.

Note: Shrimp Creole can be made 1 day in advance and refrigerated. To serve, reheat over medium heat, stirring occasionally (do not boil).

Taste of the South

Creole is a flavor fusion of French, Spanish, and African cuisines, whereas Cajun cooking stems from French Acadians (Cajuns) now living in Louisiana. Both Creole and Cajun foods boast significant usage of the culinary "holy trinity" of chopped onion, celery, and green bell pepper, but Creole foods are characteristic of more tomatoes, as in Shrimp Creole.

Hearty Cioppino

MAKES 6 SERVINGS
Prep: 20 min.; Cook: 1 hr., 20 min.

*Four types of succulent seafood mingle with spices and peppers
in fish stock for robust flavor. Make it a day or two in advance so it can chill overnight for the
flavor to develop. Wait to add cream or garnishes until just before reheating.*

1 red onion, chopped
1 fennel bulb, cored and
    chopped
2 serrano chile peppers,
    seeded and chopped
3 Tbsp. olive oil
1 orange or yellow bell
    pepper, chopped
2 garlic cloves, minced

1 (28-oz.) can crushed
    tomatoes, undrained
1 bay leaf
¼ tsp. dried thyme
¼ tsp. dried oregano
2 cups fish stock or chicken
    broth
1 cup dry white wine

2 medium zucchini, cubed
1½ tsp. dried rosemary
½ tsp. salt
⅛ tsp. freshly ground
    pepper

1 lb. sea or bay scallops
12 jumbo shrimp, peeled
    and deveined
12 mussels, scrubbed and
    debearded
1 lb. red snapper or other
    firm, white fish, cut into
    large chunks

1. Cook onion, fennel, and serrano chile peppers in oil over medium heat in a Dutch oven until onion is tender. Add bell pepper and garlic; cook, stirring constantly, 3 minutes.
2. Stir in tomatoes and next 5 ingredients. Bring to a boil; cover, reduce heat, and simmer 45 minutes.
3. Stir in zucchini and rosemary; bring to a simmer, and simmer 10 minutes. Remove and discard bay leaf. Stir in salt and pepper.
4. Add scallops and shrimp, and cook 3 minutes. Add mussels and fish; cook 4 more minutes or until mussels open and fish flakes easily when tested with a fork. Serve with garlic bread or grilled focaccia.

Taste of the South

Bouillon cubes or granules work in a pinch, but making your own fish stock is simple and really makes a difference in the flavor of this recipe. You need only a pot of simmering water, a few trimmings (including fish heads, shells, and bones), and some vegetables and seasonings. You can also make a specialty seafood stock from just shrimp shells and heads. Add a couple of celery ribs, carrots, a sliced onion, a bay leaf, and anything else that sounds appealing. After simmering to extract flavors, strain the mixture, and discard solids.

Cream Cheese Lasagna

MAKES 6 SERVINGS
Prep: 40 min., Cook: 30 min., Other: 10 min.

*Cream cheese may seem an unexpected ingredient in lasagna, but it makes the
layers of four types of cheese in this dish velvety and smooth.*

1 lb. ground beef
1 small onion, chopped
1 (8-oz.) can tomato sauce
1 (8-oz.) can tomato paste
¼ cup water
1 Tbsp. dried parsley flakes
2 tsp. dried Italian
   seasoning
1 tsp. beef bouillon
   granules
¼ tsp. garlic powder

1 (8-oz.) package cream
   cheese, softened
1 cup cottage cheese
¼ cup sour cream
2 large eggs, beaten

½ (16-oz.) package lasagna
   noodles, cooked and
   drained
1 (4-oz.) packaged sliced
   pepperoni
2 cups (8 oz.) shredded
   mozzarella cheese
½ cup grated Parmesan
   cheese

Garnish: bell pepper rings

1. Cook ground beef and onion in a large skillet, stirring
until it crumbles and is no longer pink; drain. Stir in
tomato sauce and next 6 ingredients; cook over low heat
10 minutes.

2. Combine cream cheese, cottage cheese, sour cream, and
eggs; stir well.

3. Spoon a small amount of meat sauce into a lightly
greased 13- x 9-inch baking dish. Layer with half each of
lasagna noodles, cheese mixture, pepperoni, meat sauce,
and mozzarella cheese; repeat layers. Sprinkle with
Parmesan cheese.

4. Cover and bake at 350° for 30 minutes. Let stand
10 minutes before serving. Garnish, if desired.

Vegetable Cheddar Chowder

MAKES 10 CUPS
Prep: 10 min., Cook: 25 min.

An entire pound of cheese smothers chunks of potatoes as this chowder bubbles.
A bit of hot sauce adds a punch.

3 cups water
3 chicken bouillon cubes
4 medium potatoes, peeled
    and diced
1 medium onion, sliced
1 cup thinly sliced carrot
½ cup diced green bell
    pepper

⅓ cup butter or margarine
⅓ cup all-purpose flour
3½ cups milk
4 cups (1 lb.) shredded
    sharp Cheddar cheese

1 (2-oz.) jar diced pimiento,
    drained
¼ tsp. hot sauce (optional)
Garnish: fresh parsley sprigs

1. Combine water and bouillon cubes in a Dutch oven; bring to a boil. Add diced potato and next 3 ingredients. Cover; simmer 12 minutes or until vegetables are tender.
2. Melt butter in a heavy saucepan over low heat; add flour, stirring until smooth. Cook 1 minute, stirring constantly. Gradually add milk; cook over medium heat, stirring constantly, until thickened and bubbly. Add cheese, stirring until melted.
3. Stir cheese sauce, pimiento, and, if desired, hot sauce into vegetable mixture. Cook chowder over low heat until thoroughly heated (do not boil). Garnish, if desired.

Taste of the South

Chowders developed in the coastal colonies as a way to enjoy the gifts of the sea. Fish chowders are popular all the way down to Florida; clam and cod chowders are favored farther north. Fresh water trout became a chowder ingredient for inlanders. Vegetable and corn chowders are found across the South due to the abundance of fresh vegetables; made with milk, these deluxe dishes may be thickened with flour or potatoes.

Southern
classics

Cornbread, greens, fried chicken, and peach cobbler—all favorites we grew up with that are dear to our hearts. Find the classics just like Grandma used to make along with updated versions while you peruse these pages of Southern gems.

our best
40 years
recipes

HOT-WATER CORNBREAD, PAGE 100

Watermelon Granita

MAKES 7 CUPS
Prep: 20 min.; Other: 8 hrs.,15 min.

*This recipe earned its perfect score three years ago.
It's so simple, yet so refreshing.*

8 cups seeded and cubed
    watermelon

1 (6-oz.) can frozen orange
    juice concentrate,
    thawed
1½ cups lemon-lime soft
    drink (we tested with
    7UP soft drink)

1. Process watermelon in a blender or food processor until smooth.

2. Stir together watermelon puree and remaining ingredients. Pour mixture into a 2-qt. glass bowl. Cover and freeze 8 hours, stirring occasionally.

3. Remove from freezer 15 minutes before serving. Stir with a fork, and spoon into glasses. Serve immediately.

From Our Kitchen

When looking for the perfect melon, choose one with no bruises, cuts, or dents; it should feel heavy for its size. If you don't have room in your refrigerator for a whole melon, cut it in halves or quarters, cover tightly with plastic wrap, and chill for up to one week.

Quick Buttermilk Biscuits

MAKES 8 BISCUITS
Prep: 5 min., Cook: 14 min.

We printed our favorite biscuit recipe in February 1988 and haven't found one since that tops it in terms of flavor, texture, or simplicity. It's the Southern-produced soft wheat flour that gives these biscuits their light-as-a-feather interior. The three basic ingredients are a snap to stir together, and if you pat the dough instead of rolling it, you can have the South's best biscuits ready for the oven in 5 minutes flat.

⅓ cup butter or margarine
2 cups self-rising soft wheat flour (we tested with White Lily Self-Rising Soft Wheat Flour)
¾ cup buttermilk

Butter or margarine, melted

1. Cut ⅓ cup butter into flour with a pastry blender until mixture is crumbly; add buttermilk, stirring until dry ingredients are moistened.

2. Turn dough out onto a lightly floured surface; knead 3 or 4 times.

3. Pat or roll dough to ¾-inch thickness; cut with a 2½-inch round cutter, and place on a baking sheet.

4. Bake at 425° for 12 to 14 minutes. Brush with melted butter.

Spoon Rolls

MAKES 14 ROLLS
Prep: 10 min., Cook: 20 min., Other: 5 min.

As with cornbread, baking these rolls in cast iron creates a wonderfully crisp crust. If you're a fan of muffin tops, bake these rolls in drop biscuit pans. They can also be baked in well-greased metal muffin pans.

1 (¼-oz.) envelope active
    dry yeast
2 cups warm water (100° to
    110°)

4 cups self-rising flour
¼ cup sugar
¾ cup butter or margarine,
    melted
1 large egg, lightly beaten

1. Combine yeast and 2 cups warm water in a large bowl; let stand 5 minutes.

2. Stir in flour and remaining ingredients until blended. Spoon into well-greased cast-iron muffin pans, filling two-thirds full, or into well-greased cast-iron drop biscuit pans, filling half full.

3. Bake at 400° for 20 minutes or until rolls are golden brown.

Note: Store unused batter in an airtight container in the refrigerator up to 1 week.

Taste of the South

Imagine a warm winter kitchen filled with the aroma of hot homemade rolls. If you think you don't have time for such a luxury, take heart. Comfort food doesn't always require a huge amount of time or effort. You can have these delicious rolls from *A Skillet Full of Traditional Southern Lodge Cast Iron Recipes and Memories*, a community cookbook benefiting our friends in the Historic Preservation Society of South Pittsburg, Tennessee, ready for the oven in 10 minutes. South Pittsburgh is home of the National Cornbread Festival and Lodge Manufacturing Company, makers of cast-iron cookware.

Hot-Water Cornbread

MAKES 9 SERVINGS
Prep: 5 min., Cook: 6 min. per batch

When Cynthia Ann Briscoe, a former staff member, wrote about her childhood memory of making crisp, pancakelike Hot-Water Cornbread in the January 2001 issue, some of us felt we'd had a deprived childhood! We voted this recipe a 25-year winner as we commemorated the silver anniversary of the publication of Southern Living Annual Recipes *in 2003. The pones are especially handy to have on hand as you sit down to a bowl of greens. The secret to their golden crispness? Why, the cast-iron skillet, of course, which keeps an even heat of the hot oil as you fry.*

2 cups white cornmeal
¼ tsp. baking powder
1¼ tsp. salt
1 tsp. sugar
¼ cup half-and-half
1 Tbsp. vegetable oil
1 to 2 cups boiling water

Vegetable oil

Softened butter

1. Combine cornmeal, baking powder, salt, and sugar in a large bowl; stir in half-and-half and 1 Tbsp. vegetable oil. Gradually add 1 to 2 cups boiling water to mixture, stirring until batter is the consistency of grits.
2. Pour vegetable oil to a depth of ½ inch into a large cast-iron skillet over medium-high heat.
3. Drop batter by ¼-cupfuls into hot oil; fry cornbread, in batches, 2 to 3 minutes on each side or until golden. Drain on paper towels. Serve with softened butter.

Taste of the South

Some Southern foods just wouldn't be the same cooked in anything except cast iron. Cast iron's ability to evenly distribute heat, as well as to stand up to high temperatures, makes it an admirable addition to any kitchen. If you haven't baked cornbread in cast iron before, give it a try. For the best crust, heat the pan first and add a small amount of bacon grease or oil. It's likely you'll never go back to using a baking pan again.

Chicken-Fried Steak

MAKES 4 SERVINGS
Prep: 10 min., Cook: 19 min.

Chicken-Fried Steak might just be the national entrée of Texas, so we challenged Lone Star State native Vanessa McNeil Rocchio from our Test Kitchens to develop the definitive version for our February 2001 issue. That she did, and our discriminating taste panel for this book tipped their hats to her recipe again. Vanessa recommends using an electric skillet to keep the frying temperature even, and she says the breading works well with chicken, too. Leftovers make great sandwiches; her dad piles chopped jalapeños on his.

2¼ tsp. salt, divided
1¾ tsp. black pepper, divided
4 (4-oz.) cube steaks
38 saltine crackers (1 sleeve), crushed
1¼ cups all-purpose flour, divided
½ tsp. ground red pepper
½ tsp. baking powder
4¾ cups milk, divided
2 large eggs

3½ cups peanut oil

Garnish: chopped fresh parsley

1. Sprinkle ¼ tsp. salt and ¼ tsp. black pepper evenly over steaks. Combine cracker crumbs, 1 cup flour, 1 tsp. salt, ½ tsp. black pepper, red pepper, and baking powder. Whisk together ¾ cup milk and eggs. Dredge steaks in cracker mixture; dip in milk mixture, and dredge again in cracker mixture.

2. Pour oil into a 12-inch skillet; heat to 360°. (Do not use a nonstick skillet.) Fry steaks 3 to 4 minutes. Turn and fry 2 to 3 minutes or until golden brown. Remove steaks to a wire rack in a jelly-roll pan. Keep steaks warm in a 225° oven. Carefully drain hot oil, reserving cooked bits and 1 Tbsp. drippings in skillet.

3. Whisk together remaining 4 cups milk, remaining ¼ cup flour, remaining 1 tsp. salt, and remaining 1 tsp. black pepper. Add milk mixture to reserved drippings in skillet; cook, whisking constantly, over medium-high heat 10 to 12 minutes or until thickened. Serve gravy with steaks. Garnish, if desired.

Taste of the South

The secret to Vanessa's Chicken-Fried Steak is in the breading. "Saltine crackers make a great crust," she says. To achieve maximum flavor, Vanessa suggests firmly pushing the cracker crumbs into the cube steaks to fill the crevices and to keep the steaks from shrinking as they cook.

Our Best Southern Fried Chicken

MAKES 4 SERVINGS
Prep: 25 min., Cook: 30 min. per batch, Other: 8 hrs.

This dish really lives up to its name. It was the brainchild of Nashville author and food historian John Egerton, who fried it up in our Test Kitchens for the September 1995 issue. He combined techniques from several respected sources to create this version. Don't skip the overnight soak in salty water because that's the secret to making the chicken extra tender and juicy. Buy a chicken that hasn't been injected with a salty solution or your chicken may be too salty. Our homemade brine is more effective and easy to do. Just refrigerate the chicken overnight in a large pitcher; then drain and pat it dry before breading.

3 qt. water
1 Tbsp. salt
1 (2½- to 3-lb.) whole
　chicken, cut up

1 tsp. salt
1 tsp. pepper
1 cup all-purpose flour

2 cups vegetable oil
¼ cup bacon drippings

1. Combine water and 1 Tbsp. salt; add chicken. Cover and chill 8 hours. Drain chicken; rinse chicken with cold water, and pat dry.

2. Combine 1 tsp. salt and 1 tsp. pepper; sprinkle half of pepper mixture over chicken. Combine remaining pepper mixture and flour in a large zip-top freezer bag. Place 2 pieces of chicken in bag; seal. Shake to evenly coat. Remove chicken, and repeat procedure with remaining chicken, 2 pieces at a time.

3. Combine oil and bacon drippings in a 12-inch cast-iron skillet or chicken fryer; heat to 360°. Add chicken, skin sides down, a few pieces at a time. Cover and cook 6 minutes; uncover and cook 9 minutes. Turn chicken pieces; cover and cook 6 minutes. Uncover and cook 5 to 9 minutes, turning pieces during the last 3 minutes for even browning, if necessary. Drain on paper towels.

Chicken Cobbler Casserole

MAKES 4 SERVINGS
Prep: 35 min., Cook: 15 min.

This dish combines the robust flavors and cheesy bread topping of French onion soup with chicken pot pie. We created it in our kitchens to marry the favorite crusty topping of a classic Southern dessert with a savory sensation.

6 Tbsp. melted butter, divided
4 cups cubed sourdough rolls
⅓ cup grated Parmesan cheese
2 Tbsp. chopped fresh parsley

2 medium-size sweet onions, sliced
1 (8-oz.) package sliced fresh mushrooms

1 cup white wine
1 (10¾-oz.) can cream of mushroom soup
½ cup drained and chopped jarred roasted red bell peppers
2½ cups shredded cooked chicken

1. Toss 4 Tbsp. melted butter with next 3 ingredients; set aside.

2. Sauté onions in remaining 2 Tbsp. butter in a large skillet over medium-high heat 15 minutes or until golden brown. Add mushrooms, and sauté 5 minutes.

3. Stir in wine and remaining 3 ingredients; cook, stirring constantly, 5 minutes or until bubbly. Spoon mixture into a lightly greased 9-inch square baking dish; top evenly with bread mixture.

4. Bake at 400° for 15 minutes or until golden brown.

Chicken and Dumplings

MAKES 8 SERVINGS
Prep: 30 min.; Cook: 1 hr., 30 min.

Southerners are both passionate and opinionated about the various recipes for Chicken and Dumplings. The dumplings must be rolled, or they must be dropped. Celery is either the salvation or the ruination of the broth. And don't even think about asking if you could use a package of chicken breasts instead of the whole bird. These dumplings are dropped and there's no celery in sight, but the extra flavor generated from starting with a whole chicken made us unanimously adore this version.

1 (2½-lb.) whole chicken,
   cut up
2½ tsp. salt, divided
¾ tsp. black pepper, divided
½ tsp. garlic powder
½ tsp. dried thyme
¼ tsp. ground red pepper

1 tsp. chicken bouillon
   granules

3 cups self-rising flour
½ tsp. poultry seasoning
⅓ cup shortening
2 tsp. bacon drippings
1 cup milk

Freshly ground black pepper

1. Cover chicken with water, and bring to a boil in a large Dutch oven. Add 1½ tsp. salt, ½ tsp. black pepper, and next 3 ingredients; cover, reduce heat, and simmer 1 hour. Remove chicken, reserving broth in Dutch oven; cool chicken. Skim fat from broth; bring to a simmer.

2. Skin, bone, and coarsely chop chicken. Add chopped chicken, bouillon, remaining 1 tsp. salt, and remaining ¼ tsp. pepper to broth. Return to simmer.

3. Combine flour and poultry seasoning in a bowl. Cut in shortening and bacon drippings with a pastry blender until mixture is crumbly. Add milk, stirring until dry ingredients are moistened.

4. Turn dough out onto a lightly floured surface. Roll out to ⅛-inch thickness; cut into 1-inch pieces.

5. Bring broth mixture to a boil. Drop dumplings, a few at a time, into boiling broth, stirring gently. Reduce heat, cover, and simmer, stirring often, for 25 minutes. Top each serving with freshly ground black pepper.

From Our Kitchen

• Skimming off fat from warm broth can be tricky. If you boil the chicken the night before and refrigerate it in the broth, all the fat will collect on the surface, making it easy to remove. Plus, the chicken will be cool when you're ready to pull it off the bone.
• The even distribution of ingredients is key to dumpling success. Break shortening into small pieces, and use solidified bacon drippings.
• The more you handle the dough, the tougher your dumplings are likely to be. So as soon as you have a moist ball of dough, resist the urge to keep working it.

Classic Fried Catfish

MAKES 6 TO 8 SERVINGS
Prep: 15 min., Cook: 6 min. per batch

For an extra-crispy crust, use stone-ground yellow cornmeal, if available.

1 cup yellow cornmeal
⅓ cup all-purpose flour
1¼ tsp. ground red pepper
½ tsp. garlic powder
2½ tsp. salt
12 catfish fillets (about
    3¾ lb.)

Vegetable oil

1. Combine first 4 ingredients and 2 tsp. salt in a large shallow dish. Sprinkle catfish fillets evenly with remaining ½ tsp. salt, and dredge in cornmeal mixture, coating evenly.

2. Pour vegetable oil to a depth of 2 inches into a Dutch oven; heat to 350°. Fry fillets, in batches, 5 to 6 minutes or until golden; drain on paper towels.

Note: For a quick weeknight version, skip the deep fryer. Cook catfish in 2 Tbsp. hot oil, per batch, in a nonstick skillet 5 minutes on each side.

Then & Now

Growing up on the Tennessee River, *Southern Living* Test Kitchens Director Lyda Jones Burnette learned that every Friday night meant one thing: a catfish fry at her family's cabin. "Grandmommy served up perfect fried catfish with all the trimmings. Carrying on the tradition, I prepare these recipes at my family's get-togethers," she says.

Fried Okra Salad

MAKES 6 SERVINGS
Prep. 20 min., Cook: 2 min. per batch

*Drizzled with tangy Lemon Dressing, this salad
transforms even the fussiest eaters into okra lovers.*

1½ cups self-rising yellow
    cornmeal
1 tsp. salt
1 lb. fresh okra
1½ cups buttermilk

Peanut oil

1 head Bibb lettuce
1 large tomato, chopped
    (about 1 cup)
1 medium-size sweet
    onion, thinly sliced
    (about ¾ cup)
1 medium-size green bell
    pepper, chopped
Lemon Dressing
3 bacon slices, cooked
    and crumbled

1. Combine cornmeal and salt. Dip okra in buttermilk; dredge in cornmeal mixture.

2. Pour peanut oil to a depth of 2 inches into a Dutch oven or deep cast-iron skillet; heat to 375°. Fry okra, in batches, 2 minutes or until golden, turning once. Drain on a wire rack over paper towels.

3. Arrange lettuce leaves on a serving platter; top with tomato, onion slices, and bell pepper. Drizzle with Lemon Dressing. Top with fried okra, and sprinkle with crumbled bacon. Serve immediately.

Lemon Dressing

MAKES ¾ CUP
Prep: 5 min.

This dressing also makes a tangy dipping sauce for steamed artichokes or asparagus.

¼ cup fresh lemon juice
3 Tbsp. chopped fresh
    basil
1 tsp. salt
1 tsp. paprika
½ tsp. pepper
¼ cup olive oil

1. Combine first 5 ingredients in a bowl. Add oil, whisking until combined.

Fried Okra

MAKES 4 SERVINGS
Prep: 11 min., Cook: 3 min. per batch

We'd almost forgotten about this fried okra recipe from our May 1987 issue, but two folks on our staff who still make it for their families refreshed our memories. The sliced okra is folded in beaten egg whites and breaded with homemade soft breadcrumbs before being fried into the crispiest morsels you'll ever taste. Add a light sprinkling of salt, and your family will devour these golden nuggets.

1 lb. fresh okra
3 Tbsp. all-purpose flour

2 egg whites
1½ cups soft breadcrumbs
(fresh)

Vegetable oil
Salt

1. Wash okra, and drain well. Remove tips and stem ends; cut okra into ½-inch slices. Place flour and okra in a zip-top freezer bag. Seal bag, and shake until okra is coated.

2. Beat egg whites at high speed with an electric mixer until stiff peaks form; fold in okra. Stir in breadcrumbs, coating well.

3. Pour oil to a depth of 2 inches into a large skillet or Dutch oven; heat to 375°. Fry okra, in batches, 3 minutes or until golden brown, stirring as little as necessary for even browning. Drain on paper towels. Sprinkle with salt.

From Our Kitchen

We fry okra in batches to make sure not to crowd the nuggets. Plenty of room to sizzle in the hot oil generates extra-crispy crust.

Barbecue Beans

MAKES 10 SERVINGS
Prep: 25 min., Cook: 1 hr.

When we ran this recipe in 1994, it called for 10 slices of bacon. It's still great that way, but you can use half the bacon—or opt for turkey bacon—and still get fabulous results.

½ medium onion, chopped

½ lb. ground beef
  (optional)

10 bacon slices, cooked and
  crumbled

⅔ cup firmly packed brown
  sugar

¾ cup barbecue sauce

1 (15-oz.) can butterbeans,
  rinsed and drained

1 (15-oz.) can kidney beans,
  rinsed and drained

1 (15-oz.) can pork and
  beans, undrained

2 Tbsp. molasses

2 tsp. Dijon mustard

½ tsp. salt

½ tsp. pepper

½ tsp. chili powder

1. Cook onion and, if desired, ground beef in a Dutch oven, stirring until meat crumbles and is no longer pink; drain. Stir in bacon and remaining ingredients; spoon into a lightly greased 2½-qt. baking dish. Chill 8 hours, if desired.

2. Bake bean mixture at 350° for 1 hour, stirring once.

Grits and Greens

MAKES 4 TO 6 SERVINGS
Prep: 8 min., Cook: 34 min.

Stone-ground grits add a more pronounced corn flavor to this dish, as well as a heartier texture. If you prefer, sprinkle chopped cooked ham instead of bacon over the grits before serving.

1 cup whipping cream
1 (32-oz.) container chicken
    broth, divided
1 cup stone-ground grits

½ (1-lb.) package chopped
    fresh collard greens

¼ cup butter
1 cup freshly grated
    Parmesan cheese
½ tsp. freshly ground black
    pepper
6 slices bacon, cooked and
    crumbled

1. Combine whipping cream and 3 cups chicken broth in a large saucepan; bring to a boil. Gradually stir in grits. Cook over medium heat until mixture returns to a boil; cover, reduce heat, and simmer, stirring occasionally, 25 minutes, or until creamy.

2. While grits cook, pour remaining 1 cup chicken broth into a large skillet; add greens. Bring to a boil; cover, reduce heat, and simmer 15 minutes or until greens are tender and broth is absorbed.

3. Add butter, cheese, and pepper to grits, stirring well. Stir in cooked greens. Cook 1 minute or until grits and greens are thoroughly heated. Sprinkle with crumbled bacon, and serve immediately.

Then & Now

Collards are a country classic—a staple of true Southern cuisine. Today, we cook them faster and serve them in new and different ways.

Inexpensive fresh collards are available much of the year. In this recipe, we take the simplest route by using the prewashed and cut variety. If you choose to use fresh collard greens, start with a 1-lb. bunch with crisp, dark green leaves. Remove and discard stems and any discolored spots; wash the leaves in plenty of cold water. Roughly chop leaves to reduce the cooking time.

Vidalia Onion Pie with Mushrooms

MAKES 4 TO 6 SERVINGS
Prep: 20 min., Cook: 45 min.

1 large Vidalia onion,
    halved and thinly sliced
2 cups sliced shiitake
    mushrooms
1 Tbsp. olive oil

4 large eggs
1 cup whipping cream
1 Tbsp. chopped fresh
    thyme
1½ tsp. salt
1 tsp. pepper
⅛ tsp. ground nutmeg
1 frozen (9-inch) deep-dish
    pastry shell, thawed

1. Sauté onion and mushrooms in hot oil in a large skillet over medium heat 15 minutes or until tender.

2. Stir together eggs and next 5 ingredients in a large bowl; stir in onion mixture. Spoon mixture into pastry shell, and place on a baking sheet.

3. Bake on lower oven rack at 350° for 45 minutes or until done.

Taste of the South

The Vidalia onion took root in Toombs County, Georgia, when in the spring of 1931 a farmer named Mose Coleman discovered that the onions he had planted were not hot but sweet. The onions were popular and sold so quickly that by the 1970s they had become a major crop in the area. Georgia's state legislature gave Vidalia onions legal status by limiting their production to 20 counties.

Hearty Black-Eyed Peas

MAKES 8 SERVINGS
Prep: 20 min., Cook: 1 hr.

*These are not your grandmother's black-eyed peas.
You'll love the bite from the jalapeño peppers.*

1 (16-oz.) package dried
    black-eyed peas
4 cups water
1 medium onion, chopped
½ tsp. pepper
¾ tsp. salt
1 (1-lb.) ham steak, cut into
    ½-inch cubes, or 1 ham
    hock
4 whole jalapeño peppers
    (optional)

1. Bring first 6 ingredients and, if desired, jalapeños to a boil in a Dutch oven; cover, reduce heat, and simmer 1 hour or until peas are tender.

Creamy Mashed Potatoes

MAKES 4 SERVINGS
Prep: 5 min., Cook: 10 min., Other: 5 min.

These quick potatoes with a hint of garlic pair perfectly with Chicken-Fried Steak (page 102).

3 Tbsp. butter
1 large garlic clove, minced

1 (22-oz.) bag frozen
    mashed potatoes
2⅓ cups milk

½ tsp. salt
¼ tsp. pepper

1. Melt butter in a small saucepan over medium-low heat; add garlic, and sauté until tender. Remove from saucepan, and set aside.

2. Prepare mashed potatoes in saucepan according to package directions, using 2⅓ cups milk and stirring with a wire whisk.

3. Stir in garlic mixture, salt, and pepper. Let potatoes stand 5 minutes before serving.

Old-Fashioned Gingerbread

MAKES 12 TO 15 SERVINGS
Prep: 15 min., Cook: 35 min., Other: 10 min.

Never mind if you don't have Southern Living Our Best Recipes, *published in 1970. We couldn't resist publishing in this collection this gem from that book. We retested it, and we found no need to change a thing—except perhaps to suggest serving it with ice cream.*

⅓ cup shortening
1 cup sugar
2 large eggs
½ cup molasses
1 (8-oz.) carton sour cream

2 cups all-purpose flour
1 tsp. baking soda
½ tsp. salt
1½ tsp. ground ginger
¼ tsp. ground cloves

1. Beat shortening and sugar at medium speed with an electric mixer until creamy. Add eggs, 1 at a time, beating well after each addition. Stir in molasses and sour cream.

2. Combine flour and remaining 4 ingredients; stir into molasses mixture. Beat 2 minutes at medium speed. Pour batter into a lightly greased 13- x 9-inch pan.

3. Bake at 350° for 32 to 35 minutes or until a wooden pick inserted in center comes out clean. Cool in pan on a wire rack 10 minutes. Serve warm.

Cream Cheese Pound Cake

MAKES 10 TO 12 SERVINGS
Prep: 15 min.; Cook: 1 hr., 45 min.; Other: 15 min.

Postman Eddy McGee, of Elkin, North Carolina, bakes Cream Cheese Pound Cake every Christmas for the lucky folks on his route and shared it with us in our November 1995 issue. We gave it our highest rating then in a tube pan and again in November 2001 when submitted by Yolanda Powers, of Decatur, Alabama, baked in a shapely Bundt pan and with a brazen double the amount of vanilla extract. The baking time is the same in either pan, so take your pick.

1½ cups butter, softened
1 (8-oz.) package cream
   cheese, softened
3 cups sugar
6 large eggs

3 cups all-purpose flour
⅛ tsp. salt
1 Tbsp. vanilla extract

1. Beat butter and cream cheese at medium speed with an electric mixer until creamy. Gradually add sugar, beating well. Add eggs, 1 at a time, beating just until yellow disappears.
2. Combine flour and salt; gradually add to butter mixture, beating at low speed just until blended. Stir in vanilla. Spoon batter into a greased and floured 10-inch Bundt or tube pan.
3. Bake at 300° for 1 hour and 45 minutes or until a long wooden pick inserted in center comes out clean. Cool in pan on a wire rack 15 minutes; remove from pan, and cool completely on wire rack.

From Our Kitchen

Make the Perfect Pound Cake
• Use name-brand ingredients. Store brands of sugar are often more finely ground than name brands, yielding more sugar per cup, which can cause a cake to fall. Store brands of butter can contain more liquid fat; flours can have more hard wheat, making the cake heavy.
• Measure accurately. Extra sugar or leavening causes a cake to fall; extra flour makes it dry.
• For maximum volume, use ingredients at room temperature. We like to premeasure our ingredients and line them up in the order listed. That way, if interrupted, we're less likely to make a mistake when we return to the recipe.
• Beat softened butter (and cream cheese or vegetable shortening) at medium speed with an electric mixture until creamy. This can take from 1 to 7 minutes, depending on the power of your mixer. Gradually add sugar, continuing to beat until light and fluffy. These steps are important because they whip air into the batter so the cake will rise during baking.
• Add the eggs one at a time, beating the batter just until the yellow yolk disappears. Overbeating the eggs can cause the batter to overflow the sides of the pan when baked, or it can create a fragile crust that crumbles and separates from the cake as it cools.
• To prevent the batter from curdling, always add the dry ingredients alternately with the liquid, beginning and ending with the dry ingredients. Mix just until blended after each addition. Overmixing the batter once the flour has been added creates a tough and rubbery cake.

Brown Sugar Pound Cake

MAKES 12 SERVINGS
Prep: 20 min.; Cook: 1 hr., 15 min.; Other: 45 min.

1 cup shortening
½ cup butter, softened
1 (16-oz.) box light brown
   sugar
5 large eggs

3 cups all-purpose flour
½ tsp. salt
½ tsp. baking powder
1 cup evaporated milk
1 tsp. maple flavoring or
   vanilla extract

Brown Sugar Glaze

1. Beat shortening, butter, and brown sugar at medium speed with an electric mixer 2 minutes or until creamy. Add eggs, 1 at a time, beating well after each addition.
2. Combine flour, salt, and baking powder; add alternately with milk, beginning and ending with flour mixture. Stir in flavoring. Pour batter into a greased and floured 12-cup Bundt pan.
3. Bake at 300° for 1 hour and 15 minutes or until a long wooden pick inserted in center comes out clean. Cool in pan on a wire rack 15 minutes; remove from pan, and cool completely on a wire rack. Pour Brown Sugar Glaze over cake. Let cake stand 30 minutes or until glaze is firm.

Brown Sugar Glaze

MAKES 2 CUPS
Prep: 3 min., Cook: 6 min.

½ cup butter
1 cup firmly packed brown
   sugar

¼ cup milk
3 cups powdered sugar
1 tsp. vanilla extract

1. Melt butter in a medium saucepan over medium heat. Whisk in brown sugar, and cook 1 minute.
2. Add milk, powdered sugar, and vanilla; whisk until creamy. Remove from heat and immediately pour over cooled cake.

Then & Now

After debuting in an early issue of *Southern Living*, this recipe was prominently featured in *Southern Living Our Best Recipes Cookbook*, published in 1970. The original recipe used margarine, but we preferred butter in our recent recipe test to confirm the "wow" factor of this pound cake.

Sour Cream Pound Cake

MAKES 10 TO 12 SERVINGS
Prep: 20 min.; Cook: 1 hr., 30 min.; Other: 10 min.

Leavened with a smidgen of baking soda, the fine-crumb texture and delicate lemon-almond flavor of Sour Cream Pound Cake pairs perfectly with summer fruits. We especially love it with fresh peaches, but feel free to substitute nectarines or berries if you'd like.

1½ cups butter, softened
3 cups sugar
6 large eggs

3 cups all-purpose flour
½ tsp. salt
¼ tsp. baking soda
1 (8-oz.) container sour cream
1 tsp. lemon extract
¼ tsp. almond extract

Whipped Cream
Peach slices

1. Beat butter at medium speed with an electric mixer until creamy. Gradually add sugar, beating at medium speed until light and fluffy. Add eggs, 1 at a time, beating just until yolk disappears.

2. Sift together flour, salt, and baking soda. Add to butter mixture alternately with sour cream, beginning and ending with flour mixture. Beat batter at low speed just until blended after each addition. Stir in extracts. Pour into a greased and floured 12-cup tube pan.

3. Bake at 325° for 1 hour and 20 minutes to 1½ hours or until a long wooden pick inserted in center of cake comes out clean. Cool in pan on a wire rack 10 minutes. Remove cake from pan, and cool completely on wire rack. Serve with Whipped Cream and peaches.

Whipped Cream

MAKES ABOUT 2 CUPS
Prep: 5 min.

Try replacing the tsp. of vanilla extract with a Tbsp. of your favorite liqueur. Almond-flavored liqueur is a perfect match for peaches; orange liqueur pairs especially well with berries.

1 cup whipping cream
2 Tbsp. powdered sugar
1 tsp. vanilla extract

1. Beat whipping cream at low speed with an electric mixer until foamy; increase speed to medium-high, and gradually add powdered sugar, beating until soft peaks form. Stir in vanilla.

From Our Kitchen

Bake this delicious cake, and store it at room temperature up to three days; or place it in a large zip-top freezer bag, and store it in the freezer up to two months.

Classic Strawberry Shortcake

MAKES 8 SERVINGS
Prep: 20 min., Cook: 15 min., Other: 2 hrs.

Don't let the thought of making biscuits scare you. We created this streamlined version in our kitchens so there's no rolling or cutting involved—it's just a tender dough that you drop onto a baking sheet. Fresh berries and a lavish crown of whipped cream make the biscuits irresistible.

2 (16-oz.) containers fresh
  strawberries, quartered
¾ cup sugar, divided
¼ tsp. almond extract
  (optional)

1 cup whipping cream
2 Tbsp. sugar

2¾ cups all-purpose flour
4 tsp. baking powder
¾ cup cold butter, cut up

2 large eggs, lightly beaten
1 (8-oz.) container sour
  cream
1 tsp. vanilla extract

Garnish: fresh mint sprigs

1. Combine strawberries, ½ cup sugar, and, if desired, almond extract. Cover berry mixture, and let stand 2 hours.

2. Beat whipping cream at medium speed with an electric mixer until foamy; gradually add 2 Tbsp. sugar, beating until soft peaks form. Cover and chill up to 2 hours.

3. Combine flour, remaining ¼ cup sugar, and baking powder in a large bowl; cut butter into flour mixture with a pastry blender until crumbly.

4. Whisk together eggs, sour cream, and vanilla until blended; add to flour mixture, stirring just until dry ingredients are moistened. Drop dough by lightly greased ⅓-cupfuls onto a lightly greased baking sheet. (Coat cup with vegetable cooking spray after each drop.)

5. Bake at 450° for 12 to 15 minutes or until golden.

6. Split shortcakes in half horizontally. Spoon about ½ cup berry mixture onto each shortcake bottom; top each with 1 rounded Tbsp. chilled whipped cream, and cover with tops. Serve with remaining whipped cream. Garnish, if desired.

Strawberry Jam Shortcakes: Prepare recipe as directed. Before topping shortcake bottoms with strawberry mixture, stir together ¼ cup strawberry jam and 2 Tbsp. chopped fresh mint. Spread cut sides of bottom shortcake halves evenly with jam mixture. Proceed with recipe as directed.

From Our Kitchen

You can bake the biscuits ahead and freeze them, wrapped in foil and stored in a zip-top freezer bag. Defrost them the morning of the day you plan to serve them. Cut and sugar berries in the morning as well, and store them in the fridge until you're ready for them. Whip the cream up to 2 hours before serving. (If you prefer your shortcake warm, reheat the biscuits in a 350° oven for 5 to 7 minutes.) Assemble everything at the table for a dazzling presentation.

Chocolate-Praline Cake

MAKES 12 SERVINGS
Prep: 30 min., Cook: 18 min., Other: 10 min.

Chocolate and pralines are perfect partners in this delightfully Southern cake.

1 cup boiling water
1 cup butter or margarine
¼ cup unsweetened cocoa,
   cut into pieces

½ cup buttermilk
2 large eggs
1 tsp. baking soda
1 tsp. vanilla extract
2 cups sugar
2 cups all-purpose flour
½ tsp. salt

Chocolate Frosting
Praline Topping
Garnish: pecan halves

1. Pour boiling water over butter and cocoa, stirring until butter melts and mixture is smooth.

2. Beat buttermilk, eggs, baking soda, and vanilla at medium speed with an electric mixer until smooth. Add butter mixture to buttermilk mixture, beating until well blended. Combine sugar, flour, and salt; gradually add to buttermilk mixture, beating until blended.

3. Coat 3 (9-inch) round cakepans with cooking spray; line with wax paper. Pour batter evenly into pans. Bake at 350° for 16 to 18 minutes or until a wooden pick comes out clean and cake pulls away from sides of pan. Cool in pans on wire racks 10 minutes. Remove from pans, and cool completely on wire racks.

4. Spread about ½ cup Chocolate Frosting between cake layers; spread remaining on sides of cake. Pour warm Praline Topping slowly over the center of cake, spreading to edges, allowing some topping to run over sides. Freeze, if desired; thaw at room temperature 4 to 6 hours. Garnish, if desired.

Chocolate Frosting

MAKES ABOUT 2 CUPS
Prep: 5 min., Other: 15 min.

1 (12-oz.) package semi-
    sweet chocolate
    morsels
⅓ cup whipping cream
¼ cup butter or margarine,
    cut into pieces

1. Microwave chocolate morsels and whipping cream in a glass bowl at HIGH 1 minute or until morsels are melted. Whisk until smooth. Gradually add butter, whisking until smooth. Cool, whisking often, 10 to 15 minutes or until spreading consistency.

Praline Topping

MAKES ABOUT 1¾ CUPS
Prep: 10 min., Cook: 3 min.

Do not prepare this frosting ahead because it'll harden very quickly.

¼ cup butter or margarine
1 cup firmly packed brown
    sugar
⅓ cup whipping cream

1 cup powdered sugar
1 tsp. vanilla extract
1 cup chopped pecans,
    toasted

1. Bring first 3 ingredients to a boil in a 2-qt. saucepan over medium heat, stirring often; boil 1 minute. Remove from heat.
2. Whisk in powdered sugar and vanilla until smooth. Stir in toasted pecans, stirring gently 2 minutes or until mixture begins to cool and thicken slightly. Pour over cake immediately.

Pecan Pie Cheesecake

MAKES 16 SERVINGS
Prep: 15 min., Cook: 50 min., Other: 9 hrs.

We put this $100,000 grand-prize-winning cheesecake from our first annual Reader Recipe Cook-off in 2002 up against our most memorable dessert recipes, and it maneuvered to the top tier. Ginnie Prater, of Anniston, Alabama, started with a frozen pecan pie to keep it simple and deftly stirred up a cheesecake batter that marries the two flavors in Southern bliss.

1 (2-lb., 4-oz.) package frozen pecan pie (we tested with Mrs. Smith's Special Recipe Southern Pecan Pie)
2 cups graham cracker crumbs
½ cup granulated sugar
½ cup butter, melted
¼ tsp. ground cinnamon

2 (8-oz.) packages cream cheese, softened
2 large eggs
⅔ cup sour cream
½ cup half-and-half
1 tsp. vanilla extract

1 cup powdered sugar
1 Tbsp. all-purpose flour
16 pecan halves

1. Thaw pecan pie according to package directions. Cut into 20 thin slices, keeping wedges intact; set aside. Stir together cracker crumbs and next 3 ingredients; press mixture onto bottom and 1½ inches up sides of a 10-inch springform pan.

2. Arrange 10 pecan pie wedges in a spoke design in prepared pan, placing 1 cut side of each wedge on crust with narrow end toward center of pan. Reserve remaining pecan pie wedges for another use.

3. Beat cream cheese until smooth; add eggs, 1 at a time, beating after each addition. Add sour cream, half-and-half, and vanilla; beat until blended.

4. Fold in powdered sugar and flour. Carefully pour cream cheese mixture evenly over pecan pie wedges in pan, making sure wedges remain in place. Arrange pecan halves evenly around edge of cheesecake.

5. Bake at 325° for 45 to 50 minutes. Turn off oven, and let cheesecake stand in oven 1 hour. Remove to a wire rack, and cool completely. Chill at least 8 hours or overnight before serving.

Blackberry Cobbler

MAKES 6 TO 8 SERVINGS
Prep: 10 min., Cook: 45 min.

Serve Sugared Piecrust Sticks alongside this juicy dessert to delight the cobbler crust fans in your family.

1⅓ cups sugar
½ cup all-purpose flour
½ cup butter or margarine, melted
2 tsp. vanilla extract
2 (14-oz.) bags frozen blackberries, unthawed

½ (15-oz.) package refrigerated piecrusts
1 Tbsp. sugar

Vanilla ice cream (optional)
Sugared Piecrust Sticks (optional)

1. Stir together first 4 ingredients in a large bowl. Gently stir in blackberries until sugar mixture is crumbly. Spoon fruit mixture into a lightly greased 11- x 7-inch baking dish.

2. Cut 1 piecrust into ½-inch-wide strips, and arrange strips diagonally over blackberry mixture. Sprinkle top with 1 Tbsp. sugar.

3. Bake at 425° for 45 minutes or until crust is golden brown and center is bubbly. Serve with ice cream and Sugared Piecrust Sticks, if desired.

Sugared Piecrust Sticks: Cut 1 refrigerated piecrust into ½-inch-wide strips. Sprinkle strips with 1 Tbsp. sugar; place on a lightly greased baking sheet. Bake at 425° for 6 to 8 minutes or until golden brown.

Double-Crust Peach Cobbler

MAKES 8 SERVINGS
Prep: 30 min., Cook: 38 min.

8 cups sliced fresh peaches
(about 5 lb. peaches) or
2 (20-oz.) packages
frozen unsweetened
peach slices, thawed
2 cups sugar
3 Tbsp. all-purpose flour
½ tsp. ground nutmeg
1 tsp. almond or vanilla
extract
⅓ cup butter or margarine

Double-Crust Pastry

1. Stir together first 4 ingredients in a Dutch oven; set aside until syrup forms. Bring peach mixture to a boil; reduce heat to low, and cook 10 minutes or until tender. Remove from heat; add almond extract and butter, stirring until butter melts.

2. Roll half of Double Crust Pastry to ⅛-inch thickness on a lightly floured surface; cut into a 9-inch square. Spoon half of peaches into a lightly buttered 9-inch square pan; top with pastry square. Bake at 475° for 12 minutes or until lightly browned. Spoon remaining peaches over baked pastry square.

3. Roll remaining pastry to ⅛-inch thickness, and cut into 1-inch strips; arrange in lattice design over peaches. Bake 15 to 18 more minutes or until browned.

Double-Crust Pastry

MAKES 1 DOUBLE-CRUST PASTRY
Prep: 8 min.

2 cups all-purpose flour
1 tsp. salt
⅔ cup shortening
4 to 6 Tbsp. ice water

1. Combine flour and salt; cut in shortening with a pastry blender until mixture resembles small peas. Sprinkle with ice water, 1 Tbsp. at a time, stirring with a fork until dry ingredients are moistened. Shape into a ball. Wrap in plastic wrap, and chill until ready to use.

Then & Now

Double-Crust Peach Cobbler debuted in our June 1977 issue, before the *Southern Living® Annual Recipes* book series started. The recipe made such an impression on our staff in 1990 that we shared it in that December issue as an All-Time Best Desserts, marking the 25th anniversary of *Southern Living*. Its double crust and perfectly sweetened and spiced peach filling made it a winner in this race, too.

Sweet Potato-Apple Cobbler

MAKES 12 SERVINGS
Prep: 40 min.; Cook: 1 hr., 45 min.

This fall-friendly recipe makes a scrumptious finale to a fine meal. Tart Granny Smith apples are enhanced by sweet potatoes, a blend of sugars, and cool-weather spices. An entire cup of pecans and a finishing touch of Bourbon Whipped Cream make it a genuine Southern gem.

4 medium-size sweet potatoes

2 Granny Smith apples,
    peeled and thinly sliced

1½ cups orange juice
½ cup granulated sugar
¼ cup firmly packed dark
    brown sugar
3 Tbsp. all-purpose flour
½ tsp. ground cinnamon
¼ tsp. ground nutmeg
¼ tsp. salt
½ cup butter or margarine,
    divided

1 cup chopped pecans, toasted
1 (15-oz.) package
    refrigerated piecrusts

2 tsp. granulated sugar

Bourbon Whipped Cream
    (optional)

1. Pierce sweet potatoes several times with a fork, and place on an aluminum foil-lined baking sheet.
2. Bake at 400° for 1 hour or until done; cool slightly. Peel and cut crosswise into ¼-inch-thick slices.
3. Place apple slices in an even layer in a lightly greased 13- x- 9-inch baking dish; top with sweet potato slices.
4. Stir together 1½ cups orange juice and next 6 ingredients. Pour over sweet potato mixture. Dot with 6 Tbsp. butter.
5. Sprinkle ½ cup chopped pecans on a cutting board. Unfold 1 piecrust, and place on pecans; gently roll piecrust dough into pecans. Cut with a leaf-shaped cookie cutter; place leaves over sweet potato mixture. Repeat procedure with remaining ½ cup chopped pecans and piecrust.
6. Microwave remaining 2 Tbsp. butter in a 1-cup glass measuring cup at HIGH 20 to 30 seconds or until melted. Brush butter over crust, and sprinkle with 2 tsp. granulated sugar.
7. Bake at 400° for 45 minutes or until golden. Serve warm with Bourbon Whipped Cream, if desired.

Bourbon Whipped Cream

MAKES ABOUT 2 CUPS
Prep: 5 min.

1 cup whipping cream
2 Tbsp. granulated sugar
1 Tbsp. bourbon

1. Beat whipping cream and sugar at medium speed with an electric mixer until stiff peaks form; stir in bourbon.

Warm Apple-Buttermilk Custard Pie

MAKES 8 SERVINGS
Prep: 30 min.; Cook: 1 hr., 10 min.; Other: 1 hr.

½ (15-oz.) package
    refrigerated piecrusts

½ cup butter or margarine,
    divided
2 Granny Smith apples,
    peeled and sliced
½ cup granulated sugar
¾ tsp. ground cinnamon,
    divided

1⅓ cups granulated sugar
4 large eggs
2 Tbsp. all-purpose
    flour
1 tsp. vanilla extract
¾ cup buttermilk

3 Tbsp. butter or
    margarine, softened
¼ cup granulated sugar
¼ cup firmly packed light
    brown sugar
½ cup all-purpose flour

1. Fit piecrust into a 9-inch pieplate according to package directions; fold edges under, and crimp. Prick bottom and sides of piecrust with a fork.

2. Melt ¼ cup butter in a large skillet over medium heat; add apple, ½ cup granulated sugar, and ½ tsp. cinnamon. Cook, stirring occasionally, 3 to 5 minutes or until apple is tender; set aside.

3. Beat remaining ¼ cup butter and 1⅓ cups granulated sugar at medium speed with an electric mixer until creamy. Add eggs, 1 at a time, beating just until yellow disappears. Add 2 Tbsp. flour and vanilla, beating until blended. Add buttermilk, beating until smooth.

4. Spoon apple mixture into piecrust; pour buttermilk mixture over apple mixture.

5. Bake at 300° for 30 minutes. Stir 3 Tbsp. butter, ¼ cup granulated sugar, brown sugar, ½ cup flour, and remaining ¼ tsp. cinnamon until crumbly. Sprinkle over pie. Bake 40 more minutes or until a knife inserted in center comes out clean. Let stand 1 hour before serving.

Then & Now

Pairing apples and a custard pie is an old Southern custom that's as yummy today as it was in days of old.

Lemon Meringue Pie

MAKES 8 TO 10 SERVINGS
Prep: 40 min., Cook: 20 min., Other: 10 min.

*Sealing meringue to the outer edge of the crust over a hot filling ensures
that the meringue topping cooks completely without shrinking.*

1 (15-oz.) package
    refrigerated piecrusts

1 cup sugar
¼ cup cornstarch
⅛ tsp. salt

4 large egg yolks
2 cups milk
⅓ cup fresh lemon juice
3 Tbsp. butter or margarine
1 tsp. grated lemon rind
½ tsp. vanilla extract

6 large egg whites
6 Tbsp. sugar

1. Unroll and stack piecrusts on a lightly floured surface. Roll into 1 (12-inch) circle. Fit piecrust into a 9-inch pieplate (about 1-inch deep); fold edges under, and crimp. Prick bottom and sides of piecrust with a fork. Freeze 10 minutes. Line piecrust with parchment paper; fill with pie weights or dried beans.

2. Bake at 425° for 10 minutes. Remove weights and parchment paper; bake 12 more minutes or until crust is lightly browned. (Shield edges with aluminum foil if they brown too quickly.)

3. Whisk together 1 cup sugar, cornstarch, and salt in a heavy, nonaluminum medium saucepan.

4. Whisk together egg yolks, milk, and lemon juice in a bowl; whisk into sugar mixture in pan over medium heat. Bring to a boil, and boil, whisking constantly, 1 minute. Remove pan from heat; stir in butter, lemon rind, and vanilla extract until smooth. Cover hot filling in saucepan with lid. (Proceed immediately with next step to ensure that the meringue is spread over the pie filling while filling is still hot.)

5. Beat egg whites at high speed with an electric mixer until foamy. Add sugar, 1 Tbsp. at a time, and beat 2 minutes or until soft peaks form and sugar dissolves.

6. Reheat filling just until it begins to bubble. Pour hot filling into hot crust, and quickly spread meringue evenly over hot filling, sealing to edge of pastry.

7. Bake at 325° for 20 minutes or until golden brown. Cool pie completely on a wire rack. Store leftovers in the refrigerator.

Favorite Pecan Pie

MAKES 8 SERVINGS
Prep: 15 min., Cook: 55 min.

We've featured over five dozen variations of pecan pie since this version first appeared in Southern Living *in 1975. It's simply a classic.*

½ cup butter or margarine,
   melted
1 cup sugar
1 cup light corn syrup
4 large eggs, beaten
1 tsp. vanilla extract
¼ tsp. salt

1 unbaked 9-inch pastry
   shell
1 to 1¼ cups pecan halves

1. Combine butter, sugar, and corn syrup in a medium saucepan; cook over low heat, stirring constantly, until sugar dissolves. Cool slightly. Add eggs, vanilla, and salt to mixture; mix well.

2. Pour filling into unbaked pastry shell, and top with pecan halves. Bake at 325° for 50 to 55 minutes. Serve warm or cold.

Rum Pecan Pie: Prepare recipe as directed above, adding 3 Tbsp. rum with the eggs; mix well.

Banana Pudding

MAKES 8 TO 10 SERVINGS
Prep: 25 min., Cook: 25 min.

*This recipe takes you back to Grandma's kitchen with proof that you
can't improve on perfection.*

3½ Tbsp. all-purpose flour
1⅓ cups sugar
Dash of salt
3 cups milk
3 large eggs, separated
2 tsp. vanilla extract,
  divided

1 (12-oz.) package vanilla
  wafers
6 medium bananas
½ tsp. cream of tartar
6 Tbsp. sugar

1. Combine flour, 1⅓ cups sugar, and salt in a heavy saucepan. Slowly stir in milk. Cook over medium heat, stirring constantly, 12 minutes or until mixture thickens. Remove from heat. Beat egg yolks; whisk about one-fourth of hot mixture into egg yolks. Return hot mixture to saucepan. Cook 3 minutes. Remove from heat; stir in 1 tsp. vanilla.

2. Layer one-third of wafers (about 32 cookies) in a 3-qt. baking dish. Slice 2 bananas, and layer over wafers. Pour one-third (about 1⅓ cups) of custard over bananas. Repeat layers twice. Beat egg whites and cream of tartar at high speed with an electric mixer until foamy. Gradually add 6 Tbsp. sugar, 1 Tbsp. at a time, beating until stiff peaks form. Add remaining 1 tsp. vanilla, and beat until blended. Spread meringue over warm custard, sealing to edge of dish. Bake at 325° for 25 minutes or until golden brown.

Pound Cake Banana Pudding

MAKES 10 TO 12 SERVINGS
Prep: 30 min., Cook: 15 min., Other: 6 hrs.

This recipe is inspired by the daily dessert combo served at the famous Mrs. Wilkes' Dining Room, in Savannah, Georgia. Look for pound cake in the frozen dessert case of the supermarket.

4 cups half-and-half
4 egg yolks
1½ cups sugar
¼ cup cornstarch
¼ tsp. salt
3 Tbsp. butter
2 tsp. vanilla extract
1 (1-lb.) pound cake, cubed
   (we tested with Sara
   Lee Family Size All
   Butter Pound Cake)
4 large ripe bananas, sliced

Meringue

1. Whisk together first 5 ingredients in a saucepan over medium-low heat; cook, whisking constantly, 13 to 15 minutes or until thickened. Remove from heat; stir in butter and vanilla until butter melts. Layer half of pound cake cubes, half of bananas, and half of pudding mixture in a 3-qt. round baking dish. Repeat layers. Cover pudding, and chill 6 hours.
2. Spread Meringue over pudding.
3. Bake at 375° for 15 minutes or until golden brown.

Meringue

MAKES ABOUT 3½ CUPS
Prep: 10 min.

¼ cup sugar
⅛ tsp. salt

4 egg whites
¼ tsp. vanilla extract

1. Combine sugar and salt.
2. Beat egg whites and vanilla at high speed with an electric mixer until foamy. Add sugar mixture, 1 Tbsp. at a time, and beat 2 to 3 minutes or until stiff peaks form and sugar dissolves.

Blastin' Banana-Blueberry Pudding

MAKES 10 TO 12 SERVINGS
Prep: 10 min.; Cook: 20 min.; Other: 4 hrs., 10 min.

We loved the color and crunch the blueberries added to this creamy dessert.
If you prefer a less-sweet banana pudding, omit the powdered sugar from the whipped cream.

4 cups milk
4 egg yolks
1½ cups granulated sugar
⅓ cup all-purpose flour
2 Tbsp. butter
1 Tbsp. vanilla extract

1 (12-oz.) box vanilla
   wafers
4 large ripe bananas, sliced
2 cups frozen blueberries

1½ cups whipping cream
3 Tbsp. powdered
   sugar

1. Whisk together first 4 ingredients in a large saucepan over medium-low heat. Cook, whisking constantly, 20 minutes or until thickened. Remove from heat; stir in butter and vanilla until butter melts. Let stand 10 minutes.
2. Arrange half of vanilla wafers evenly in a 13- x 9-inch baking dish; top with half of banana slices and half of blueberries. Spoon half of pudding mixture evenly over fruit. Repeat layers. Cover and chill 4 hours.
3. Beat whipping cream at high speed with an electric mixer until foamy; gradually add powdered sugar, beating until soft peaks form. Spread evenly over chilled pudding. Serve immediately.

Morning
miracles

A hearty breakfast is just the right way to start your day. If you have ample time, sit down to a fresh batch of waffles or an omelet casserole. If you're running late, grab a smoothie and a slice of grits bread on your way out the door.

our best
40years
recipes

OAT BRAN WAFFLES, PAGE 161

Sparkling Orange Punch

MAKES 8 SERVINGS
Prep: 5 min.; Other: 2 hrs., 5 min.

*Champagne, stirred in just before serving, lends a celebratory note
to this colorful brunch beverage.*

4 cups boiling water
4 regular size tea bags
½ cup sugar
1 (6-oz.) can orange juice
   concentrate, thawed

1 (750-milliliter) bottle
   Champagne or
   sparkling wine, chilled

1. Pour 4 cups boiling water over tea bags; cover and steep 5 minutes. Remove and discard tea bags. Stir in sugar and juice concentrate, stirring until sugar dissolves. Cover and chill 2 hours.

2. Stir together chilled tea mixture and Champagne. Serve immediately.

White Chocolate Latte

MAKES 4 CUPS
Prep: 5 min., Cook: 5 min.

*Enjoy a coffee shop sensation in your own home
with a mug of white chocolate-inspired joe.*

2 cups milk
1 cup half-and-half
⅔ cup white chocolate
   morsels
2 Tbsp. instant coffee
   granules

1 tsp. vanilla extract
¼ tsp. almond extract
Whipped cream (optional)
Garnish: cinnamon sticks

1. Stir first 4 ingredients together in a small saucepan over low heat until white chocolate morsels melt.
2. Stir in vanilla and almond extracts; pour evenly into 4 mugs. Top with whipped cream, if desired. Garnish, if desired, and serve immediately.

Yogurt-Fruit Smoothie

MAKES 5 CUPS
Prep: 5 min.

This quick and easy smoothie is the perfect breakfast for you to drink on your way to work or for children to enjoy on the way to school. It's also a great source of calcium. Blend in other fruits for a variety of flavors.

2 cups fat-free milk
1 (8-oz.) container vanilla
    low-fat yogurt
½ cup thawed pineapple-
    orange juice
    concentrate
2 cups frozen strawberries
1 banana, coarsely chopped

1. Process all ingredients in a blender until smooth, stopping to scrape down sides. Serve immediately.

Bacon-Cheddar Grits Bread

MAKES 3 LOAVES
Prep: 15 min.; Cook: 40 min.; Other: 2 hrs., 25 min.

Combine three of the South's favorite ingredients to make a showstopping morning bread. Toasted and topped with butter, a slice is so good that you'll think you've gone to heaven.

2 cups milk
¾ cup quick-cooking grits, uncooked
2 tsp. salt
1 (10-oz.) package white Cheddar cheese, shredded (we tested with Cracker Barrel Vermont Sharp White Cheddar)

1 cup warm water (100° to 110°)
¼ cup sugar
2 (¼-oz.) envelopes rapid-rise yeast

5 to 6 cups bread flour

½ cup cooked, crumbled bacon
¾ cup shredded sharp Cheddar cheese

1. Bring milk to a boil in a large saucepan over medium heat; stir in grits, and cook, stirring often, 5 minutes (mixture will be very thick). Remove from heat; add salt and cheese, stirring until cheese is melted. Let stand 25 minutes, stirring occasionally.

2. Combine 1 cup warm water, sugar, and yeast in the mixing bowl of a heavy-duty stand mixer; let stand 5 minutes. Add grits mixture, beating at medium-low speed with the dough hook attachment until well blended.

3. Add 4 cups flour, 1 cup at a time, beating until blended after each addition and stopping to scrape down sides as necessary. Gradually add enough flour to make a stiff but slightly sticky dough. Dough will form a ball around mixer attachment.

4. Shape dough into a ball with well-floured hands, and place in a well-greased bowl, turning to coat top. Cover and let rise in a warm place (85°), free from drafts, 1 hour or until doubled in bulk.

5. Punch dough down, and divide into thirds; roll each third into a 14- x 9-inch rectangle on a lightly floured surface. Sprinkle each dough rectangle evenly with bacon and ¾ cup shredded sharp Cheddar cheese. Roll up, jelly-roll fashion, starting with each short side and ending at middle of dough; form 2 rolls per loaf. Place into lightly greased 9- x 5-inch loafpans; cover and let rise in a warm place (85°), free from drafts, 45 minutes or until doubled in bulk.

6. Bake at 350° for 35 to 40 minutes or until golden. Cool in pans on wire racks 10 minutes. Remove from pans, and cool completely on wire racks.

Whole Wheat Nut Bread

MAKES 8 SERVINGS
Prep: 15 min.; Cook: 1 hr., 15 min.

Don't be surprised by the heavy weight of this hearty bread when you remove it from the pan.
Even though the batter has no egg or oil, it still produces a moist and tender loaf.

2 cups whole wheat flour
1 cup all-purpose flour
1 cup chopped pecans,
    toasted
½ cup sugar
1 tsp. salt

1 tsp. baking soda
1½ cups milk
½ cup molasses

1. Combine first 5 ingredients in a large bowl; make a well in center of mixture.

2. Dissolve baking soda in milk; stir in molasses. Add to flour mixture, stirring just until dry ingredients are moistened. Spoon into a greased and floured 9- x 5-inch loafpan.

3. Bake at 325° for 1 hour to 1 hour and 15 minutes or until a wooden pick inserted in center comes out clean. Remove from pan, and cool on a wire rack.

Swedish Rye Bread

MAKES 2 LOAVES
Prep: 20 min.; Cook: 35 min.; Other: 1 hr., 35 min.

This rye bread has stood the test of time since its first publishing in 1965. It stands out as an editor's favorite for its tender dough and slightly sweet rye flavor.

2 (¼-oz.) envelopes active
    dry yeast
¼ cup warm water
    (100° to 110°)

⅓ cup butter
½ cup molasses
1¾ cups beer (we tested
    with Corona)
2 tsp. salt
1 Tbsp. caraway seeds

3½ cups stone-ground rye
    flour
3 to 4 cups all-purpose
    flour, divided
2 Tbsp. butter, melted

1. Dissolve yeast in warm water in a 1-cup glass measuring cup; let stand 5 minutes.

2. Place ⅓ cup butter in a large microwave-safe bowl; microwave at HIGH 30 seconds or until butter melts. Stir in molasses and beer. Add dissolved yeast, salt, and caraway seeds.

3. Add rye flour, stirring until smooth. Stir in about 3 cups all-purpose flour to make a soft dough. Brush top of dough with 2 Tbsp. melted butter. Cover and let rise in a warm (85°) place, free from drafts, 45 minutes or until doubled in bulk.

4. Punch dough down, turn out onto a lightly floured board, and knead about 8 minutes, adding additional all-purpose flour, 1 Tbsp. at a time, as necessary to prevent sticking.

5. Shape into loaves, and place in 2 greased 8- x 4-inch loafpans. Cover and let rise in a warm place (85°), free from drafts, 45 minutes or until doubled in bulk.

6. Bake at 350° for 35 minutes. Remove from pans immediately. Cool completely before slicing.

From Our Kitchen

Fresh bread is best enjoyed the day it's made. If you expect to have some left over, simply freeze it up to one month.

Basic Buttery Biscuits

MAKES 2 DOZEN
Prep: 10 min., Cook: 9 min.

Whether you top these flaky gems with Honey Butter or Sausage Gravy (page 177), they'll remind you of the buttery classics Grandma used to make.

2¼ cups all-purpose baking mix (we tested with Bisquick)
⅓ cup buttermilk
6 Tbsp. unsalted butter, melted and divided

Honey Butter (optional)

1. Stir together baking mix, buttermilk, and 5 Tbsp. melted butter just until blended.
2. Turn dough out onto a lightly floured surface, and knead 1 or 2 times. Pat to ½-inch thickness; cut with a 1½-inch round cutter, and place on lightly greased baking sheets.
3. Bake at 450° for 7 to 9 minutes or until lightly browned. Brush tops evenly with remaining 1 Tbsp. melted butter. Serve with Honey Butter, if desired.

To Make Ahead: Freeze unbaked biscuits on a lightly greased baking sheet 30 minutes or until frozen. Store biscuits in a zip-top freezer bag up to 3 months. Bake as directed for 8 to 10 minutes or until lightly browned. Proceed with recipe as directed.

Honey Butter

MAKES 6 TBSP.
Prep: 3 min.

¼ cup butter, softened
2 Tbsp. honey

1. Combine butter and honey until blended.

Cinnamon Rolls

MAKES 2 DOZEN
Prep: 44 min., Cook: 18 min., Other: 56 min.

*Nothing compares to the aroma of just-baked cinnamon rolls.
Since this recipe makes enough for two pans, you'll have plenty to share with friends.*

½ cup water
½ cup milk
⅓ cup butter

3½ to 4 cups all-purpose
   flour, divided
1 tsp. salt
¼ cup firmly packed brown
   sugar
1 (¼-oz.) envelope rapid-
   rise yeast
2 large eggs

1 cup firmly packed brown
   sugar
⅓ cup butter, softened
2 tsp. ground cinnamon

2 cups sifted powdered
   sugar
3½ to 4 Tbsp. milk
¼ tsp. vanilla extract

From Our Kitchen

Using floss to cut the rolls for baking makes perfect rounds. Just slide the floss under the dough, cross over, and pull across to the opposite sides to easily cut.

1. Combine water, ½ cup milk, and ⅓ cup butter in a saucepan over medium heat; cook until butter almost melts, stirring occasionally. Cool to 125° to 130°.
2. Combine 2 cups flour and next 3 ingredients in a large mixing bowl. Gradually add warm milk mixture to flour, beating at low speed of a heavy-duty electric mixer. Add eggs, and beat 2 minutes at medium speed.
3. Gradually add 1½ cups flour, beating 2 minutes. Gradually stir in enough remaining flour to make a soft dough.
4. Turn dough out onto a well-floured surface, and knead 5 minutes or until smooth and elastic. Cover and let rest 10 minutes. Divide dough in half. Working with half of dough at a time and keeping other half covered, roll each half into a 12-inch square.
5. Combine 1 cup brown sugar, ⅓ cup butter, and cinnamon; spread evenly over both squares of dough. Roll up dough, jelly-roll fashion, starting at long end; pinch seams to seal.
6. Cut each roll into 1-inch slices. Place rolls, cut sides down, in 2 lightly greased 9-inch square pans.
7. Cover and let rise in a warm place (85°), free from drafts, 40 minutes or until doubled in bulk. Bake at 375° for 18 minutes or until golden.
8. Combine powdered sugar, 3½ to 4 Tbsp. milk, and vanilla; drizzle glaze over warm rolls.

Note: Baked Cinnamon Rolls can be frozen without glaze. Cover with aluminum foil; freeze up to 3 months. Thaw in refrigerator overnight, and bake in foil at 375° for 10 to 15 minutes or until thoroughly heated. Drizzle with glaze.

Lemon-Orange Rolls

MAKES 4 DOZEN
Prep: 20 min., Cook: 10 min., Other: 20 min.

Citrus notes elevate these rolls to premier morning status.

1 (16-oz.) package hot roll mix (we tested with Pillsbury Hot Roll Mix)

¼ cup butter, softened and divided

⅔ cup granulated sugar
2 Tbsp. grated orange rind
1 Tbsp. grated lemon rind

2 cups powdered sugar
¼ cup orange juice

1. Prepare hot roll dough according to package directions.
2. Divide dough into 2 equal portions. Roll 1 portion of dough into a 12- x 8-inch rectangle on a lightly floured surface. Spread with 2 Tbsp. butter.
3. Stir together granulated sugar and grated rinds; sprinkle half of sugar mixture evenly over butter on rectangle. Roll up rectangle, jelly-roll fashion, starting at a long edge. Repeat procedure with remaining half of dough, 2 Tbsp. butter, and remaining half of sugar mixture.
4. Cut each roll into ½-inch-thick slices, and place in lightly greased miniature muffin pans.
5. Cover and let rise in a warm place (85°), free from drafts, 20 minutes.
6. Bake at 375° for 8 to 10 minutes or until golden. Remove from pans, and place on wire racks.
7. Stir together powdered sugar and orange juice until smooth; spoon evenly over tops of rolls.

From Our Kitchen

If you don't have four miniature muffin pans, you can let these little rolls rise and bake them in batches; just be sure to keep the extra portions of dough in the refrigerator until you're ready to fill the pans again. These rolls can be baked up to a month ahead and frozen in zip-top freezer bags. Thaw at room temperature, and reheat, uncovered, at 350° for 3 to 5 minutes.

Breakfast Muffins

MAKES 1 DOZEN
Prep: 10 min., Cook: 18 min.

Transform a leisurely Sunday morning treat into a hectic Monday morning breakfast-on-the-go by individually wrapping one of these delicious muffins. Chill leftovers in the refrigerator.

2 cups self-rising flour
¾ cup shredded Parmesan
    cheese
2 Tbsp. sugar
1 cup cooked and crumbled
    ground pork sausage

1 cup milk
¼ cup vegetable oil
2 large eggs

1. Combine first 4 ingredients in a large bowl; make a well in center of mixture.

2. Whisk together milk, oil, and eggs until well blended. Add to flour mixture, and stir just until dry ingredients are moistened.

3. Spoon mixture into a lightly greased muffin pan, filling two-thirds full.

4. Bake at 400° for 15 to 18 minutes or until golden brown.

Cream Cheese-Banana-Nut Bread

MAKES 2 LOAVES
Prep: 15 min., Cook: 1 hr., Other: 40 min.

*Warm bread is yummy, but to get perfect slices,
cool this bread 30 minutes and cut with a serrated or electric knife.*

¾ cup butter, softened
1 (8-oz.) package cream
    cheese, softened
2 cups sugar
2 large eggs

3 cups all-purpose flour
½ tsp. baking powder
½ tsp. baking soda
½ tsp. salt
1½ cups mashed bananas
    (1¼ lb. unpeeled
    bananas, about
    4 medium)
1 cup chopped pecans,
    toasted
½ tsp. vanilla extract

1. Beat butter and cream cheese at medium speed with an electric mixer until creamy. Gradually add sugar, beating until light and fluffy. Add eggs, 1 at a time, beating just until blended after each addition.
2. Combine flour and next 3 ingredients; gradually add to butter mixture, beating at low speed just until blended. Stir in bananas, pecans, and vanilla. Spoon batter into 2 greased and floured 8- x 4-inch loaf pans.
3. Bake at 350° for 1 hour or until a long wooden pick inserted in center comes out clean and sides pull away from pan, shielding with aluminum foil during last 15 minutes to prevent browning, if necessary. Cool bread in pans on wire racks 10 minutes. Remove from pans, and cool 30 minutes on wire racks before slicing.

Toasted Coconut-Topped Cream Cheese-Banana-Nut Bread: Prepare and bake bread or muffins in desired pans. While bread is baking, stir together ¼ cup butter, ¼ cup granulated sugar, ¼ cup firmly packed brown sugar, and ¼ cup milk in a small saucepan over medium-high heat; bring to a boil, stirring constantly. Remove from heat. Stir in 1 cup sweetened flaked coconut; 1 cup toasted, chopped pecans; and 2 tsp. vanilla extract. Remove baked bread or muffins from oven, and immediately spread tops with coconut mixture. Broil 5½ inches from heat 2 to 3 minutes or just until topping starts to lightly brown. Cool in pans on wire racks 20 minutes. Remove from pans, and cool 30 minutes on wire racks before slicing.

From Our Kitchen

The perfect bananas for this bread don't look so perfect. Let them get ripe, almost black or very speckled. It takes a week to go from green to ready. To hasten ripening, place bananas in a paper bag with a bruised apple. Once ripe, refrigerate or freeze unpeeled bananas in zip-top freezer bags; thaw before mashing. We tried freezing mashed bananas but once thawed they were not suitable for use.

Oat Bran Waffles

MAKES 1 DOZEN
Prep: 10 min., Cook: 5 min. per waffle

These good-for-you waffles offer a fluffy way to start your day. The combination of oat bran, whole wheat, and all-purpose flour make them hearty yet light in texture.

¾ cup oat bran
½ cup whole wheat flour
½ cup all-purpose flour
2 tsp. baking powder
½ tsp. salt
1½ cups skim milk
3 Tbsp. safflower or
    vegetable oil
1 egg yolk, beaten
2 egg whites

Toppings: butter, syrup,
    powdered sugar, fresh
    blueberries

1. Combine first 5 ingredients in a medium bowl. Combine milk, oil, and egg yolk; add to dry ingredients, stirring just until moistened. Beat egg whites at high speed with an electric mixer until stiff peaks form; gently fold into batter.
2. Coat a waffle iron with cooking spray, and allow waffle iron to preheat. Spoon 1⅓ cups batter onto hot waffle iron, spreading batter to edges. Bake until lightly browned. Repeat procedure with remaining batter. Serve immediately with desired toppings.

Overnight Refrigerator Pancakes

MAKES 2½ DOZEN
Prep: 15 min.; Cook: 10 min.; Other: 8 hrs., 5 min.

If you think there's no time to make breakfast, think again. Stir up this batter the night before, and all you have to do in the morning is pour it on the griddle.

1 (¼-oz.) envelope active
    dry yeast
¼ cup warm water
    (100° to 110°)

4 cups all-purpose flour
2 Tbsp. baking powder
2 tsp. baking soda
1 tsp. salt
2 tsp. sugar
6 large eggs
4 cups buttermilk
¼ cup vegetable oil

1. Combine yeast and warm water in a 1-cup glass measuring cup; let stand 5 minutes.

2. Combine flour and next 4 ingredients in a large bowl; make a well in center. Combine eggs, buttermilk, and oil; add to flour mixture, stirring just until dry ingredients are moistened. Stir in yeast mixture. Cover and chill 8 hours.

3. Remove from refrigerator; stir well.

4. Preheat griddle to 350°; lightly grease griddle. Pour about ¼ cup batter for each pancake onto hot griddle. Cook pancakes until tops are covered with bubbles and edges look cooked; turn and cook other side.

Note: You can store pancake batter in refrigerator up to 1 week.

Triple-Chocolate Coffee Cake

MAKES 2 (9-INCH) COFFEE CAKES
Prep: 15 min., Cook: 30 min.

You have our permission to enjoy all the chocolate you'd like for breakfast in this coffee cake.

1 (18.25-oz.) package devil's
  food cake mix
1 (3.9-oz.) package
  chocolate instant
  pudding mix
2 cups sour cream
1 cup butter or margarine,
  softened
5 large eggs
1 tsp. vanilla extract
3 cups semisweet chocolate
  morsels, divided

1 cup white chocolate
  morsels
1 cup chopped pecans,
  toasted

1. Beat first 6 ingredients at low speed with an electric mixer 30 seconds or just until moistened; beat at medium speed 2 minutes. Stir in 2 cups semisweet chocolate morsels; pour batter evenly into 2 greased and floured 9-inch square cake pans.

2. Bake at 350° for 25 to 30 minutes or until a wooden pick inserted in center comes out clean. Cool completely in pans on wire racks.

3. Microwave white chocolate morsels in a glass bowl at HIGH 30 to 60 seconds or until morsels melt; stirring at 30-second intervals until smooth. Drizzle evenly over cakes; repeat procedure with remaining 1 cup semisweet morsels. Sprinkle pecans evenly over cakes.

Sour Cream-Blueberry Coffee Cake

MAKES 12 SERVINGS
Prep: 15 min., Cook: 40 min., Other: 25 min.

Bring the antioxidant power of blueberries to your morning. Nestled atop this spongy coffee cake, blueberries cradle pecans and pools of powdered sugar icing.

½ cup butter or margarine, softened
½ cup granulated sugar
2 large eggs
1 (8-oz.) container sour cream
1 tsp. vanilla extract
2 tsp. grated lemon rind

1½ cups all-purpose flour
1 tsp. baking powder
½ tsp. salt

1 pt. fresh or frozen blueberries
½ cup chopped pecans
¼ cup granulated sugar
1 tsp. ground cinnamon

1 cup powdered sugar
4 tsp. milk

1. Beat butter at medium speed with an electric mixer 2 minutes or until creamy. Gradually add ½ cup granulated sugar, beating 2 to 3 minutes. Add eggs and next 3 ingredients, beating until smooth.

2. Combine flour, baking powder, and salt. Gradually add to butter mixture, beating until blended. Pour batter into a lightly greased 9-inch springform pan.

3. Combine blueberries and next 3 ingredients. Sprinkle over batter.

4. Bake at 350° for 35 to 40 minutes or until a wooden pick inserted in center comes out clean. Cool in pan on a wire rack 10 to 15 minutes; remove from pan, and cool on wire rack 10 minutes.

5. Whisk together powdered sugar and milk until smooth. Drizzle over cake.

Croissant French Toast with Fresh Strawberry Syrup

MAKES 4 SERVINGS
Prep: 15 min., Cook: 4 min. per batch

Replacing the typical sandwich bread in French toast with butter-laden puff pastry creates a luxurious morning delicacy guaranteed to awaken all your senses.

4 large day-old croissants

¾ cup milk
2 large eggs
1 tsp. vanilla extract

2 Tbsp. butter
3 Tbsp. powdered sugar
Sweetened Whipped Cream
Fresh Strawberry Syrup

1. Slice croissants in half lengthwise.
2. Whisk together milk, eggs, and vanilla. Pour into a shallow dish. Dip croissant halves into egg mixture, coating well.
3. Melt 1 Tbsp. butter in a large nonstick skillet over medium heat. Add 4 croissant halves, and cook about 2 minutes on each side or until golden brown. Repeat procedure with remaining 1 Tbsp. butter and remaining 4 croissant halves. Sprinkle with powdered sugar; top with Sweetened Whipped Cream and Fresh Strawberry Syrup.

Sweetened Whipped Cream

MAKES ABOUT 1 CUP
Prep: 5 min

½ cup whipping cream
1½ Tbsp. powdered sugar

1. Beat cream at medium speed with an electric mixer until soft peaks form. Add powdered sugar, beating until stiff peaks form.

Fresh Strawberry Syrup

MAKES ABOUT 2 CUPS
Prep: 10 min., Cook: 5 min., Other: 30 min.

1 qt. fresh strawberries, sliced
½ cup sugar
1 tsp. grated orange rind
¼ cup orange liqueur or orange juice

1. Combine all ingredients in a saucepan, and let stand 30 minutes or until sugar dissolves.
2. Cook over low heat, stirring occasionally, 5 minutes or until warm.

Open-Faced Bacon and Potato Omelet

MAKES 4 TO 6 SERVINGS
Prep: 25 min., Cook: 30 min.

This newfangled omelet is a meal in itself. Enjoy the combo of bacon, hash browns, tomatoes, eggs, and cheese for breakfast or dinner.

4 bacon slices, chopped

2 cups frozen Southern-style
   cubed hash browns,
   thawed
4 green onions, thinly sliced

2 tsp. butter or margarine
1 large tomato, seeded and
   chopped
2 Tbsp. chopped fresh
   flat-leaf parsley

6 large eggs
½ tsp. salt
¼ tsp. pepper
4 drops of hot sauce
   (optional)
1 cup shredded sharp
   Cheddar cheese

1. Cook bacon in a large ovenproof nonstick skillet over medium heat until crisp; remove bacon, and drain on paper towels, reserving 1 Tbsp. drippings in skillet. Set bacon aside.
2. Cook hash browns in hot drippings over medium heat 10 minutes or until hash browns are tender, stirring occasionally. Stir in green onions; cook 5 minutes or until tender.
3. Add butter to skillet, stirring until melted. Add tomato, and cook over medium-high heat 3 to 4 minutes. Sprinkle with bacon and parsley.
4. Whisk together eggs, salt, pepper, and, if desired, hot sauce. Pour over hash brown mixture. Gently lift edges of omelet, and tilt pan so uncooked portion flows underneath. Cook over medium heat until omelet begins to set. Sprinkle with cheese.
5. Broil 5½ inches from heat 5 minutes or until top is set and cheese melts. Slide omelet out of skillet onto platter. Cut into wedges, and serve immediately.

BLT Breakfast Sandwiches

MAKES 4 SERVINGS
Prep: 10 min., Cook: 6 min.

*Your family will appreciate a satisfying BLT
at any meal—breakfast, lunch, or supper.*

1 (0.9-oz.) envelope
   hollandaise sauce mix*

6 bacon slices, cooked and
   crumbled
2 (3-oz.) packages cream
   cheese, softened
2 Tbsp. chopped fresh
   chives
¾ tsp. seasoned pepper,
   divided
4 sourdough bread slices,
   toasted

1 Tbsp. butter or margarine
4 large eggs

4 lettuce leaves
2 small tomatoes, sliced

1. Prepare hollandaise sauce according to package directions; keep warm.

2. Stir together bacon, cream cheese, chives, and ¼ tsp. seasoned pepper; spread evenly on 1 side of each toasted bread slice.

3. Melt butter in a large nonstick skillet over medium heat. Gently break eggs into hot skillet, and sprinkle evenly with ¼ tsp. seasoned pepper. Cook 2 to 3 minutes on each side or until done.

4. Place lettuce leaves and tomatoes on top of bread slices, and top with fried eggs. Drizzle hollandaise sauce evenly over top, and sprinkle evenly with remaining ¼ tsp. seasoned pepper. Serve immediately.

*Check the hollandaise sauce package for the fresh ingredients needed to prepare it.

From Our Kitchen

• Eggs are economical, convenient, easy to prepare, and nutritious. One egg supplies 10% of our daily protein requirement. They're also a terrific source of vitamins A, D, and B$_{12}$.

• Egg substitute, such as Egg Beaters, can be used successfully in place of whole eggs (¼ cup egg substitute equals 1 egg).

• Leftovers of vegetables, beef, chicken, or pork make great fillings for omelets. Chop ingredients into bite-size pieces. Heat in the microwave; sprinkle over egg mixture just before folding the omelet.

Confetti Omelet Casserole

MAKES 8 SERVINGS
Prep: 30 min., Cook: 45 min., Other: 5 min.

Fresh parsley sprigs and flecks of pimiento make this casserole pretty enough for Christmas morning and a healthy start to a day of feasting.

6 bacon slices

½ cup chopped onion

4 cups egg substitute
2 cups (8 oz.) 2% reduced-
    fat shredded sharp
    Cheddar cheese
1 cup fat-free milk
1 (4-oz.) jar chopped
    pimiento, drained
2 Tbsp. chopped fresh
    parsley
½ tsp. salt

Garnish: fresh flat-leaf
    parsley sprigs

1. Cook bacon in a medium skillet until crisp; remove bacon, and drain on paper towels, reserving 1 tsp. drippings in skillet. Crumble bacon, and set aside.

2. Add ½ cup chopped onion to hot drippings in skillet, and sauté over medium heat 3 to 4 minutes or until tender.

3. Stir together crumbled bacon, onion, egg substitute, and next 5 ingredients in a large bowl. Pour egg mixture into a 13- x 9-inch baking dish coated with cooking spray.

4. Bake at 325° for 45 minutes or until set. Let stand 5 minutes before serving. Garnish, if desired.

Breakfast Enchiladas

MAKES 6 TO 8 SERVINGS
Prep: 20 min., Cook: 30 min.

1 (1-lb.) package hot
    ground pork sausage

2 Tbsp. butter or margarine
4 green onions, thinly sliced
2 Tbsp. chopped fresh cilantro
14 large eggs, beaten
¾ tsp. salt
½ tsp. pepper
Cheese Sauce

8 (8-inch) flour tortillas
1 cup (4 oz.) shredded
    Monterey Jack cheese
    with jalapeños

Toppings: halved grape
    tomatoes, sliced green
    onions, chopped cilantro

1. Cook sausage in a large nonstick skillet over medium-high heat, stirring until sausage crumbles and is no longer pink. Remove from pan; drain well, pressing between paper towels.

2. Melt butter in skillet over medium heat. Add thinly sliced green onions and cilantro, and sauté 1 minute. Add eggs, salt, and pepper, and cook, without stirring, until eggs begin to set on bottom. Draw a spatula across bottom of pan to form large curds. Continue to cook until eggs are thickened but still moist; do not stir constantly. Remove from heat, and gently fold in 1½ cups Cheese Sauce and sausage.

3. Spoon about ⅓ cup egg mixture down the center of each flour tortilla; roll up. Place, seam sides down, in a lightly greased 13- x- 9-inch baking dish. Pour remaining Cheese Sauce evenly over tortillas; sprinkle evenly with Monterey Jack cheese.

4. Bake at 350° for 30 minutes or until sauce is bubbly. Serve with desired toppings.

Cheese Sauce

MAKES ABOUT 4 CUPS
Prep: 10 min., Cook: 8 min.

⅓ cup butter
⅓ cup flour
3 cups milk
2 cups (8 oz.) shredded
    Cheddar cheese
1 (4.5-oz.) can chopped
    green chiles, undrained
¾ tsp. salt

1. Melt butter in a heavy saucepan over medium-low heat; whisk in flour until smooth. Cook, whisking constantly, 1 minute. Gradually whisk in milk; cook over medium heat, whisking constantly, 5 minutes or until thickened. Remove from heat, and whisk in remaining ingredients.

Brie-and-Sausage Breakfast Casserole

MAKES 8 TO 10 SERVINGS
Prep: 20 min., Cook: 1 hr., Other: 8 hrs.

The rich, savory Brie sensation adds unique flavor to this hearty casserole.

1 (8-oz.) Brie round*

1 lb. ground hot pork
    sausage

6 white sandwich bread
    slices
1 cup grated Parmesan
    cheese

7 large eggs, divided
3 cups whipping cream,
    divided
2 cups fat-free milk
1 Tbsp. chopped fresh sage
    or 1 teaspoon dried
    rubbed sage
1 tsp. seasoned salt
1 tsp. dry mustard

Garnishes: chopped green
    onions, shaved
    Parmesan cheese

1. Trim rind from Brie, and discard; cut cheese into cubes, and set aside.

2. Cook sausage in a large skillet over medium-high heat, stirring until it crumbles and is no longer pink; drain well.

3. Cut crusts from bread slices, and place crusts evenly in bottom of a lightly greased 13- x 9-inch baking dish. Layer evenly with bread slices, sausage, Brie, and Parmesan cheese.

4. Whisk together 5 eggs, 2 cups whipping cream, milk, and next 3 ingredients; pour evenly over cheeses. Cover and chill mixture for 8 hours.

5. Whisk together remaining 2 eggs and remaining 1 cup whipping cream; pour evenly over chilled mixture.

6. Bake at 350° for 1 hour or until casserole is set. Garnish, if desired.

*Substitute 2 cups (8 ounces) shredded Swiss cheese, if desired.

Sausage-Filled Crêpes

MAKES 6 TO 8 SERVINGS
Prep: 10 min., Cook 20 min.

1 lb. ground pork sausage
1 small onion, diced
2 cups (8 oz.) shredded
    Cheddar cheese, divided
1 (3-oz.) package cream
    cheese
½ tsp. dried marjoram

Crêpes

½ cup sour cream
¼ cup butter or margarine,
    softened
¼ cup chopped fresh parsley
Sliced tomato

1. Cook sausage and onion in a large skillet over medium heat, stirring until sausage crumbles and is no longer pink; drain well. Return sausage to skillet; add 1 cup Cheddar cheese, cream cheese, and marjoram, stirring until cheeses melt.

2. Spoon 3 tablespoons filling down center of each crêpe. Roll up, and place, seam sides down, in a lightly greased 13- x 9-inch baking dish.

3. Bake, covered, at 350° for 15 minutes. Stir together sour cream and butter; spoon over Crêpes. Bake 5 more minutes. Sprinkle with remaining 1 cup Cheddar cheese and parsley. Serve with sliced tomato.

Crêpes

MAKES 12 (7-INCH) CRÊPES
Prep: 5 min., Cook: 20 min., Other: 1 hr.

3 large eggs
1 cup milk
1 Tbsp. vegetable oil
1 cup all-purpose flour
½ tsp. salt

Melted butter

1. Beat first 3 ingredients at medium speed with an electric mixer until blended. Gradually add flour and salt, beating until smooth. Cover and chill 1 hour.

2. Coat bottom of a 7-inch nonstick skillet with melted butter; place skillet over medium heat until hot.

3. Pour 3 Tbsp. batter into skillet; quickly tilt in all directions so batter covers bottom of skillet.

4. Cook 1 minute or until crêpe can be shaken loose from skillet. Turn crêpe over, and cook about 30 seconds. Place on a dish towel to cool. Repeat procedure with remaining batter.

5. Stack Crêpes between sheets of wax paper.

From Our Kitchen

Crêpes can be assembled and frozen. To reheat, let stand 30 minutes at room temperature. Bake, covered, at 350° for 40 minutes. Proceed as directed.

Sausage Gravy

MAKES 2 CUPS
Prep: 15 min., Cook 10 min.

Indulge in a truly Southern breakfast with Sausage Gravy served over Basic Buttery Biscuits (page 155). For some kick, use spicy sausage.

8 oz. pork sausage

¼ cup all-purpose flour
2⅓ cups milk
½ tsp. salt
½ tsp. pepper

1. Cook sausage in a large skillet over medium heat, stirring until it crumbles and is no longer pink. Remove sausage, and drain on paper towels, reserving 1 Tbsp. drippings in skillet.

2. Whisk flour into hot drippings until smooth; cook, whisking constantly, 1 minute. Gradually whisk in milk, and cook, whisking constantly, 5 to 7 minutes or until thickened. Stir in sausage, salt, and pepper. Serve over buttermilk biscuits or grits.

Party
starters

Chilled drinks, savory snacks, and irresistible appetizers are Southern party essentials. Get your gathering started on the right foot with an array of these delectable choices.

BRANDY VELVET, PAGE 191

Blackberry Spritzer

MAKES 2 SERVINGS
Prep: 5 min., Other: 1 hr.

To create a refreshing drink that looks—and tastes—like the essence of summer, turn blackberries into luscious "ice cubes" that flavor water as they thaw.

1 pt. fresh blackberries
2 (6-inch) wooden skewers

1 to 2 Tbsp. corn syrup
1 Tbsp. grated lime rind
(about 2 limes)

2 (8.45-oz.) bottles sparkling
water, chilled
Garnish: fresh mint sprigs

1. Thread fresh blackberries onto 6-inch wooden skewers. Freeze 1 hour.

2. Dip rims of glasses into corn syrup, and roll in grated lime rind.

3. Place frozen blackberry skewers in prepared glasses. Pour chilled sparkling water over skewers, and garnish, if desired.

From Our Kitchen

Don't have sparkling water on hand? These skewers work just as well in lemonade, iced tea, or any flavored fruit juice.

Cool Lavender Lemonade

MAKES ABOUT 8 CUPS
Prep: 5 min., Cook: 5 min., Other: 2 hrs.

Lavender sprigs add a refreshing twist to this Southern sipper. Adjust the intensity of lavender and mint flavors by adding more or less herbs or by steeping for a longer or shorter period of time.

7 cups water
1 cup sugar
1½ cups frozen lemon
    juice from concentrate,
    thawed
4 fresh mint sprigs
3 fresh lavender sprigs*

Garnishes: lemon slices,
    fresh lavender and mint
    sprigs

1. Bring 7 cups water to a boil over medium-high heat. Stir in 1 cup sugar, and cook, stirring constantly, 1 to 2 minutes or until sugar dissolves; remove from heat. Stir in lemon juice, 4 mint sprigs, and 3 lavender sprigs; let stand at least 2 hours.

2. Pour lemonade mixture through a wire-mesh strainer into a large pitcher, discarding herbs. Serve over ice. Garnish, if desired.

*Substitute 2 Tbsp. dried lavender flowers, if desired.

From Our Kitchen

Chances are, you have fruit juices and concentrates in your freezer. If not, grab some on your next grocery run, and stir up this cooling quencher. Got leftovers? Save unused juices and concentrates to flavor iced tea, blend a tropical smoothie, or perk up a marinade.

Cool Lavender Lemonade (front)
and White Sangría (page 186)

Fruited Mint Tea

MAKES 10 CUPS
Prep: 11 min., Cook: 4 min., Other: 5 min.

Fresh mint and citrus liven up tea for a refreshing summer beverage.

3 cups boiling water
4 regular size tea bags
12 fresh mint sprigs
1 cup sugar
5 cups water
1 cup orange juice
¾ cup lemon juice (about
    3 lemons)
Garnishes: fresh mint sprigs,
    orange slices

1. Pour boiling water over tea bags and 12 mint sprigs; cover and steep 5 minutes. Remove tea bags and mint, squeezing gently. Stir in sugar and next 3 ingredients. Serve over ice. Garnish, if desired.

Taste of the South

Long considered a symbol of hospitality, mint plays a major role in the South's two most famous beverages: mint tea and mint juleps. Crush the pretty herb leaves in a beverage to release their intense flavor, or simply garnish a glass with a bouquet of the vibrant herb to relish the aroma with every sip. Choose leaves that are evenly colored, with no signs of wilting. Store a bunch of mint, stems down, in a glass of water with a plastic bag over the leaves. Refrigerate up to a week, changing the water every two days.

Cranberry-Pineapple Punch

MAKES 26 CUPS
Prep: 10 min., Other: 8 hrs.

Tart cranberry meets sweet pineapple in this punch that's perfect for a large party.
A touch of almond flavoring tantalizes the taste buds.

1 (48-oz.) bottle cranberry
   juice drink
1 (48-oz.) can pineapple
   juice
½ cup sugar
2 tsp. almond extract

1 (2-liter) bottle ginger ale,
   chilled

1. Stir together first 4 ingredients until sugar dissolves. Cover mixture, and chill 8 hours.

2. Stir in ginger ale just before serving. Serve immediately.

White Sangría

MAKES ABOUT 8 CUPS
Prep: 20 min.
(pictured on page 183)

Sangría, Spanish for "bleeding," got its name from the beverage being made with red wine. This version is made with white wine and accented beautifully with orange, lemon, and lime slices.

1 (750-milliliter) bottle dry white wine
1 cup orange juice concentrate
⅓ cup lemonade concentrate
⅓ cup limeade concentrate
1 navel orange, sliced
1 lemon, sliced
1 lime, sliced

3 cups club soda, chilled

1. Stir together first 4 ingredients. Stir in half of fruit slices. Cover and chill until ready to serve.
2. Stir in club soda just before serving. Serve immediately over ice with remaining fruit slices.

From Our Kitchen

Citrus juice concentrates rarely freeze solid, so it's easy to spoon out and measure just the amount you need and leave the remainder frozen to use another time. If the concentrates are too firm to measure, just let them stand at room temperature 10 minutes or so to soften; then spoon out what you need and refreeze the rest.

Margarita Granita

MAKES 5 CUPS
Prep: 15 min., Other: 8 hrs.

This frozen concoction takes a pucker-inducing drink to a sweeter level.
We garnish the glasses with sugar instead of salt.

3 cups water
1 cup sugar

½ cup fresh lime juice
⅓ cup fresh lemon juice
6 Tbsp. orange liqueur
6 Tbsp. gold tequila
2 tsp. grated lime rind

Additional sugar

1. Bring 3 cups water and 1 cup sugar to a boil in a saucepan, stirring mixture constantly.

2. Pour sugar mixture into a large bowl; add lime juice and next 4 ingredients. Cover and freeze 8 hours.

3. Process frozen mixture in a blender or food processor until slushy.

4. Dip margarita glass rims into water; dip rims into sugar. Spoon granita into glasses, and serve immediately.

Note: For a nonalcoholic version, omit liquors and add ¾ cup fresh orange juice.

Tequila Mojitos

MAKES 5 CUPS
Prep: 10 min., Cook: 8 min., Other: 2 hrs.

Make the simple syrup needed for this beverage up to 1 week ahead,
and store it in the refrigerator.

1 cup water
¾ cup sugar
1 cup fresh mint sprigs

2 cups lemon-lime soft
  drink, chilled
1 cup fresh lime juice
½ cup tequila
Garnishes: fresh mint sprigs,
  lime slices

1. Bring 1 cup water and sugar to a boil in a medium saucepan. Boil, stirring often, until sugar dissolves. Remove from heat; add 1 cup mint sprigs, and let stand 2 hours or until mixture is completely cool.

2. Pour mixture through a wire-mesh strainer into a pitcher, discarding mint. Stir in lemon-lime soft drink, lime juice, and tequila. Serve immediately over ice. Garnish, if desired.

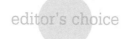

Brandy Velvet

MAKES 2¼ CUPS
Prep: 5 min.

*Coffee ice cream, brandy, and coffee combine to make this
drink as smooth as its name implies.*

½ tsp. instant coffee
   granules
¼ cup hot water
1 pt. coffee ice cream
¼ cup brandy
¼ cup chocolate syrup
Garnish: grated chocolate

1. Stir together coffee granules and hot water. Process coffee and next 3 ingredients in a blender until smooth. Garnish, if desired. Serve immediately.

make ahead

Date-Orange-Nut Spread

MAKES 2 CUPS
Prep: 20 min., Other: 8 hrs.

The addition of honey makes this spread ideal for Jewish holiday gatherings.

1½ cups chopped dates (we tested with Sunsweet)
½ cup raisins
½ cup sweet white wine (we tested with Mogen David)

½ tsp. grated orange rind
1 large navel orange, peeled and cut into chunks
⅓ cup honey
½ cup almonds, toasted
½ cup walnuts, toasted
½ tsp. ground cinnamon
¼ tsp. ground cardamom

1. Combine first 3 ingredients in a bowl. Cover and chill 8 hours.
2. Process date mixture, orange rind, and remaining ingredients in a food processor until slightly chunky and spreadable, adding more wine if needed.

Goat Cheese Spread

MAKES 4 CUPS
Prep: 30 min., Other: 8 hrs.

This creamy spread packs a flavor punch—basil pesto and dried tomatoes give it holiday color.

2 (8-oz.) packages cream
    cheese, softened
8 oz. goat cheese
2 garlic cloves, minced
4 tsp. chopped fresh or
    1¼ tsp. dried oregano
⅛ tsp. freshly ground
    pepper
¼ cup basil pesto
½ cup dried tomatoes in
    oil, drained and
    chopped

Garnishes: dried tomato
    slivers, fresh oregano
    sprigs

1. Process first 5 ingredients in a food processor until smooth. Spread one-third of cheese mixture in a plastic wrap-lined 8- x 4-inch loafpan. Top with pesto; spread one-third cheese mixture over pesto. Sprinkle with ½ cup dried tomatoes; top with remaining cheese mixture. Cover and chill 8 hours.

2. Invert spread onto a serving plate, discarding plastic wrap. Garnish, if desired. Serve with French bread slices or crackers.

From Our Kitchen

To garnish, cut a dried tomato into slivers. Gently press fresh oregano sprigs and tomato slivers in a decorative pattern over the top of the cheese after it's inverted.

Pimiento Cheese

MAKES 4 CUPS
Prep: 15 min.

1½ cups mayonnaise
1 (4-oz.) jar diced pimiento, drained
1 tsp. Worcestershire sauce
1 tsp. finely grated onion
¼ tsp. ground red pepper
1 (8-oz.) block extra-sharp Cheddar cheese, finely shredded
1 (8-oz.) block sharp Cheddar cheese, shredded

1. Stir together first 5 ingredients in a large bowl; stir in cheeses. Store in refrigerator up to 1 week.

Jalapeño Pimiento Cheese: Add 2 seeded and minced jalapeño peppers.

Cream Cheese-and-Olive Pimiento Cheese: Reduce mayonnaise to ¾ cup. Stir together first 5 ingredients, 1 (8-oz.) package softened cream cheese, and 1 (5¾-oz.) jar drained sliced salad olives. Proceed with recipe as directed.

Pecan Pimiento Cheese: Stir in ¾ cup toasted chopped pecans.

Taste of the South

Barbecue, catfish, and grits are all true Southern culinary icons, as is pimiento cheese. Since these favorite Southern recipes survive by way of oral tradition, a cookbook containing the one true recipe for each—let alone the many regional variations—is almost impossible to find.

In our search for the definitive pimiento cheese, we asked Mary Allen Perry of our Test Kitchens to share her recipe. She drew upon childhood memories to record this fabulous formula, so you should feel confident with this terrific version and its variations.

Her secret? Using a regular shred for the sharp Cheddar and a fine shred for the extra-sharp Cheddar creates a pleasing texture variation.

Strawberry-Cheese Horseshoe

MAKES 6 CUPS
Prep: 20 min., Other: 8 hrs.

This tangy-sweet cheese spread first ran in Southern Living *in 1986 shaped in a ring with a small bowl of the preserves in the center. In 2000 it graced our pages shaped as a horseshoe for a Kentucky Derby party. It's an addictive spread no matter how you shape it.*

1 (1-lb.) block sharp
  Cheddar cheese,
  shredded
1 cup mayonnaise
½ cup chopped onion
¼ tsp. salt
¼ tsp. black pepper
¼ to ½ tsp. ground red
  pepper
1 cup chopped pecans,
  toasted

1 (12-oz.) jar strawberry
  preserves

1. Beat first 6 ingredients at medium speed with an electric mixer until blended; stir in pecans. Shape mixture into a horseshoe shape, or spoon into a 5-cup mold. Cover and chill at least 8 hours or up to 2 days.

2. Spoon preserves over cheese mixture, and serve immediately with crackers or bread rounds.

Layered Nacho Dip

MAKES ABOUT 8 CUPS
Prep: 10 min.

Serving this classic from 1981 has been a time-honored party tradition. The combination of beans, avocado, tomatoes, and chiles creates an instant Southwestern fiesta.

1 (16-oz.) can refried beans
½ (1.25-oz.) package taco
   seasoning mix

1 (6-oz.) carton avocado dip
1 (8-oz.) container sour
   cream
1 (4.5-oz.) can chopped
   black olives
2 large tomatoes, diced
1 small onion, finely
   chopped
1 (4.5-oz.) can chopped
   green chiles
1½ cups (6 oz.) shredded
   Monterey Jack cheese

1. Combine beans and seasoning mix; spread bean mixture in an 8-inch square dish.
2. Layer remaining ingredients on top of bean mixture in order listed. Serve with corn chips or tortilla chips.

Spinach and Artichokes in Puff Pastry

MAKES 4 DOZEN
Prep: 20 min., Cook: 20 min., Other: 30 min.

*These rich little treats are packed with such goodies as spinach and Parmesan cheese.
Flaky puff pastry shells make them irresistible.*

1 (10-oz.) package frozen
    chopped spinach,
    thawed

1 (14-oz.) can artichoke
    hearts, drained and
    chopped
½ cup mayonnaise
½ cup grated Parmesan
    cheese
1 tsp. onion powder
1 tsp. garlic powder
½ tsp. pepper

1 (17.3-oz.) package frozen
    puff pastry sheets

1. Drain spinach well, pressing between layers of paper towels.

2. Stir together spinach, artichoke hearts, and next 5 ingredients.

3. Thaw puff pastry at room temperature 30 minutes. Unfold pastry, and place on a lightly floured surface or heavy-duty plastic wrap. Spread one-fourth spinach mixture evenly over pastry sheet, leaving a ½-inch border. Roll up pastry, jelly-roll fashion, pressing to seal seam; wrap in heavy-duty plastic wrap. Repeat procedure with remaining pastry and spinach mixture. Freeze 30 minutes; cut into ½-inch-thick slices. (Rolls can be frozen up to 3 months.)

4. Bake at 400° for 20 minutes or until golden brown.

Catfish Poppers with Spicy Dipping Sauce

MAKES 15 APPETIZER SERVINGS (ABOUT 45 POPPERS)
Prep: 10 min., Cook: 6 min. per batch

You can make a splash at a party by serving these poppers on individual forks placed in a bud vase. Just pierce each popper with the tines of a fork, and place forks, handle end down, in the vase for a stylish presentation.

½ tsp. salt
½ tsp. Cajun seasoning
⅔ cup all-purpose flour
1 large egg
¼ cup milk
1¾ lb. catfish fillets, cut into 1½-inch pieces
1½ cups Japanese bread-crumbs (panko)

Vegetable oil
Spicy Dipping Sauce

1. Combine first 3 ingredients; whisk together egg and milk. Dredge catfish pieces in flour mixture, and dip in egg mixture. Dredge in breadcrumbs.
2. Pour oil to a depth of ½ inch in a large skillet; heat to 375°. Fry catfish pieces, in batches, 2 to 3 minutes on each side or until golden brown. Drain on paper towels. Serve with Spicy Dipping Sauce.

Spicy Dipping Sauce

MAKES 1 CUP
Prep: 5 min.

¾ cup mayonnaise
¼ cup spicy cocktail sauce
2 tsp. fresh lemon juice
¼ tsp. ground red pepper
Old Bay seasoning (optional)

1. Stir together first 4 ingredients. Cover and chill until ready to serve. Sprinkle with Old Bay seasoning, if desired.

Shrimp 'n' Grits Tarts

MAKES 36 TARTS
Prep: 45 min., Cook: 35 min.

Most folks would agree that hot cooked grits rank high among adored Southern sides. The addition of cheese and eggs over the years has made them a must-serve at brunch. This recipe pairs an old favorite with unique ingredients to create a delightfully different memory. So have fun serving this down-home side in a new and clever way.

3½ cups chicken broth, divided
1 cup milk
¼ cup butter or margarine, divided
½ tsp. white pepper
1 cup uncooked coarse-ground or regular grits
⅔ cup shredded Parmesan cheese

⅔ cup diced smoked ham
3 Tbsp. all-purpose flour

3 Tbsp. chopped fresh parsley
¾ tsp. white wine Worcestershire sauce
36 medium-size peeled cooked shrimp

Garnish: chopped parsley

1. Bring 2 cups chicken broth, milk, 2 Tbsp. butter, and white pepper to a boil in a large saucepan over medium-high heat. Gradually whisk in grits; return to a boil. Reduce heat, and simmer, stirring occasionally, 5 to 10 minutes or until thickened. Add Parmesan cheese, and whisk until melted and blended.

2. Spoon 1 rounded tablespoonful of grits-and-cheese mixture into each lightly greased cup of 3 (12-cup) miniature muffin pans.

3. Bake at 350° for 20 to 25 minutes or until lightly browned. Make an indentation in centers of warm grits tarts, using the back of a spoon. Cool completely in pans. Remove tarts from muffin pans, and place tarts on a 15- x 10-inch jelly-roll pan.

4. Melt remaining 2 Tbsp. butter in a medium saucepan over medium-high heat; add ham, and sauté 1 to 2 minutes. Sprinkle 3 Tbsp. flour evenly over ham, and cook, stirring often, 1 to 2 minutes or until lightly brown. Gradually add remaining 1½ cups chicken broth, stirring until smooth.

5. Reduce heat, and cook, stirring often, 5 to 10 minutes or until thickened. Stir in 3 Tbsp. chopped parsley and white wine Worcestershire sauce, and spoon evenly into tarts. Top each with 1 shrimp.

6. Bake at 350° for 5 to 10 minutes or just until warm. Garnish, if desired.

Starry Snack Mix

MAKES 15 CUPS
Prep: 5 min., Cook: 8 min.

Stir it together, and pack it up! Serving this snack mix is the perfect solution for grumbling tummies on a hiking trip or a long car ride—little and big kids eat it up.

2 (8-oz.) packages crispy cereal squares snack mix (we tested with Bold Party Blend Chex Mix)
1 (16-oz.) package raisins
1 (12-oz.) jar honey-roasted peanuts
1 (9.5-oz.) package fish-shaped Cheddar cheese crackers

1. Combine all ingredients in a very large bowl. Store in an airtight container.

Spicy Pecans

MAKES 1½ CUPS
Prep: 5 min., Cook: 8 min.

Tame the heat of these sweet and spicy pecans by adjusting the amounts of chili powder and pepper.

2 Tbsp. brown sugar
2 Tbsp. orange juice concentrate
1½ Tbsp. butter or margarine
½ tsp. salt
½ tsp. chili powder
¼ tsp. pepper
1½ cups coarsely chopped pecans

1. Cook first 6 ingredients in a skillet over medium-high heat, stirring until brown sugar dissolves. Remove from heat, and stir in pecans. Transfer to a lightly greased baking sheet.
2. Bake at 350° for 8 minutes or until toasted. Cool and store in an airtight container.

Prissy Pecans

MAKES 3 CUPS
Prep: 2 min., Cook: 20 min.

Our Test Kitchens staff loves the kick of coffee these nuts provide—hence the fun name.
Sugar and cinnamon combine with toasty pecans for complexity of flavor
that your adult guests will appreciate.

2 cups pecan halves

2 tsp. instant coffee
   granules
2 Tbsp. hot water

¼ cup sugar
¼ tsp. ground cinnamon
Dash of salt

1. Place pecans in a large skillet; cook over medium-high heat, stirring occasionally, 5 minutes or until pecans are toasted. Remove from heat.

2. Combine instant coffee granules and hot water, stirring until coffee dissolves; set aside.

3. Place sugar in a heavy, medium-size saucepan. Cook, without stirring, 6 minutes or until sugar melts; stir. Add coffee, cinnamon, and salt. (Mixture will bubble and some of the sugar will firm into a ball.) Reduce heat to low; cook, stirring constantly, 6 minutes or until smooth. Bring to a boil over medium heat; boil 3 minutes, stirring constantly. Remove from heat; add pecans, stirring well to coat pecans. Spoon coated pecans on wax paper to cool.

Blue Cheese Thumbprints

MAKES ABOUT 5 DOZEN
Prep: 15 min., Cook: 15 min. per batch, Other: 2 hrs.

Pair these cherry preserves-filled bites with sparkling white wine.

2 (4-oz.) packages crumbled
    blue cheese
½ cup butter, softened
1⅓ cups all-purpose flour
3 Tbsp. poppy seeds
¼ tsp. ground red
    pepper

⅓ cup cherry preserves

1. Beat blue cheese and butter at medium speed with an electric mixer until fluffy. Add flour, poppy seeds, and red pepper, beating just until combined. Roll dough into ¾-inch round balls; cover and chill 2 hours.
2. Arrange balls on ungreased baking sheets, and press thumb into each ball of dough, leaving an indentation.
3. Bake at 350° for 15 minutes or until golden. Transfer to wire racks to cool completely. Place about ¼ tsp. preserves in each indentation.

Blue Cheese Crisps: Combine ingredients for dough as directed. Shape dough into 2 (9-inch) logs. Wrap each log in plastic wrap, and chill 2 hours. Cut each log into ¼-inch-thick slices, and place on ungreased baking sheets. Bake at 350° for 10 to 12 minutes or until golden brown. Transfer to wire racks to cool completely. Omit cherry preserves. Store crisps in an airtight container up to 1 week.

Taste of the South

Cheese straws are like deviled eggs in that every Southern cook wants to make great ones. They make perfect snacks whether you prefer thumbprints or wafers cut into round or square slices, or choose to put the dough through a cookie press to make the traditional straws. Cheese straws can also go solo with a glass of Champagne or beer. No matter the shape, that's an idea worth toasting.

Cheddar Cheese Straws

MAKES ABOUT 10 DOZEN
Prep: 30 min., Cook: 12 min. per batch

If you don't have a heavy-duty stand mixer, you can use a handheld mixer. Just divide the ingredients in half, and work with two batches.

1½ cups butter, softened
1 (1-lb.) block sharp
    Cheddar cheese,
    shredded
1½ tsp. salt
1 to 2 tsp. ground red
    pepper
½ tsp. paprika
4 cups all-purpose flour

1. Beat first 5 ingredients at medium speed with a heavy-duty stand mixer until blended. Gradually add flour, beating just until combined.

2. Use a cookie press with a star-shaped disk to shape mixture into long ribbons, following manufacturer's instructions, on parchment paper-lined baking sheets. Cut ribbons into 2-inch pieces.

3. Bake at 350° for 12 minutes or until lightly browned. Remove to wire racks to cool.

Cheese Wafers: Combine ingredients as directed; chill dough 2 hours. Shape dough into 4 (8-inch) logs; wrap each in plastic wrap, and chill 8 hours. Cut each log into ¼-inch-thick slices; place on parchment paper-lined baking sheets. Bake at 350° for 13 to 15 minutes or until lightly browned. Remove to wire racks to cool. Store in an airtight container 1 week.

From Our Kitchen

Tips for Cheese Straws

• Shred your own cheese; it's stickier and blends better than preshredded cheese.

• Refrigerate unbaked dough between batches to keep wafers from spreading too thin when baked.

• Store baked cheese straws in an airtight container for up to 1 week. Store unbaked dough in the fridge for up to 1 week or in the freezer for up to 1 month.

• Bake stored cheese straws in the oven at 350° for 3 to 4 minutes to make them crispy again.

Pull-Away Bread

MAKES 12 SERVINGS
Prep: 15 min., Cook: 30 min., Other: 3 hrs.

This tender bread breaks away to expose caverns of buttery cheese trails.
Once you give it a try, you won't be able to pull yourself away.

¼ cup grated Parmesan
 cheese
3 Tbsp. sesame seeds
1 tsp. dried basil

1 (25-oz.) package
 frozen roll dough,
 thawed
3 Tbsp. butter or
 margarine, melted

1. Combine first 3 ingredients. Sprinkle one-third of cheese mixture into a greased 12-cup Bundt pan.

2. Place half of roll dough in pan, and drizzle with 1½ Tbsp. butter. Sprinkle with half of remaining cheese mixture. Repeat procedure with remaining dough, butter, and cheese mixture.

3. Let rise in a warm place (85°), free from drafts, 2 to 3 hours or until doubled in bulk.

4. Bake at 350° for 30 minutes, shielding with aluminum foil after 20 minutes to prevent excessive browning. Loosen bread from sides of pan with a knife. Immediately invert onto a serving plate. Serve warm.

Chocolate Chess Tartlets

MAKES ABOUT 6 DOZEN
Prep: 20 min., Cook: 25 min.

Serve these tartlets on kiwifruit slices, and dot the serving platter with raspberry puree for a playful, colorful presentation.

1½ cups sugar
3 Tbsp. unsweetened cocoa
1½ Tbsp. cornmeal
1 Tbsp. all-purpose flour
2 tsp. white vinegar
½ cup butter, melted
Dash of salt

3 large eggs, lightly beaten
5 (2.1-oz.) packages frozen mini phyllo pastry shells, thawed (we tested with Athens Mini Fillo Shells)

Garnishes: thawed frozen whipped topping, kiwifruit slices

1. Stir together first 7 ingredients until blended.

2. Add eggs, stirring well. Spoon about 1 heaping tsp. chocolate mixture into each pastry shell, and place on 2 large ungreased baking sheets.

3. Bake at 350° for 25 minutes or just until set. Remove to wire racks, and cool completely. Garnish, if desired.

Note: Store tartlets in an airtight container up to 3 days.

Easy weeknight favorites

Even if you're short on time, you don't have to skimp on flavor. Choose from one of these fresh selections to have a memorable meal on the table with little hands-on time.

our best
40 years
recipes

TOMATO-PESTO TART, PAGE 226

Easy Cheddar Biscuits

MAKES 1½ DOZEN
Prep: 20 min., Cook: 20 min.

1½ cups all-purpose flour
1 Tbsp. baking powder
½ tsp. salt
1 Tbsp. sugar

1 cup (4 oz.) shredded sharp
   Cheddar cheese
⅓ cup shortening
½ cup milk

1. Pulse first 4 ingredients in a food processor 4 or 5 times or until dry ingredients are thoroughly combined.
2. Add shredded cheese and shortening, and pulse 4 or 5 times or until mixture is crumbly. With processor running, gradually add milk, and process until dough forms a ball and leaves sides of bowl.
3. Turn dough out onto a lightly floured surface; shape into a ball.
4. Pat or roll dough to ½-inch thickness; cut with a 2-inch round cutter, and place on lightly greased baking sheets.
5. Bake biscuits at 425° for 10 minutes or until golden.

Taste of the South

A biscuit is a small, flaky quick bread—leavened with baking soda or baking powder—that has a light, tender texture. Most Southerners pat the biscuits into little circles, but the dough can be rolled and cut with a biscuit cutter or dropped from a spoon before baking. Tender biscuits are delicious split and spread with butter, honey, and jam, or filled with slivers of ham or steak. In the South, some cooks swear soft wheat flour makes the most tender, flaky biscuits. White Lily and Martha White are the most popular brands of soft wheat flour in the South. If they aren't available in your area, use equal amounts of all-purpose and cake flour. Mix only until the ingredients just hold together. Overmixing the dough will develop the gluten in the flour and toughen the biscuits.

Breakaway Vegetable Bread

MAKES 8 TO 10 SERVINGS
Prep: 15 min., Cook: 45 min.

3 (10-oz.) cans refrigerated buttermilk biscuits
½ cup butter or margarine, melted

½ lb. bacon, cooked and crumbled
½ cup grated Parmesan cheese
1 small onion, finely chopped
1 small green bell pepper, finely chopped

1. Cut biscuits into quarters; dip each piece in butter, and layer one-third in a lightly greased 10-inch Bundt pan.
2. Sprinkle with half each of bacon, cheese, onion, and bell pepper. Repeat layers until all ingredients are used, ending with biscuits. Bake at 350° for 40 to 45 minutes or until done.

Taste of the South

This bread was the first savory version of what began as a sweet rage: monkey bread. Made by piling small balls of dough in a tube pan, monkey breads in sweet *and* savory form became popular in the early 1980s. Today, they're still popular because of quick assembly offered by convenience products and pull-apart characteristics that make them easy to serve and fun to eat at all sorts of gatherings.

Bacon Pasta

MAKES 8 SERVINGS
Prep: 3 min., Cook: 27 min.

1 (16-oz.) package penne
   pasta

15 bacon slices

1 cup sliced fresh
   mushrooms
2 garlic cloves, minced
1 cup grated fresh
   Parmesan cheese
2 cups whipping cream
½ tsp. freshly ground
   pepper

½ cup sliced green onions

1. Cook pasta according to package directions; set aside.
2. Meanwhile, cook bacon in a large skillet over medium heat until crisp; remove bacon, and drain on paper towels, reserving 2 Tbsp. drippings in skillet. Crumble bacon, and set aside.
3. Sauté sliced mushrooms and garlic in reserved drippings 3 minutes or until tender. Stir in pasta, Parmesan cheese, whipping cream, and pepper; simmer over medium-low heat until sauce is thickened, stirring often.
4. Stir in crumbled bacon and green onions; serve immediately.

Taste of the South

It hisses, it sputters, it sends an aromatic waft through the house. Sizzling bacon announces the salty pleasure it delivers long before it's brought to the table. Whether served with eggs, in pasta, or on a sandwich, bacon is a flavor enhancer that adds a distinct, sassy note to any dish.

Fresh Pesto Pasta Salad

MAKES 8 SERVINGS
Prep: 20 min.

*Create a sassy room-temperature side or main dish when you toss
hot pasta with cool vinaigrette and cheese.*

1 (16-oz.) package small
    shell pasta

⅓ cup red wine vinegar
1 Tbsp. sugar
1 tsp. seasoned pepper
½ tsp. salt
1 tsp. Dijon mustard
1 garlic clove, pressed
¾ cup olive oil

1 cup chopped fresh basil
1 (3-oz.) package shredded
    Parmesan cheese
½ cup toasted pine nuts
Garnishes: gourmet mixed
    baby salad greens;
    grape tomatoes; small,
    yellow pear-shaped
    tomatoes

1. Prepare pasta according to package directions; drain.
2. Whisk together vinegar and next 5 ingredients.
Gradually whisk in olive oil.
3. Add vinaigrette to pasta. Add basil, cheese, and pine
nuts; toss to combine. Garnish, if desired.

Greek Pasta Salad

MAKES 4 TO 6 SERVINGS
Prep: 30 min., Cook: 8 min.

This simply seasoned salad is a make-ahead pleaser. Lemon juice offers characteristic Greek flair in a bed of mushroom- and black olive-studded pasta.

1 (8-oz.) package sliced
    fresh mushrooms
4 to 5 shallots, chopped
    (about ½ cup)
6 Tbsp. olive oil, divided

2 Tbsp. lemon juice
3 Tbsp. mayonnaise
1 Tbsp. Greek seasoning

1 (8-oz.) package penne
    pasta, cooked
2 (2.5-oz.) cans sliced
    ripe black olives,
    drained
1 (4-oz.) jar diced
    pimiento, drained

1. Sauté sliced mushrooms and chopped shallot in 2 Tbsp. hot olive oil in a large skillet over medium-high heat 7 to 8 minutes or until tender. Remove from heat.

2. Whisk together remaining 4 Tbsp. oil, juice, mayonnaise, and seasoning in a large bowl, blending well.

3. Add cooked pasta, mushroom mixture, olives, and pimiento, tossing to coat. Cover and chill 8 hours, if desired.

Tomato-Basil-Asparagus Pasta Salad

MAKES 8 SERVINGS
Prep: 10 min., Cook: 14 min., Other: 1 hr.

Leave it to Southern ingenuity to create this quick and flavorful salad. An explosion of chopped fresh basil personalizes a bottled vinaigrette to dress this make-ahead salad.

1 (16-oz.) package bow tie
   pasta
1 lb. asparagus, cut into
   2-inch pieces

1 cup lemon vinaigrette (we
   tested with Wish-Bone
   Lemon Garlic & Herb
   Vinaigrette)
1 (1-oz.) package fresh basil,
   chopped (about ¾ cup)

1 pt. grape tomatoes,
   halved
Salt and pepper to taste

Garnish: chopped fresh basil

1. Cook pasta according to package directions, adding asparagus during the last 2 minutes of cooking time. Drain and rinse under cool water.

2. Stir together lemon vinaigrette and fresh basil; pour ¾ cup dressing mixture over pasta mixture.

3. Stir in tomatoes and salt and pepper to taste. Cover and chill 1 hour.

4. Toss pasta mixture with remaining ¼ cup dressing just before serving. Garnish, if desired.

From Our Kitchen

When it comes to summer meals, nothing beats quick, easy, light, and delicious.
• Add sliced grilled chicken or tuna to turn this into a main-dish salad. Double the serving size for a main dish.
• To save time, prep the tomatoes, asparagus, and basil while the pasta water comes to a boil.

Black Bean and Black-Eyed Pea Salad

MAKES 6 SERVINGS
Prep: 20 min., Other: 30 min.

This recipe was originally submitted using only black beans; we added black-eyed peas for Southern flavor. You can top this salad with grilled or deli rotisserie chicken, leftover steak strips, or canned albacore tuna.

1 tsp. grated lime rind
½ cup fresh lime juice
   (about 4 limes)
¼ cup olive oil
1 tsp. brown sugar
1 tsp. chili powder
½ tsp. ground cumin
½ to 1 tsp. salt

1 (15-oz.) can black beans,
   rinsed and drained
1 (15.5-oz.) can black-eyed
   peas, rinsed and
   drained
1½ cups frozen whole
   kernel corn, thawed
½ small green bell pepper,
   chopped
⅓ cup chopped fresh
   cilantro

Romaine lettuce
2 large avocados, sliced
Garnishes: lime wedges,
   fresh cilantro sprigs

1. Whisk together first 7 ingredients in a large bowl.
2. Add black beans and next 4 ingredients, tossing to coat. Cover and chill 30 minutes.
3. Serve over lettuce; arrange avocado slices around salad. Garnish, if desired.

Lentil and Orzo Salad

MAKES 4 SERVINGS
Prep: 15 min., Other: 2 hrs.

This mouthwatering recipe combines familiar favorites, such as lemon juice, onion, and bell pepper, with global ingredients, like lentils, cumin, and orzo. If you've never cooked orzo before, don't worry—it couldn't be easier. It boils up just like regular pasta, only faster.

¼ cup vinaigrette dressing
2 Tbsp. fresh lemon
    juice
½ tsp. ground cumin
½ tsp. salt
½ tsp. freshly ground black
    pepper
¼ tsp. dried crushed
    red pepper

2 cups cooked lentils
1 cup cooked orzo
½ red bell pepper, diced
½ small red onion, diced
1½ Tbsp. chopped
    fresh cilantro

1. Whisk together first 6 ingredients in a large bowl.

2. Add lentils and remaining ingredients, tossing gently to coat. Cover and chill 2 hours.

Potato Salad

MAKES 8 SERVINGS
Prep: 15 min., Cook: 40 min., Other: 2 hrs.

4 lb. red potatoes (about
   8 large)

5 hard-cooked eggs,
   separated
1 tsp. salt, divided
3 green onions, sliced
   (optional)

1 cup mayonnaise
2 Tbsp. sweet pickle
   relish
1 Tbsp. prepared mustard
½ tsp. pepper

1. Cook potatoes in boiling water to cover 40 minutes or until tender; drain and cool. Peel potatoes, and cut into 1-inch cubes.

2. Chop egg whites. Stir together potato cubes, egg whites, ½ tsp. salt, and, if desired, green onions.

3. Mash egg yolks; add remaining ½ tsp. salt, mayonnaise, and remaining 3 ingredients, stirring until blended. Gently stir into potato mixture. Cover and chill 2 hours.

Taste of the South

In a traditional potato salad, cooked, sliced, or diced potatoes are bound with mayonnaise or sour cream dressing and flavored with ingredients ranging from onion to pickle relish to hard-cooked eggs. Red potatoes lend uplifting color to this traditional version.

Southern-Style Cobb Salad

MAKES 6 SERVINGS
Prep: 30 min.

½ to 1 lb. fresh sugar snap
    peas

2 heads iceberg lettuce
3 hard-cooked eggs
4 plum tomatoes
1 large avocado

1 bunch fresh watercress,
    torn
2 skinned and boned
    chicken breasts,
    cooked and sliced
12 bacon slices, cooked and
    crumbled
Blue Cheese-Buttermilk
    Dressing
Freshly ground pepper

1. Cook peas in boiling water to cover 2 to 3 minutes; drain. Plunge into ice water to stop the cooking process; drain and set aside.

2. Cut iceberg lettuce into 6 wedges. Coarsely chop eggs. Remove and discard pulp from tomatoes, and cut into thin strips. Dice avocado.

3. Arrange watercress evenly on 6 salad plates. Top with peas, chopped eggs, tomato strips, avocado, and chicken; sprinkle with bacon. Place a lettuce wedge on each plate. Drizzle with Blue Cheese-Buttermilk Dressing; sprinkle with pepper.

Blue Cheese-Buttermilk Dressing

MAKES 6 SERVINGS
Prep: 5 min.

1 (4-oz.) package crumbled
    blue cheese
1 cup nonfat buttermilk
½ to ⅔ cup reduced-fat
    mayonnaise
3 to 4 Tbsp. lemon juice
1 garlic clove, minced

1. Stir together all ingredients in a bowl. Serve over salad.

Taste of the South

Sugar snap peas lend a Southern accent to this classic salad. Whether raw or lightly cooked, these bright green pods complement salads, stir-fries, and dips. Like snow peas, you can enjoy the entire pod. Their sweetness and crunchy texture make sugar snap peas a vegetable your kids will actually eat without coaxing.

Tomato-Pesto Tart

MAKES 4 SERVINGS
Prep: 30 min., Cook: 25 min., Other: 15 min.

*Pesto, a sauce originating in Genoa, Italy, traditionally combines fresh basil,
garlic, pine nuts, Parmesan cheese, and olive oil. It's a perfect complement to tomatoes
and makes this tart ultimately rich and savory.*

½ (15-oz.) package
   refrigerated piecrusts

2 cups (8 oz.) shredded
   mozzarella cheese,
   divided
5 plum tomatoes, sliced

½ cup mayonnaise
¼ cup grated Parmesan
   cheese
2 Tbsp. basil pesto
½ tsp. freshly ground
   pepper

3 Tbsp. chopped
   fresh basil

1. Unroll piecrust on a lightly greased baking sheet. Roll into a 12-inch circle. Brush outer 1 inch of crust with water. Fold edges up and crimp. Prick bottom.

2. Bake at 425° for 8 to 10 minutes. Remove from oven. Sprinkle with 1 cup mozzarella cheese; cool 15 minutes. Arrange tomato slices over cheese.

3. Stir together remaining 1 cup mozzarella cheese, mayonnaise, and next 3 ingredients. Spread over tomato slices.

4. Bake at 375° for 20 to 25 minutes. Remove from oven; sprinkle with basil.

Summer Garden Pie

MAKES 4 TO 6 SERVINGS
Prep: 1 hr., Cook: 30 min., Other: 35 min.

We salted the tomato slices and let them stand for 30 minutes to draw out any excess moisture that could make this pie soggy.

3 large tomatoes, peeled, seeded, and sliced
1 tsp. salt, divided

½ (15-oz.) package refrigerated piecrusts

4 bacon slices

3 medium-size sweet onions, halved and thinly sliced

1 cup (4 oz.) shredded sharp Cheddar cheese
1 cup mayonnaise
¼ tsp. pepper
⅓ cup grated Parmesan cheese
2 Tbsp. fine, dry breadcrumbs

1. Place tomato slices on paper towels, and sprinkle with ½ tsp. salt; let stand 30 minutes.

2. Unroll piecrust, and fit into a 9-inch deep-dish pieplate. Fold edges of piecrust under, and crimp. Line with aluminum foil, and fill with pie weights or dried beans.

3. Bake at 425° for 10 to 12 minutes or until lightly browned. Remove pie weights and foil.

4. Cook bacon in a large skillet until crisp; remove bacon, and drain on paper towels, reserving 1 tsp. drippings in skillet. Crumble bacon, and set aside.

5. Sauté onion in hot drippings in skillet over medium-high heat 8 to 10 minutes or until tender. Spoon onion over prepared piecrust, and top with tomato slices.

6. Stir together Cheddar cheese, mayonnaise, pepper, and remaining ½ tsp. salt. Spread mixture over tomato slices. Combine Parmesan cheese and breadcrumbs; sprinkle over top.

7. Bake at 350° for 30 minutes or until golden. Let stand 5 minutes before serving. Sprinkle with bacon.

Broccoli and Cauliflower Gratin

MAKES 8 SERVINGS
Prep: 15 min., Cook: 25 min.

Gratin dishes offer a great way to incorporate vegetables into menus. By definition, a gratin is any dish topped with cheese or breadcrumbs and then heated in the oven until browned and crispy. Shed new light on broccoli and cauliflower with this cheesy dish.

2 (16-oz.) packages fresh broccoli and cauliflower florets

1½ cups reduced-fat mayonnaise
1 cup (4 oz.) shredded reduced-fat Cheddar cheese
1 (3-oz.) package shredded Parmesan cheese
4 green onions, sliced
2 Tbsp. Dijon mustard
¼ tsp. ground red pepper
3 Tbsp. Italian-seasoned breadcrumbs

1. Arrange florets in a steamer basket over boiling water. Cover and steam for 6 to 8 minutes or until crisp-tender. Drain well.
2. Arrange florets in a lightly greased 2-qt. baking dish.
3. Stir together mayonnaise and next 5 ingredients. Spoon over florets. Sprinkle with breadcrumbs.
4. Bake at 350° for 20 to 25 minutes or until golden.

Au Gratin Potato Casserole

MAKES 10 TO 12 SERVINGS
Prep: 10 min.; Cook: 1 hr., 20 min.

Crushed cornflakes cereal adds eye-popping crunch to this creamy casserole.

1 (32-oz.) package
   frozen Southern-style
   hash browns (we tested
   with Ore-Ida Southern
   Style Hash Browns)
1 (16-oz.) container sour
   cream
2 cups (8 oz.) shredded
   Cheddar cheese
1 (10¾-oz.) can cream
   of mushroom soup
1 small onion, finely
   chopped
¼ tsp. pepper

2 cups crushed cornflakes
   cereal
¼ cup butter, melted

1. Stir together first 6 ingredients in a large bowl.

2. Spoon potato mixture into a lightly greased 13- x 9-inch baking dish. Sprinkle evenly with crushed cornflakes, and drizzle evenly with butter.

3. Bake at 325° for 1 hour and 20 minutes or until bubbly.

From Our Kitchen

You'll love the ease of this casserole. You can make it ahead of time, refrigerate it, and then bake it just before dinner. Let a chilled casserole sit at room temperature 20 minutes before you bake it.

Butternut Squash Casserole

MAKES 6 TO 8 SERVINGS
Prep: 10 min., Cook: 45 min.

2 cups cooked, mashed
  butternut squash
3 large eggs
¾ cup sugar
⅓ cup butter or margarine,
  softened
⅓ cup milk
1 tsp. ground ginger
½ tsp. coconut flavoring

Crunchy Cereal Topping

1. Combine first 7 ingredients; pour into a lightly greased 8-inch square baking dish.

2. Bake at 350° for 35 minutes. Sprinkle with Crunchy Cereal Topping, and bake 10 more minutes.

Crunchy Cereal Topping

MAKES 1½ CUPS
Prep: 3 min.

1½ cups cornflake cereal
  crumbs
¾ cup firmly packed
  brown sugar
½ cup chopped pecans
¼ cup butter or margarine,
  melted

1. Combine all ingredients in a medium-size bowl.

From Our Kitchen

You'll discover sweet flavor inside a club-shaped golden butternut squash. Bake and then freeze the cooked, mashed pulp for up to six months. This way, you can easily create this version of squash casserole at any time of year.

Taco Soup

MAKES 10 CUPS
Prep: 13 min., Cook: 40 min.

This beefy soup is chock-full of good-for-you foods. Beans, corn, and tomatoes make it an easy meal-in-one dish.

1 lb. ground beef

1 (15-oz.) can pinto beans
1 (15.25-oz.) can whole kernel corn
1 (14.5-oz.) can green beans
1 (15-oz.) can ranch beans, undrained
1 (14½-oz.) can stewed tomatoes
1 (12-oz.) can beer
1 (10-oz.) can diced tomatoes and green chiles
1 (1.25-oz.) package taco seasoning mix
1 (1-oz.) envelope Ranch dressing mix

5 (6-inch) corn tortillas
Salt

1. Brown beef in a stockpot, stirring until it crumbles and is no longer pink; drain. Return beef to pot.

2. Rinse and drain pinto beans, corn, and green beans; stir into beef. Stir in ranch beans and next 5 ingredients; bring to a boil. Reduce heat; simmer 30 minutes.

3. Meanwhile, cut tortillas into ¼-inch strips. Place on a baking sheet; coat with cooking spray. Sprinkle with salt.

4. Bake at 400° for 5 to 8 minutes. Ladle soup into bowls, and top with tortilla strips.

Pot Liquor Soup

MAKES 19 CUPS
Prep: 40 min., Cook: 45 min.

You can't get much more Southern than pot liquor soup. This version has been a hit in our Test Kitchens since the mid-1990s. We've since streamlined it by calling for prewashed and chopped collard greens.

1 (16-oz.) package fresh
   chopped collard greens

1 (2-lb.) ham steak, chopped
2 Tbsp. hot sauce
3 Tbsp. olive oil
3 medium onions, chopped
1 garlic clove, minced

6 red potatoes, diced
3 (14.5-oz.) cans chicken
   broth
2 (16-oz.) cans field peas,
   drained
2 (16-oz.) cans crowder
   peas, drained
2 cups water
½ cup vermouth
1 Tbsp. white vinegar
½ tsp. salt

1. Bring collard greens and water to cover to a boil in a large Dutch oven. Remove from heat; drain. Repeat procedure if boiling in batches.

2. Toss together ham and hot sauce; cook in hot oil in Dutch oven over medium-high heat 8 to 10 minutes or until browned. Add onion and garlic; sauté until tender.

3. Stir in greens, potato, and remaining ingredients; bring to a boil. Reduce heat; simmer, stirring occasionally, 45 minutes.

Chicken Tetrazzini

MAKES 6 SERVINGS
Prep: 20 min., Cook: 25 min.

This casserole is ideal for making use of leftover chicken or chopped cooked chicken. The secret to the supercreamy indulgence is the Alfredo sauce.

3 cups chopped cooked
   chicken
1 cup shredded Parmesan
   cheese, divided
1 (10¾-oz.) can cream
   of mushroom soup*
1 (10-oz.) container
   refrigerated Alfredo
   sauce*
1 (3½-oz.) can sliced
   mushrooms, drained
½ cup slivered almonds,
   toasted
½ cup chicken broth
¼ cup dry sherry
¼ tsp. freshly ground
   pepper
7 oz. vermicelli, cooked

1. Stir together chicken, ½ cup Parmesan cheese, and next 7 ingredients; gently stir in pasta.
2. Spoon mixture into 6 lightly greased 6-oz. baking dishes or a lightly greased 11- x 7-inch baking dish.
3. Sprinkle with remaining ½ cup Parmesan cheese.
4. Bake at 350° for 25 minutes or until thoroughly heated.

*Substitute reduced-sodium, reduced-fat cream of mushroom soup and light Alfredo sauce, if desired.

Oven-Fried Parmesan Chicken Strips

MAKES 5 SERVINGS
Prep: 15 min., Cook: 30 min.

Dunk this perfect finger food into barbecue sauce or sweet honey mustard.

2 Tbsp. butter

⅓ cup reduced-fat baking
   mix (we tested with
   Bisquick Heart Smart)
⅓ cup grated Parmesan
   cheese
1½ tsp. Old Bay seasoning
⅛ tsp. pepper
2 lb. chicken breast strips

1. Melt butter in a 15- x 10-inch jelly-roll pan in a 425° oven.

2. Place baking mix and next 3 ingredients in a large zip-top plastic bag; shake well to combine. Add chicken, several pieces at a time, shaking well to coat. Arrange chicken in melted butter in hot jelly-roll pan.

3. Bake at 425° for 30 minutes or until chicken is done, turning once. Serve immediately.

To Freeze: Place uncooked coated chicken strips on a baking sheet in the freezer. Once frozen, place strips in a zip-top freezer bag and return to freezer until ready to prepare. Bake frozen strips on a hot, buttered jelly-roll pan (according to previous directions) at 425° for 35 minutes, turning after 25 minutes.

From Our Kitchen

Each serving of this crunchy indulgence offers fewer than 300 calories and only 28% of calories are from fat. Baking instead of frying and using reduced-fat baking mix keeps the coveted flavor and crunch without having the excessive fat of original fried chicken.

Turkey Piccata

MAKES 4 TO 6 SERVINGS
Prep: 15 min., Cook: 15 min.

"A hot pan, poultry or meat, simple seasonings, lemon juice, and parsley, and—voilà—a scrumptious dinner," says Peg Lee, manager of the Cooking School for Central Market in Houston. We took a lesson from her with this lemon-herbed turkey. Pull out your largest nonstick skillet for this recipe. (An electric one would be great.) Don't crowd the pan, and add each turkey cutlet slowly so the temperature will stay hot.

1 lb. boneless turkey breast
   cutlets*

½ cup all-purpose flour
1 tsp. salt
1 tsp. white pepper

3 Tbsp. butter, divided
2 Tbsp. olive oil

½ cup dry white wine
⅓ cup fresh lemon juice
1 Tbsp. drained capers
6 lemon slices, halved

1 Tbsp. chopped fresh
   flat-leaf parsley

1. Place turkey between 2 sheets of heavy-duty plastic wrap, and flatten to ¼-inch thickness, using a rolling pin or the flat side of a meat mallet.

2. Combine flour, salt, and pepper in a shallow dish. Dredge turkey cutlets in flour mixture.

3. Melt 1 Tbsp. butter in 1 Tbsp. olive oil in a large non-stick skillet over medium-high heat. Add half of turkey, and cook 2 to 3 minutes on each side or until golden brown. Remove turkey from skillet, and place on a wire rack in a jelly-roll pan in a 200° oven to keep warm. Repeat with remaining turkey, 1 Tbsp. butter, and remaining 1 Tbsp. oil as needed.

4. Stir wine and next 3 ingredients into skillet, and cook over medium-high heat 2 minutes or until sauce is slightly thickened. Remove from heat; stir in remaining 1 Tbsp. butter.

5. Place turkey on a serving platter; pour sauce over turkey, and sprinkle evenly with parsley.

*Substitute 1 lb. skinned and boned chicken thighs or thinly cut boneless pork chops, if desired.

Fruitini

MAKES 6 SERVINGS
Prep: 20 min.

Helen DeFrance and Leslie Carpenter always make cooking a family affair. Their dedication to family bonding in the kitchen is so strong that they hold a series of cooking classes—Kids Are Cooking—throughout the year at the Everyday Gourmet in Jackson, Mississippi, among other locations. Look for Helen and Leslie's cookbook of delicious kid-friendly recipes, At Home Café from Basil Leaf Publications, at www.athomecafe.net. Packed with an assortment of colorful, heart-healthy fruits, the whimsical Fruitini allows little hands to help out in the kitchen. Powdered sugar-rimmed parfait glasses add pizzazz.

1 banana, peeled and sliced
   (about ½ cup)
½ cantaloupe, cut into
   ½-inch cubes (about
   3 cups)
½ lb. grapes, halved
   (about 1 cup)
2 kiwifruit, peeled and
   sliced
1 navel orange, peeled and
   sectioned
10 strawberries, sliced

¼ cup powdered sugar,
   divided
⅓ cup fresh lemon juice,
   divided (about 2 lemons)

1. Toss together first 6 ingredients in a large bowl.
2. Stir in 2 Tbsp. powdered sugar and 1 Tbsp. lemon juice.
3. Pour remaining powdered sugar and lemon juice into separate saucers. Dip rims of 6 parfait, wine, or martini glasses into lemon juice; dip rims into powdered sugar.
4. Fill glasses with fruit mixture.

Brand
name recipes

The *Southern Living* Test Kitchens Staff often creates recipes that showcase great food products and fit the tastes of the day's consumers. Here, we offer the cream of the crop.

our best
40 years
recipes

BAKED ZITI, PAGE 262

Black Bean-Corn Salsa

MAKES 3½ CUPS
Prep: 10 min., Other: 2 hrs.

*Always a hit at any party, this medley of fresh and colorful veggies
keeps guests coming back for more.*

1 (15-oz.) can black beans,
    rinsed and drained (we
    tested with Bush's Best)
1 (11-oz.) can sweet whole
    kernel corn, drained
2 medium tomatoes,
    chopped
1 red bell pepper, chopped
⅓ cup chopped fresh
    cilantro
¼ cup diced red onion
1 Tbsp. minced fresh
    jalapeño pepper
3 Tbsp. fresh lime juice
1 tsp. salt
½ tsp. freshly ground black
    pepper

1 avocado
Tortilla chips

1. Combine first 10 ingredients in a bowl. Cover and chill at least 2 hours.

2. Chop avocado, and add just before serving. Serve with tortilla chips.

Savory Tomato-Bacon Biscuit Bites

MAKES 32 APPETIZER SERVINGS
Prep: 20 min., Cook: 10 min.

These savory biscuits marry two Southern gems—tomatoes and bacon—in crumbly decadence.

2 cups all-purpose baking
    mix (we tested with
    Bisquick)
1/3 cup grated Parmesan
    cheese
1 Tbsp. sugar
1 tsp. Italian seasoning
1/4 tsp. ground red pepper
2/3 cup mayonnaise, divided
1/4 cup milk

4 large plum tomatoes,
    each cut into 8 slices
10 bacon slices, cooked and
    crumbled
Thinly sliced green onions
    (optional)

1. Combine first 5 ingredients in a medium bowl; stir in 1/3 cup mayonnaise and milk with a fork until moistened. Turn dough out onto a lightly floured surface and knead 5 or 6 times.

2. Pat or roll dough to a 1/4-inch thickness; cut with a 1 3/4-inch round cutter, and place on a lightly greased baking sheet.

3. Bake at 425° for 8 to 10 minutes or until golden brown. Cool slightly.

4. Spread each biscuit evenly with half of remaining 1/3 cup mayonnaise; top with tomato slice. Spread tomato slices with remaining mayonnaise; sprinkle with bacon and, if desired, sliced green onions.

Roasted Vegetable Quesadillas

MAKES 6 SERVINGS
Prep: 26 min., Cook: 35 min.

Quickly singeing fresh flour tortillas
gives crunchy contrast to a tender veggie filling.

Vegetable cooking spray (we tested with Pam Original)

2 medium-size sweet potatoes, peeled and cubed
1 medium-size red bell pepper, cut into ½-inch pieces
1 medium-size sweet onion, coarsely chopped
1 tsp. salt
1 tsp. ground cumin

6 (8-inch) flour tortillas
1 (8-oz.) block Monterey Jack cheese with peppers, shredded
Garnishes: sour cream, fresh cilantro sprigs, lime wedges

1. Coat a 15- x 10-inch jelly-roll pan with cooking spray.
2. Place potatoes, bell pepper, and onion in pan; sprinkle with salt and cumin, and toss until vegetables are coated with cooking spray.
3. Bake at 450° for 30 to 35 minutes or until potatoes are tender.
4. Spoon vegetable mixture evenly on half of each tortilla; sprinkle evenly with cheese. Fold each tortilla over filling. Cook quesadillas, in batches, on a hot griddle or nonstick skillet coated with cooking spray 1 minute on each side or until lightly browned and cheese is melted. Garnish, if desired. Serve immediately.

Southwestern Brunch Casserole

MAKES 8 TO 10 SERVINGS
Prep: 30 min., Cook: 55 min., Other: 25 min.

*Switch from mixed fruit salad to a simple green salad, and this casserole
doubles as a great dish for supper.*

1²/₃ cups water
1 cup milk
2 Tbsp. butter or margarine
1 tsp. salt
¼ tsp. pepper
²/₃ cup uncooked
    quick-cooking grits

2 cups (8 oz.) shredded
    Mexican cheese blend,
    divided*
2 garlic cloves, pressed
¼ tsp. dried oregano
2 large eggs

1½ cups chopped cooked
    ham
1 (4.5-oz.) can chopped
    green chiles
6 large eggs
1½ cups milk, divided

3 cups all-purpose baking
    mix (we tested with
    Bisquick)
1 (8-oz.) container sour
    cream
1 tsp. hot sauce

Salsa (optional)

1. Bring first 5 ingredients to a boil in a medium saucepan; gradually stir in grits. Cover, reduce heat, and simmer, stirring occasionally, 5 to 7 minutes.

2. Add ½ cup cheese, garlic, and oregano, stirring until cheese melts; cool 10 to 15 minutes. Stir in 2 eggs, and pour into a lightly greased 13- x 9-inch baking dish.

3. Bake at 350° for 20 minutes; remove baking dish from oven. Increase oven temperature to 400°.

4. Sprinkle remaining 1½ cups cheese, ham, and chiles evenly over grits crust. Whisk together 6 eggs and ½ cup milk; pour into baking dish.

5. Stir together remaining 1 cup milk, baking mix, sour cream, and hot sauce; spoon evenly over egg mixture, slightly spreading with back of a spoon. (Baking mix mixture will be very thick.)

6. Bake at 400° for 35 minutes. Cool 10 minutes; cut into squares. Serve with salsa, if desired.

*Substitute 2 cups (8 oz.) shredded Cheddar cheese, if desired.

Spicy Huevos Rancheros

MAKES 2 TO 4 SERVINGS
Prep: 20 min., Cook: 13 min.

*You can't have brunch without eggs. Spicy Huevos Rancheros gives
fried eggs a new look and south-of-the-border flavor.*

4 (6-inch) corn tortillas (we
    tested with Mission)
2 Tbsp. vegetable oil,
    divided

4 large eggs
½ cup (2 oz.) shredded
    Monterey Jack cheese
    with peppers

2 Tbsp. chopped fresh
    cilantro
1 (8-oz.) jar peach salsa
Garnishes: fresh fruit, fresh
    cilantro sprigs

1. Cook tortillas in 2 batches in 1 Tbsp. hot vegetable oil in a large nonstick skillet 2 minutes on each side or just until crisp. Drain on paper towels. Arrange tortillas in an even layer on an aluminum foil-lined baking sheet.

2. Break eggs in remaining 1 Tbsp. hot oil in skillet, and cook 2 minutes on each side or to desired degree of doneness. Place 1 egg in center of each tortilla; top evenly with cheese.

3. Broil 5½ inches from heat 1 minute or until cheese melts. Sprinkle evenly with chopped cilantro. Top with salsa. Garnish, if desired.

From Our Kitchen

Huevos rancheros (pronounced WAY-vohs rahn-CHEH-rohs) is Spanish for "rancher's eggs." For brunch, set up a station at your cooktop and have one person cook the tortillas while another does the eggs. They'll come out hot and cooked to order. Double or triple the recipe for the desired number of guests.

Tomato Florentine Quiche

MAKES 6 TO 8 SERVINGS
Prep: 20 min., Cook: 1 hr., Other: 20 min.

For brunch, lunch, or dinner, this quiche is a one-dish delight bursting with cheese, eggs, bacon, and veggies.

1 (10-oz.) package frozen chopped spinach, thawed

1 (14.5-oz.) can petite diced tomatoes, drained (we tested with Hunt's)
2 Tbsp. Italian-seasoned breadcrumbs

3 large eggs, lightly beaten
1 cup half-and-half
4 bacon slices, cooked and crumbled
½ cup (2 oz.) shredded sharp Cheddar cheese
½ cup (2 oz.) shredded mozzarella cheese
1 tsp. pesto seasoning or dried basil
¼ tsp. ground red pepper
1 unbaked (9-inch) frozen deep-dish piecrust*

Garnish: Italian parsley sprig

1. Drain spinach well, pressing between paper towels. Set aside.
2. Toss together diced tomatoes and Italian-seasoned breadcrumbs.
3. Stir together spinach, eggs, and next 6 ingredients in a large bowl. Gently fold in tomato mixture. Pour mixture into frozen piecrust, and place on a baking sheet.
4. Bake at 350° for 50 to 60 minutes. Remove from oven, and let stand 20 minutes before cutting. Garnish, if desired.

*Substitute ½ (15-oz.) package refrigerated piecrusts, if desired. Place in a deep-dish pieplate.

Tex-Mex Layered Salad

MAKES 8 SERVINGS
Prep: 25 min., Other: 1 hr.

This showstopper offers nine layers of color to jump-start tastebuds.

1 (10-oz.) can Mexican-
 flavored diced
 tomatoes, drained (we
 tested with Rotel)
1 (8-oz.) container sour
 cream
1 (3-oz.) package cream
 cheese, softened
1 tsp. ground cumin
1 garlic clove, pressed

4 cups shredded romaine
 lettuce
1 (15-oz.) can black beans,
 rinsed and drained
1 (15-oz.) can whole kernel
 corn, drained
1 avocado, peeled and
 chopped
1 (4-oz.) jar diced pimiento,
 drained
1 cup (4 oz.) shredded sharp
 Cheddar cheese
2 (4-oz.) cans sliced ripe
 olives, drained
Chopped green onions
 (optional)

1. Process first 5 ingredients in a blender or food processor until smooth, stopping to scrape down sides; chill.

2. Layer lettuce and next 6 ingredients in a 3-qt. bowl; spoon tomato mixture evenly over top. Sprinkle with green onions, if desired. Cover and chill 1 hour.

Spicy Okra-Tomato-Corn Sauté

MAKES 6 SERVINGS
Prep: 5 min., Cook: 15 min.

Frozen vegetables and canned tomatoes and green chiles allow you to have
Spicy Okra-Tomato-Corn Sauté ready in a flash.

½ small onion, chopped
½ Tbsp. vegetable oil
1 (16-oz.) package frozen whole okra, thawed
1 cup frozen corn, thawed
1 (10-oz.) can diced tomatoes and green chiles, undrained (we tested with Rotel)
1 tsp. sugar
¾ tsp. salt
¼ tsp. pepper

1. Sauté chopped onion in hot vegetable oil in a large nonstick skillet over medium-high heat 5 minutes or until tender. Add okra; cook, stirring occasionally, 5 minutes. Stir in corn and remaining ingredients, and cook 5 minutes or until thoroughly heated. Serve immediately.

From Our Kitchen

Unless you want to use okra for its thickening effect, don't cut the pods; just remove the tip of each stem. Also, avoid overcooking; okra cooks in 5 to 10 minutes. So if you're preparing a long-simmering dish, add it toward the end of the cooking time.

Southwestern Squash Casserole

MAKES 6 TO 8 SERVINGS
Prep: 25 min., Cook: 20 min.

This updated version of squash casserole comes together quickly and easily. Combining yellow squash and green zucchini gives it colorful appeal.

1 lb. yellow squash, sliced
1 lb. zucchini, sliced
1 cup water

1 (10¾-oz.) can Cheddar
    cheese soup (we tested
    with Campbell's)
1 cup crushed tortilla chips
1 (4.5-oz.) can chopped
    green chiles, undrained
¼ cup chopped onion
2 Tbsp. taco seasoning
1 large egg, lightly beaten
1 cup (4 oz.) shredded
    Monterey Jack and
    Cheddar cheese blend

1. Place first 3 ingredients in a large microwave-safe glass bowl, and cover tightly with plastic wrap; pierce plastic wrap with a fork several times to vent. Microwave at HIGH 8 to 9 minutes or until vegetables are tender; drain. Press between layers of paper towels to remove excess moisture.

2. Stir together cooked vegetables, Cheddar cheese soup, and next 5 ingredients until well blended; spoon into a lightly greased 11- x 7-inch baking dish. Sprinkle evenly with cheese.

3. Bake at 450° for 20 minutes or until lightly browned.

Speedy Skillet Pecan Rice

MAKES 4 SERVINGS
Prep: 10 min., Cook: 15 min.

Nuts add flair to just about any dish, and this rice dish is no exception. Pecans lend texture and a depth of flavor like no other nut when paired with sautéed bell pepper, onion, and garlic.

2 (3.5-oz.) bags quick-cooking rice (we tested with Success)

½ medium-size red bell pepper, chopped
½ small onion, chopped
1 cup sliced fresh mushrooms
2 Tbsp. vegetable oil

1 garlic clove, minced
1 tsp. Cajun seasoning
¼ tsp. salt
½ tsp. freshly ground black pepper
3 Tbsp. chopped pecans, toasted

1. Cook rice according to package directions.

2. Sauté chopped bell pepper, chopped onion, and sliced mushrooms in hot vegetable oil in a large nonstick skillet over medium-high heat 5 minutes or until tender.

3. Add garlic; sauté 2 minutes. Stir in cooked rice, Cajun seasoning, salt, and pepper; sprinkle with toasted pecans. Serve immediately.

Skillet Pepper Steak and Rice

MAKES 4 TO 6 SERVINGS
Prep: 20 min., Cook: 20 min.

*Skillet Pepper Steak and Rice gets a helpful head start from boil-in-a-bag rice.
The result is a saucy, scrumptious beef supper.*

1 (3.5-oz.) bag quick-
    cooking rice (we
    tested with Success)

1 (10½-oz.) can beef broth
3 Tbsp. cornstarch, divided
2 Tbsp. soy sauce
1 tsp. sugar
2 tsp. minced fresh or 1 tsp.
    ground ginger
½ tsp. garlic-chili sauce
    (optional)

½ tsp. salt
½ tsp. pepper
1 lb. boneless top sirloin
    steak, cut into thin
    slices

1 Tbsp. vegetable oil
2 tsp. sesame oil
1 green bell pepper, sliced
1 medium-size red onion,
    sliced
½ (8-oz.) container sliced
    fresh mushrooms
1 garlic clove, pressed

1. Prepare rice according to package directions; set aside.
2. Whisk together beef broth, 1 Tbsp. cornstarch, soy sauce, sugar, ginger, and, if desired, garlic-chili sauce; set aside.
3. Combine remaining 2 Tbsp. cornstarch, salt, and pepper; dredge steak slices in mixture.
4. Heat oils in a large skillet or wok over medium-high heat; add steak, and stir-fry 4 minutes or until browned. Add bell pepper, onion, and mushrooms; stir-fry 8 minutes or until tender. Add garlic; stir-fry 1 minute.
5. Stir in broth mixture. Bring to a boil; reduce heat, and simmer 3 to 5 minutes or until thickened. Remove from heat; stir in rice.

Then & Now

Southern Living published two recipes for pepper steak in 1981, and both dishes took twice as long to prepare as this quick and tasty version. High-flavored ingredients and convenience products pack a punch in record time for today's busy lifestyles.

Smothered Swiss Steaks

MAKES 6 SERVINGS
Prep: 40 min., Cook: 1 hr.

These delicious steaks pair well with either mashed potatoes or rice—great for soaking up cola-inspired sauce.

½ tsp. salt
6 (4-oz.) cube steaks
½ cup all-purpose flour
1 tsp. seasoned pepper

4½ Tbsp. vegetable oil

1 medium onion, diced
1 medium-size green bell
   pepper, diced

1 (14.5-oz.) can petite diced
   tomatoes (we tested
   with Hunt's)
1 (12-oz.) cola soft drink
1 Tbsp. beef bouillon
   granules
2 Tbsp. tomato paste (we
   tested with Hunt's)

1. Sprinkle salt evenly on both sides of cube steaks. Combine flour and pepper in a shallow dish. Dredge steaks in flour mixture.

2. Brown 2 steaks in 1½ Tbsp. hot oil in a large nonstick skillet over medium-high heat 3 minutes on each side; drain on paper towels. Repeat procedure with remaining steaks and remaining oil. Drain drippings from skillet, reserving 1 Tbsp. in skillet.

3. Sauté onion and bell pepper in hot drippings 7 minutes or until tender.

4. Add diced tomatoes and remaining 3 ingredients to skillet. Bring to a boil, and cook, stirring often, 5 minutes or until slightly thickened. Return steaks to skillet; cover and cook over low heat 55 to 60 minutes or until tender.

kids love it

Beefy Pizza Casserole

MAKES 8 SERVINGS
Prep: 25 min., Cook: 20 min.

Refrigerated pizza crust dough goes over the top rather than the bottom of this family-pleasing one-dish meal. In taste tests, our kitchen panel preferred this casserole with lean ground beef.

2 lb. lean ground beef
2 medium onions, chopped
½ cup chopped green bell pepper
4 tsp. dried Italian seasoning, divided

¼ cup all-purpose flour
1 (26-oz.) jar tomato-and-basil pasta sauce
2 cups (8 oz.) shredded mozzarella cheese, divided

1 (13.8-oz.) can refrigerated pizza crust dough*
1 Tbsp. olive oil
2 Tbsp. grated Parmesan cheese

1. Cook first 3 ingredients and 3 tsp. Italian seasoning in a large skillet over medium-high heat, stirring until beef crumbles and is no longer pink. Drain well, and return to skillet.

2. Add ¼ cup flour, stirring until blended. Stir in pasta sauce. Bring mixture to a boil over medium-high heat, stirring constantly. Spoon mixture into a lightly greased 13- x 9-inch baking dish. Sprinkle evenly with 1½ cups mozzarella cheese.

3. Unroll pizza crust, and place on top of cheese. (Tuck edges into baking dish, if necessary.) Brush with olive oil, and sprinkle evenly with remaining ½ cup mozzarella cheese, Parmesan cheese, and remaining 1 tsp. Italian seasoning.

4. Bake at 425° for 15 to 20 minutes or until golden brown.

*Substitute an 11.3-oz. refrigerated pizza crust, if desired.

Baked Ziti

MAKES 8 TO 10 SERVINGS
Prep: 35 min., Cook: 25 min., Other: 10 min.

Hearty comfort comes to mind when we reflect on this cheesy casserole. Pleasing to kids and adults alike, this mozzarella-topped dish boasts loads of saucy beef and perfectly tender pasta.

1 (16-oz.) box ziti pasta (we tested with Barilla)

½ medium onion, chopped
1 Tbsp. olive oil
2 garlic cloves, minced
1 lb. lean ground beef
1 (26-oz.) jar tomato-and-basil pasta sauce
¾ tsp. salt, divided

3 Tbsp. butter
3 Tbsp. all-purpose flour
3 cups milk
1 cup grated Parmesan cheese
½ tsp. pepper

1 (8-oz.) package shredded mozzarella cheese

1. Cook pasta in a large Dutch oven according to package directions. Drain and return to Dutch oven.

2. Meanwhile, sauté chopped onion in hot oil in a large skillet over medium-high heat 5 minutes or until tender. Add garlic, and sauté 1 minute. Add beef, and cook, stirring until beef crumbles and is no longer pink. Drain beef mixture, and return to pan. Stir in pasta sauce and ½ tsp. salt. Set aside.

3. Melt butter in a heavy saucepan over low heat; whisk in flour until smooth. Cook, whisking constantly, 1 minute. Gradually whisk in milk; cook over medium heat, whisking constantly, until mixture is thickened and bubbly. Stir in Parmesan cheese, remaining ¼ tsp. salt, and pepper. Pour sauce over pasta in Dutch oven, stirring until pasta is evenly coated.

4. Transfer pasta mixture to a lightly greased 13- x 9-inch baking dish. Top evenly with beef mixture; sprinkle evenly with mozzarella cheese.

5. Bake at 350° for 20 to 25 minutes or until cheese is melted. Let stand 10 minutes before serving.

Grilled Cheese Sandwiches with Tomato, Avocado, and Bacon

MAKES 4 SERVINGS
Prep: 20 min., Cook: 7 min.

Creamy avocado nestled between a duo of cheeses replaces the lettuce of a BLT for a scrumptious grilled cheese sandwich that's over the top.

8 bacon slices
2 large tomatoes, each cut into 4 slices
¼ tsp. salt
¼ tsp. pepper

¼ cup Ranch dressing
8 slices whitewheat bread (we tested with Nature's Own)
4 (1-oz.) provolone cheese slices
4 (1-oz.) sharp Cheddar cheese slices
1 large avocado, cut into 8 slices

Vegetable cooking spray

1. Prepare bacon according to package directions; drain and set aside. Sprinkle tomato slices evenly with salt and pepper.

2. Spread ½ Tbsp. dressing on 1 side of each bread slice. Top each dressing-coated side of 4 bread slices with 1 provolone slice; top each remaining 4 bread slices with 1 Cheddar slice. Top each provolone slice with 2 tomato slices, 2 bacon slices, and 2 avocado slices.

3. Cook bread slices, cheese sides up, on a hot nonstick electric griddle at 325° or in a hot nonstick skillet coated with cooking spray over medium heat 4 to 7 minutes or until browned.

4. Press together Cheddar cheese-topped bread slices and provolone-topped bread slices. Cut in half diagonally, and serve immediately.

Ranchero Catfish

MAKES 6 SERVINGS
Prep: 30 min., Cook: 12 min.

Tortilla chips are the key to the crunchy coating on Ranchero Catfish. Cutting the fillets in half lengthwise shortens cooking time and yields especially tender, crisp results.

6 (3- to 5-oz.) catfish fillets
    (we tested with U.S.
    Farm-Raised Catfish)

1 cup finely crushed tortilla
    chips
2 tsp. chili powder
½ tsp. salt
½ tsp. pepper
3 Tbsp. fresh lime juice
1 Tbsp. vegetable oil

1 cup salsa, warmed
Garnish: chopped fresh
    cilantro

1. Rinse catfish fillets, and pat dry with paper towels. Cut each fillet in half lengthwise; set aside.

2. Combine crushed tortilla chips and next 3 ingredients in a shallow dish. Stir together lime juice and oil in a separate shallow dish.

3. Dip fillets in lime juice mixture, and dredge in tortilla chip mixture, coating evenly. Place on a lightly greased rack in an aluminum foil-lined 15- x 10-inch jelly-roll pan or broiler pan. Sprinkle evenly with any remaining tortilla chip crumb mixture.

4. Bake at 450° for 10 to 12 minutes or until fillets are crisp and golden and flake with a fork. Serve with warmed salsa. Garnish, if desired.

Greek-Style Chicken

MAKES 4 SERVINGS
Prep: 35 min., Cook: 30 min.

We like Greek-Style Chicken for brunch because you have 30 minutes of hands-off cooking time to put the final touches on other dishes while the chicken bakes. Greek seasonings and a few classic ingredients make this dish simple but tasty.

½ tsp. salt
½ tsp. pepper
1½ tsp. Greek seasoning
4 (6- to 8-oz.) skinned and boned chicken breasts (we tested with Pilgrim's Pride)

2 Tbsp. olive oil

1 medium-size red bell pepper, chopped
1 small onion, thinly sliced
½ cup dry white wine
½ cup chicken broth
16 small pitted ripe black olives

Hot cooked rice
Chopped fresh flat-leaf parsley
Garnish: fresh flat-leaf parsley sprig

1. Combine first 3 ingredients; sprinkle evenly over chicken.

2. Cook chicken in hot oil in a large ovenproof skillet over medium-high heat 5 minutes on each side or until browned. Remove chicken.

3. Add bell pepper and onion to skillet; sauté 5 minutes or until tender. Stir in wine and broth, stirring to loosen particles from bottom of pan. Stir in olives. Return chicken to skillet.

4. Bring to a boil. Remove skillet from heat.

5. Bake, covered, at 350° for 30 minutes or until chicken is done. Combine rice and chopped parsley. Serve chicken over rice. Garnish, if desired.

Savory Chicken Pot Pie

MAKES 8 SERVINGS
Prep: 40 min., Cook: 35 min., Other: 15 min.

Just like mom used to make, this recipe sends the memorable aroma of bubbling pot pie beneath a flaky crust wafting through the whole house.

1 small sweet potato

12 skinned and boned chicken thighs, cut into bite-size pieces (we tested with Pilgrim's Pride)
½ tsp. seasoned salt
⅓ cup chopped onion
1 tsp. vegetable oil

¼ cup butter
⅓ cup all-purpose flour
3 cups chicken broth
1 (10¾-oz.) can cream of mushroom soup
1 (16-oz.) package frozen peas and carrots, thawed
1 Tbsp. fresh lemon juice
½ tsp. freshly ground pepper

½ (15-oz.) package refrigerated piecrust

1. Pierce sweet potato several times with a fork. Place in microwave oven, and cover with a damp paper towel. Microwave at HIGH 3 minutes or until done. Let stand 5 minutes; peel and dice. Set aside.

2. Sprinkle chicken evenly with seasoned salt. Sauté chicken and onion in hot oil in a Dutch oven over medium-high heat 5 to 8 minutes or until done. Remove chicken and onion.

3. Melt butter in Dutch oven over medium-high heat; whisk in flour, chicken broth, and soup. Reduce heat to medium-low, and cook, stirring occasionally, 3 to 4 minutes or until thickened. Stir in cooked chicken and onion, sweet potato, peas and carrots, lemon juice, and pepper. Cook, stirring often, 5 minutes or until thoroughly heated. Spoon chicken mixture into a lightly greased 13- x 9-inch baking dish.

4. Roll piecrust into 13- x 9-inch rectangle; fit over chicken mixture in baking dish. Cut several slits in top of crust for steam to escape.

5. Bake at 400° for 30 to 35 minutes or until crust is golden brown and filling is thoroughly heated. Let stand 10 minutes before serving.

Turkey Scaloppine

MAKES 6 TO 8 SERVINGS
Prep: 25 min., Cook: 40 min.

Zesty cream sauce tops thin slices of crispy turkey.

1 (1.5- to 2-lb.) package turkey tenderloins, thinly sliced
½ tsp. salt, divided
½ cup all-purpose flour

2 Tbsp. vegetable oil

2 (8-oz.) packages sliced mushrooms

¼ cup capers
4 garlic cloves, pressed
1½ cups whipping cream
¾ cup chicken broth
2 to 4 Tbsp. fresh lemon juice

1 (1-lb.) box linguine (we tested with Barilla)

Garnishes: chopped fresh parsley, fresh parsley sprigs, lemon wedges

1. Sprinkle turkey slices evenly with ¼ tsp. salt; dredge in flour.

2. Cook turkey slices, in batches, in hot vegetable oil in a large nonstick skillet over medium-high heat 3 minutes on each side.

3. Remove turkey from skillet. Add sliced mushrooms to skillet, and sauté 7 to 9 minutes or until golden brown.

4. Add capers, garlic, and remaining ¼ tsp. salt to skillet; sauté 2 minutes. Stir in whipping cream and chicken broth; reduce heat to medium, and simmer 20 minutes or until slightly thickened. Stir in lemon juice.

5. While sauce simmers, cook pasta according to package directions in a Dutch oven. Drain; return to Dutch oven.

6. Stir turkey and mushroom cream mixture into pasta in Dutch oven; cook until thoroughly heated. Garnish, if desired.

40years

Peanut-Toffee Shortbread

MAKES ABOUT 2½ TO 3 DOZEN PIECES
Prep: 30 min., Cook: 20 min., Other: 5 min.

Chocolate and honey-roasted peanuts make a perfect pair.

1 cup butter, softened
⅔ cup firmly packed light
    brown sugar
⅓ cup cornstarch
2 cups all-purpose flour
¼ tsp. salt
2 tsp. vanilla extract
2 cups coarsely chopped
    honey-roasted peanuts,
    divided

1 (12-oz.) package semi-
    sweet chocolate morsels
    (we tested with Nestlé
    Toll House)

1. Beat butter at medium speed with an electric mixer until creamy. Combine brown sugar and cornstarch; gradually add to butter, beating well. Gradually add flour and salt to butter mixture, beating at low speed just until blended. Add vanilla and 1 cup peanuts, beating at low speed just until blended.

2. Turn dough out onto a lightly greased baking sheet; pat or roll dough into an 11- x 14-inch rectangle, leaving at least a 1-inch border on all sides of baking sheet.

3. Bake at 350° for 20 minutes or until golden brown. Remove baking sheet to a wire rack; sprinkle shortbread evenly with chocolate morsels. Let stand 5 minutes; gently spread melted morsels over shortbread. Sprinkle with remaining 1 cup peanuts, and cool completely. Cut or break shortbread into 2- to 3-inch irregular-shaped pieces.

From Our Kitchen

The word *short* in shortbread describes a pastry dough that is rich, crisp, and melts in your mouth due to the high proportion of butter to flour in the recipe. Don't be tempted to substitute margarine.

Peanut Butter-Chocolate Chip Cookies

MAKES ABOUT 6 DOZEN
Prep: 20 min., Cook: 15 min. per batch

These cookies hold a surprise inside: delicious swirled morsels.
These treats are great for on-the-go energy.

½ cup butter, softened
½ cup creamy peanut
   butter
1 tsp. vanilla extract

1 (16-oz.) package dark
   brown sugar
2 large eggs
2 cups all-purpose flour
1 (10-oz.) package swirled
   milk chocolate and
   peanut butter morsels
   (we tested with Nestlé
   Toll House)

1. Beat first 3 ingredients at medium speed with an electric mixer until creamy.
2. Gradually add brown sugar, beating until well blended. Add eggs, beating until blended. Stir in flour and morsels.
3. Drop dough by level tablespoonfuls 2 inches apart onto parchment paper-lined baking sheets.
4. Bake at 350° for 13 to 15 minutes or until golden brown. Cool on baking sheets 1 minute; remove cookies to wire racks to cool completely.

From Our Kitchen

Baking cookies on parchment paper-lined baking sheets makes cleanup a snap. Flip the paper over after the first use, and bake on it again. Cookies can also be baked on lightly greased baking sheets.

Caramel-Apple Quesadillas

MAKES 4 SERVINGS
Prep: 15 min., Cook: 16 min.

Nothing goes together quite as well as apples and caramel. Wrapping each serving in a tortilla blanket and topping with ice cream makes this version of a classic irresistible.

2 Granny Smith apples, peeled and thinly sliced
½ cup coarsely chopped walnuts
1 tsp. cinnamon sugar
1 tsp. lemon juice

3 Tbsp. butter, divided

½ (8-oz.) package cream cheese, softened
¼ cup powdered sugar
4 burrito-size flour tortillas (we tested with Mission)

½ cup bottled caramel sauce
Vanilla ice cream

1. Toss together first 4 ingredients.

2. Melt 1 Tbsp. butter in a large nonstick skillet over medium-high heat; add apple mixture, and sauté 5 to 8 minutes or until apples are tender. Remove apple mixture from skillet; wipe skillet clean.

3. Stir together cream cheese and powdered sugar until smooth. Spread cream cheese mixture evenly on 1 side of each tortilla; top cream cheese mixture evenly with apple mixture. Fold tortillas in half over apple mixture.

4. Melt 1 Tbsp. butter in skillet over medium heat. Cook 2 quesadillas 2 minutes on each side or until golden brown. Repeat procedure with remaining 1 Tbsp. butter and remaining 2 quesadillas. Drizzle with caramel sauce, and top with vanilla ice cream. Serve immediately.

Fresh Fruit with Lime Syrup

MAKES 10 SERVINGS
Prep: 20 min., Cook: 5 min., Other: 2 hrs.

*Fresh Fruit with Lime Syrup turns produce into something special,
and it packs plenty of vitamin C.*

1 cup water
1 Tbsp. cornstarch
1 cup granulated sugar (we
    tested with Domino)
1 tsp. grated lime rind
¼ cup fresh lime juice

1 pineapple, peeled, cored,
    and cut into 1-inch
    pieces
2 cups red seedless grapes,
    halved
3 kiwifruit, peeled and
    sliced
2 oranges, peeled
    and sectioned
Garnish: fresh mint sprig

1. Whisk together 1 cup water and cornstarch in a small saucepan. Whisk in sugar, rind, and juice. Bring to a boil over low heat, whisking constantly; boil 1 minute. Chill at least 2 hours.

2. Combine pineapple and next 3 ingredients in a large bowl; garnish, if desired, and drizzle with chilled syrup. Serve immediately.

Splendid Strawberries

MAKES 4 SERVINGS
Prep: 5 min., Cook: 1 min.

Simple and straightforward, this quick recipe tastes divine over ice cream. With no added sugar and low-fat ice cream, it's a guilt-free indulgence.

1 Tbsp. butter
1 qt. fresh strawberries,
    halved
¼ cup no-calorie sweetener,
    granular (we tested with
    Splenda)
1 Tbsp. balsamic vinegar
Low-fat vanilla ice cream

1. Melt butter in a large skillet over medium-high heat. Stir in strawberries, no-calorie sweetener, and balsamic vinegar; cook 1 minute or until mixture is thoroughly heated. Serve over ice cream.

Outdoor
cooking

Succulent barbecue ribs, smoked brisket, and grilled chicken highlight this collection of outdoor favorites—along with some of our best sauces from over the years.

ADAMS' RIBS, PAGE 286

Easy Grilled Vegetables

MAKES 8 SERVINGS
Prep: 30 min., Cook: 14 min., Other: 30 min.

If you don't have a grill wok or a metal basket, feel free to place the tomatoes on skewers (remember to soak wooden skewers in water for at least 30 minutes before using on the grill).

2 green bell peppers
2 yellow squash
2 zucchini
10 large fresh mushrooms

¾ cup balsamic vinaigrette
1 Tbsp. lemon pepper
¼ tsp. salt

12 cherry tomatoes

1. Cut bell peppers in half, and remove seeds. Cut squash and zucchini into ¼-inch-thick slices. Place peppers, squash, zucchini, and mushrooms in a large shallow dish or large zip-top freezer bag.

2. Whisk together vinaigrette, lemon pepper, and salt until blended. Pour over vegetables. Cover and chill at least 30 minutes. Remove vegetables from marinade, reserving marinade.

3. Grill vegetables, covered with grill lid, over medium-high heat (350° to 400°), basting with reserved marinade. Grill peppers 7 minutes on each side or until tender; grill squash and zucchini 3 minutes on each side or until tender. Grill mushrooms 5 minutes or until tender. Grill tomatoes in a grill wok or metal basket 2 to 3 minutes or until skins begin to split.

Smoky Barbecue Brisket

MAKES 8 SERVINGS
Prep: 10 min., Cook: 6 hrs., Other: 8 hrs.

This brisket is even better if it stays in your refrigerator a day after cooking to absorb the flavors. Slice and reheat it in the oven or microwave.

1 (4- to 6-lb.) beef brisket, trimmed
1 (5-oz.) bottle liquid smoke
1 onion, chopped
2 tsp. garlic salt
1 to 2 tsp. salt

⅓ cup Worcestershire sauce

1 (12- to 18-oz.) bottle barbecue sauce

1. Place brisket in a large shallow dish or extra-large zip-top freezer bag; pour liquid smoke over brisket. Sprinkle evenly with onion, garlic salt, and salt. Cover or seal, and chill 8 hours, turning occasionally.
2. Remove brisket, and place on a large piece of heavy-duty aluminum foil, discarding liquid smoke mixture. Pour Worcestershire sauce evenly over brisket, and fold foil to seal; place wrapped brisket in a roasting pan.
3. Bake at 275° for 5 hours. Unfold foil; pour barbecue sauce evenly over brisket. Bake 1 more hour, uncovered.

make ahead

Ginger-Marinated Flank Steak

MAKES 4 TO 6 SERVINGS
Prep: 10 min.; Cook: 20 min.; Other: 8 hrs., 5 min.

¼ cup vegetable oil
¼ cup soy sauce
2 Tbsp. brown sugar
2 Tbsp. lime juice
2 tsp. ground ginger
1 tsp. dried crushed red pepper
2 garlic cloves, chopped
1 (2-lb.) flank steak, trimmed

1. Combine first 7 ingredients in a shallow baking dish or large zip-top freezer bag; add steak, turning to coat. Cover or seal, and chill 8 hours, turning occasionally.
2. Remove steak from marinade, discarding marinade.
3. Grill, covered with grill lid, over medium-high heat (350° to 400°) 8 to 10 minutes on each side or to desired degree of doneness. Let stand 5 minutes; cut diagonally across the grain into thin slices.

Grilled Flank Steak with Guacamole Sauce

MAKES 8 SERVINGS
Prep: 10 min., Cook: 20 min., Other: 5 min.

Dried chipotle powder can be found on the spice aisle of your supermarket.
If you serve the flank steak without the cool and creamy Guacamole Sauce,
reduce the chipotle powder to 1 tsp. to moderate the heat.

1 (2-lb.) flank steak, trimmed
2 tsp. dried chipotle powder
    (we tested with
    McCormick Gourmet
    Collection Chipotle
    Chile Pepper)
½ tsp. salt
2 tsp. minced fresh garlic

16 (8-inch) flour tortillas
    (optional)
Guacamole Sauce

1. Sprinkle steak evenly with chipotle powder and salt; rub with garlic.
2. Grill steak, covered with grill lid, over medium-high heat (350° to 400°) 8 to 10 minutes on each side or to desired degree of doneness. Cover loosely with aluminum foil, and let stand 5 minutes.
3. Cut steak diagonally across the grain into thin strips. Serve with tortillas, if desired, and Guacamole Sauce.

Guacamole Sauce

MAKES ABOUT 1½ CUPS
Prep: 15 min.

2 small ripe avocados,
    peeled and quartered
1 small jalapeño pepper,
    seeded and minced
1 green onion, sliced
½ cup fat-free sour cream
½ tsp. grated lime rind
¼ cup fresh lime juice
½ tsp. salt
½ tsp. sugar
¼ tsp. minced fresh garlic
Garnish: chopped green
    onions

1. Process first 9 ingredients in a blender or food processor 30 seconds or until smooth. Garnish, if desired.

From Our Kitchen

Prepare this sauce up to one day ahead. Cover tightly with plastic wrap, and store in the refrigerator. Let stand at room temperature at least 30 minutes before serving.

Baby Loin Back Ribs

MAKES 3 TO 4 SERVINGS
Prep: 20 min.; Cook: 2 hrs., 30 min.; Other: 3 hrs.

2 slabs baby loin back ribs
(about 4 lb.)
3 Tbsp. Dry Spices

1 cup Basting Sauce
1 cup Sweet Sauce

1. Place ribs in a large, shallow pan. Rub Dry Spices evenly over ribs. Cover and chill 3 hours.

2. Prepare a hot fire by piling charcoal or lava rocks on 1 side of grill, leaving other side empty. (For gas grill, light only 1 side.) Place food grate on grill. Arrange ribs on grate over unlit side.

3. Grill ribs, covered with grill lid, over medium heat (300° to 350°) for 2 to 2½ hours, basting every 30 minutes with Basting Sauce and turning occasionally. Brush ribs with Sweet Sauce during the last 30 minutes.

Dry Spices

MAKES 6½ TBSP.
Prep: 5 min.

3 Tbsp. paprika
2 tsp. seasoned salt
2 tsp. garlic powder
2 tsp. ground black pepper
1 tsp. dry mustard
1 tsp. ground oregano
1 tsp. ground red pepper
½ tsp. chili powder

1. Combine all ingredients in a small bowl.

Basting Sauce

MAKES 4½ CUPS
Prep: 5 min., Other: 8 hrs.

¼ cup firmly packed brown
sugar
1½ Tbsp. Dry Spices
2 cups red wine vinegar
2 cups water
¼ cup Worcestershire sauce
½ tsp. hot sauce
1 small bay leaf

1. Stir together all ingredients; let stand 8 hours. Remove bay leaf. (Sauce is for basting only.)

Sweet Sauce

MAKES 1 QT.
Prep: 10 min., Cook: 30 min.

1 cup ketchup
1 cup red wine vinegar
1 (8-oz.) can tomato sauce
½ cup spicy honey mustard
½ cup Worcestershire sauce
¼ cup butter or margarine
2 Tbsp. brown sugar
2 Tbsp. hot sauce
1 Tbsp. seasoned salt
1 Tbsp. paprika
1 Tbsp. lemon juice
1½ tsp. garlic powder
⅛ tsp. chili powder
⅛ tsp. ground red pepper
⅛ tsp. ground black pepper

1. Bring all ingredients to a boil. Reduce heat; simmer, stirring occasionally, 30 minutes.

Taste of the South

Folks in the South are passionate about barbecue. Whatever the cooking style, rubs, marinades, or sauces are the base for balanced barbecue. The key is a good seasoning rub applied and allowed to sit; then when you add just the right sauce, the experience becomes exceptional.

You can travel from the East Coast to Texas and taste four distinct sauces. Tennessee and most of Texas claim bragging rights for their thick tomato-based sauces. North Carolina is known for pungent vinegar-pepper and ketchup-based sauces. South Carolina boasts all of these types, plus a mustard-based sauce.

So turn up the heat, and enjoy this recipe—it's what many Tennesseans call their best barbecue.

Adams' Ribs

MAKES 8 TO 10 SERVINGS
Prep: 30 min.; Cook: 2 hrs., 30 min.

These ribs are the hot and spicy product of a marriage. Anne-Marie Adams' Cajun background is the source of the spicy heat. Her husband's commitment to the best equipment and a perfectly built fire contributes the smoky tenderness. A spice rub and two adapted sauces yield a taste and texture that give the ribs their signature.

Hickory wood chunks

5 lb. spareribs

1 Tbsp. garlic powder
1 Tbsp. Creole seasoning
2 Tbsp. ground pepper
1 Tbsp. Worcestershire
    sauce

Grill Basting Sauce
The Sauce

1. Soak wood chunks in water to cover for at least 30 minutes. Drain.

2. Prepare a hot fire by piling charcoal on 1 side of grill, leaving other side empty. Place wood chunks on charcoal. Place food grate on grill.

3. Remove thin membrane from back of ribs by slicing into it with a knife and then pulling.

4. Combine garlic powder and next 3 ingredients, and rub on all sides of ribs. Arrange ribs on grate over unlit side of grill.

5. Grill, covered with grill lid, 2 to 2½ hours, basting with Grill Basting Sauce during the last 30 minutes. Turn once after basting. Serve with The Sauce.

Grill Basting Sauce

MAKES 5 CUPS
Prep: 5 min., Cook: 1 hr.

2¾ cups red wine vinegar
1¾ cups water
¾ cup dry white wine
¾ cup ketchup
¼ cup firmly packed
    brown sugar
¼ cup prepared mustard
¼ cup Worcestershire
    sauce
2 to 3 Tbsp. salt
2 Tbsp. dried crushed red
    pepper
2 Tbsp. freshly ground black
    pepper

1. Cook all ingredients in a large saucepan over medium heat, stirring occasionally, 1 hour.

Note: Grill Basting Sauce can be stored in the refrigerator up to 1 week.

The Sauce

MAKES 2½ CUPS
Prep: 5 min., Cook: 18 min.

1 Tbsp. butter or margarine
1 medium onion, finely
    chopped

4 garlic cloves, minced
1 cup ketchup
½ cup white vinegar
¼ cup lemon juice
¼ cup steak seasoning (we
    tested with Dale's)
2 Tbsp. light brown sugar
1 Tbsp. Cajun seasoning (we
    tested with Luzianne
    Cajun)
2 Tbsp. liquid smoke

1. Melt butter in a large skillet over medium-high heat; add onion, and sauté until tender.

2. Add garlic and remaining ingredients; reduce heat, and simmer 15 minutes.

Then & Now

Anne-Marie Adams and her now-late husband, Oscar, shared Adams' Ribs with *Southern Living* in September 1995—Anne-Marie perfecting the sauce with her Cajun background and Oscar strategizing the grilling technique. The grilling takes time, but the distinctive spice rub and two sauces are quick to stir together so the recipe's definitely worth the time investment. Leftover sauce keeps in the refrigerator up to a week and is great on chicken and beef. Be sure to keep separate the portion you use to baste the raw meat to make sure the leftover portion is free of meat juices.

Hoppin' John with Grilled Pork Medallions

MAKES 4 SERVINGS
Prep: 10 min., Cook: 50 min.

The wild rice in this recipe gives a new twist to traditional hoppin' John.

¾ cup chopped onion
½ cup chopped celery
1 tsp. olive oil
2 (14-oz.) cans chicken
    broth
1 tsp. dried thyme

½ cup uncooked wild rice
1 cup frozen black-eyed
    peas

½ cup uncooked long-grain
    rice
¾ cup chopped tomato
2 tsp. lemon juice
2 Tbsp. chopped fresh
    parsley
½ tsp. salt
⅛ to ¼ tsp. ground red
    pepper
¼ tsp. freshly ground black
    pepper
1 Red Delicious apple, cored
    and cut into 12 wedges
Grilled Pork Medallions
Garnish: fresh thyme sprigs

1. Cook onion and celery in olive oil in a large saucepan over medium heat, stirring constantly, until tender. Add chicken broth and dried thyme; bring mixture to a boil.
2. Rinse wild rice in 3 changes of hot water; drain. Add wild rice and black-eyed peas to broth mixture. Cover, reduce heat, and cook 20 minutes.
3. Add long-grain rice and next 6 ingredients; cover and cook 30 minutes or until rice is tender and all liquid is absorbed. Serve with apple wedges and Grilled Pork Medallions. Garnish, if desired.

Grilled Pork Medallions

MAKES 4 SERVINGS
Prep: 10 min.; Cook: 24 min.; Other: 8 hrs., 5 min.

¼ cup lemon juice
2 Tbsp. soy sauce
2 garlic cloves, pressed
¼ tsp. salt
1 (1-lb.) pork tenderloin, trimmed

1. Combine first 4 ingredients in a shallow container or large zip-top freezer bag. Add tenderloin; cover or seal, and refrigerate 8 hours, turning occasionally.

2. Remove tenderloin from marinade, discarding marinade. Coat food grate with cooking spray; place on grill over medium-high heat (350° to 400°). Place tenderloin on grate, and grill, covered with grill lid, 10 to 12 minutes on each side or until a meat thermometer inserted in thickest portion registers 155°. Let pork stand 5 minutes or until it reaches 160°.

Taste of the South

Several stories exist about how hoppin' John got its name, so pick your favorite: One theory is that children loved the dish so much that they hopped around the table in eager anticipation. Another story surmises that hoppin' John was a busy waiter who served the dish. Another theory credits a man named John who loved the dish so much he would hurry, or hop, to the table when it was on the menu.

Peppercorn-Crusted Lamb Chops

MAKES 4 SERVINGS
Prep: 17 min., Cook: 14 min.

A Dijon mustard coating and peppercorn crust dress these chops for entertaining.

8 (4-oz.) 1-inch-thick lean
  lamb chops
2 Tbsp. coarse grained Dijon
  mustard
1 Tbsp. cracked black
  pepper
1 Tbsp. soy sauce
1 green onion, finely
  chopped
1 garlic clove, minced

1. Trim excess fat from lamb chops. Combine mustard and remaining 4 ingredients; coat 1 side of each chop.

2. Coat food grate with cooking spray; place on grill over medium-high heat (350° to 400°). Place chops, coated sides up, on grate; grill, covered with grill lid, 5 to 7 minutes on each side or until done.

From Our Kitchen

Purchase lamb with a bright pink color, pink bones, and white fat. If the meat and bones are dark red, it usually means the meat is older.

Smoked Lemon-Chipotle Chickens

MAKES 12 TO 16 SERVINGS
Prep: 45 min., Cook: 4 hrs., Other: 40 min.

On a chilly day, the chicken will take longer to cook—up to 45 minutes more.
Don't skip the step of tying the chicken with string;
the more compact the chicken, the better the smoking results.

1 small sweet onion,
    quartered
8 large garlic cloves, peeled
¾ cup fresh lemon juice
¼ cup olive oil
3 Tbsp. white vinegar
3 chicken bouillon cubes
3 canned chipotle peppers
    in adobo sauce
2 Tbsp. adobo sauce from
    can
2 tsp. salt, divided

3 (4½-lb.) whole chickens

2½ cups hickory or oak
    wood chips

1. Process first 8 ingredients and ¾ tsp. salt in a food processor or blender until smooth, stopping to scrape down sides. Set mixture aside.

2. Remove excess skin from necks and cavities of chickens, if desired. Starting at large cavities, loosen skin from breasts and legs by inserting fingers and gently pushing between skin and meat. (Do not completely detach skin.)

3. Place chickens in a large roasting pan. Using a bulb baster, squeeze lemon-chipotle mixture evenly into chicken cavities and under skin on breasts and legs.

4. Sprinkle chickens evenly with remaining 1¼ tsp. salt. Tuck wings under, if desired. Position the center of a 3-foot piece of kitchen string under back of 1 chicken near tail. Wrap string around legs and around body of chicken. Tie securely at neck. Repeat with remaining chickens.

5. Soak wood chips in water for at least 30 minutes. Set aside.

6. Prepare smoker according to manufacturer's directions. Bring internal temperature to 225° to 250°, and maintain temperature for 15 to 20 minutes. Place chickens on upper food grate; cover with smoker lid.

7. Cook chickens, maintaining the temperature inside the smoker between 225° and 250°, for 1½ hours. Drain reserved wood chips, and place on coals. Cover with smoker lid; smoke chickens 2 hours to 2½ hours more or until a meat thermometer inserted into thighs registers 170°. Remove chickens from smoker; cover loosely with aluminum foil, and let stand 10 minutes or to desired doneness before slicing.

Lime-Grilled Chicken

MAKES 4 SERVINGS
Prep: 10 min., Cook: 12 min., Other: 1 hr.

Peanut oil and soy sauce give this zesty chicken Asian flair.

⅓ cup lime juice
1 Tbsp. peanut oil
1½ tsp. soy sauce
1 garlic clove, minced
1 bay leaf
4 skinned and boned
    chicken breasts

1. Combine first 5 ingredients in a shallow dish or zip-top freezer bag; add chicken. Cover or seal, and chill 1 hour.
2. Remove chicken from marinade, discarding marinade.
3. Grill, covered with grill lid, over medium-high heat (350° to 400°) 4 to 6 minutes on each side or until done.

Then & Now

Prior to the 1980s, if you wanted boneless chicken breasts you had to bone them yourself or beg your butcher to do it. Today, boneless, skinless breasts are a mainstay at the meat counter. They're a healthy source of protein and a boon for busy cooks.

Orange-Ginger Grilled Chicken Thighs

MAKES 8 SERVINGS
Prep: 13 min., Cook: 8 min., Other: 1 hr.

*A whole tablespoon of minced fresh ginger contributes signature
flavor to these tangy chicken thighs.*

⅓ cup orange juice

3 Tbsp. rice wine vinegar

3 Tbsp. soy sauce

1 Tbsp. minced garlic

1 Tbsp. minced fresh ginger

1 Tbsp. sesame oil

8 skinned and boned
  chicken thighs

Garnishes: fresh cilantro
  sprigs, orange slices

1. Combine first 6 ingredients in a shallow dish or large zip-top freezer bag; add chicken. Cover or seal, and chill at least 1 hour, turning occasionally.

2. Remove chicken thighs from marinade, and discard marinade.

3. Grill, covered with grill lid, over medium-high heat (350° to 400°) 4 minutes on each side or until done. Garnish, if desired.

Mesquite-Smoked Cornish Hens

MAKES 6 SERVINGS
Prep: 40 min.; Cook: 2 hrs., 20 min.; Other: 8 hrs., 30 min.

Rome apples lend a sweet accent to these herb-studded hens.

3 (1½-lb.) Cornish hens
3 small Rome apples, cored
   and quartered (about
   ¾ lb.)

1 cup fresh thyme leaves
2 Tbsp. chopped fresh
   parsley
½ tsp. freshly ground
   pepper
¼ tsp. salt

1 cup unsweetened apple
   juice
¼ cup soy sauce

Mesquite wood chips

Garnishes: Fresh cilantro
   sprigs, apple slices

1. Remove giblets and neck from hens, and discard. Rinse hens with cold water; pat dry. Stuff hens with apple quarters.

2. Loosen skin from hen breasts without totally detaching skin. Combine thyme and next 3 ingredients. Rub half of herb mixture evenly under and over skin. Tie ends of legs together with string; close body cavities, and secure with wooden picks.

3. Place hens in a 13- x 9-inch baking dish. Combine apple juice, soy sauce, and remaining herb mixture; pour evenly over hens, turning to coat. Cover and chill 4 to 8 hours, turning occasionally.

4. Soak mesquite chips in water for at least 30 minutes. Set aside.

5. Prepare charcoal fire in smoker; let burn 20 minutes.

6. Meanwhile, drain hens, reserving marinade.

7. Drain mesquite chips, and place on coals. Place water pan in smoker; add reserved marinade and hot water to depth of fill line. Coat food grate with cooking spray. Place hens on food grate.

8. Cook, covered, 2 hours or until a meat thermometer inserted into meaty part of thigh registers 170° or desired doneness. Garnish, if desired.

Taste of the South

When it comes to smoking, choose between hickory and mesquite woods to impart the best flavor to meat and poultry. Add pecan shells or maple, cherry, apple, or alder woods to your options for delicately flavoring fish and shellfish.

Grilled Catfish over Mixed Greens

MAKES 2 SERVINGS
Prep: 20 min., Cook: 10 min., Other: 30 min.

Tarragon has a lovely fragrance, but a little of this spice goes a long way. Out of balsamic vinegar? Use apple cider vinegar with a pinch or two of sugar whisked in.

2 (6- to 7-oz.) catfish fillets

½ cup olive oil
3 Tbsp. balsamic vinegar
1 small shallot, diced
1 Tbsp. chopped fresh or
　　1 tsp. dried tarragon
¾ tsp. freshly ground
　　pepper, divided
½ tsp. salt, divided

4 cups gourmet mixed salad
　　greens
¼ lb. fresh button
　　mushrooms, thinly
　　sliced

1. Rinse catfish fillets; pat dry with paper towels, and place in a large shallow dish.

2. Whisk together olive oil, next 3 ingredients, ½ tsp. pepper, and ¼ tsp. salt; pour ¼ cup marinade over fillets, turning to coat. Reserve remaining marinade. Cover and chill fillets 30 minutes.

3. Remove fillets from marinade, discarding marinade; sprinkle evenly with remaining ¼ tsp. pepper and remaining ¼ tsp. salt.

4. Coat food grate with cooking spray; place over medium-high heat (350° to 400°). Place fillets on grate; grill 5 minutes on each side or until fish flakes with a fork.

5. Toss together salad greens, mushrooms, and reserved marinade; serve on individual plates, topped with grilled fillets.

Then & Now

Fish has come a long way since the first issues of *Southern Living* in the 1960s. Back then, catfish was always fried and salmon was commonly found canned. Today, we enjoy all types of fish, fresher than ever and prepared in new and different ways, such as grilling.

Grilled Salmon with Tangy Dill Sauce

MAKES 4 SERVINGS
Prep: 5 min., Cook: 10 min.

Colorful grilled vegetables make a great side with this dish. Cut vegetables, such as squash and zucchini, into ¼-inch-thick slices and red bell peppers into 1-inch-wide strips. Brush each cut side with mayonnaise, and sprinkle with salt and pepper. Grill 2 to 4 minutes or until crisp-tender, turning once.

4 (8-oz.) salmon fillets
½ tsp. salt
½ tsp. pepper
2 Tbsp. mayonnaise

1 Tbsp. fresh lemon juice
Garnishes: lemon wedges,
    fresh dill sprig
Tangy Dill Sauce

1. Sprinkle fillets evenly with salt and pepper; lightly brush with mayonnaise. Place on food grate.
2. Grill, covered with grill lid, over medium-high heat (350° to 400°) 10 minutes or just until fish flakes with a fork. Sprinkle with lemon juice; garnish, if desired. Serve with Tangy Dill Sauce.

Tangy Dill Sauce

MAKES 1 CUP
Prep: 10 min., Other: 1 hr.

½ cup sour cream
½ cup mayonnaise
2 Tbsp. chopped fresh dill
¼ tsp. grated lemon rind
1 Tbsp. fresh lemon juice
½ tsp. ground red pepper

1. Stir together all ingredients. Cover and chill at least 1 hour.

Light &
loving it

Indulge in flavor with these unbelievably great-tasting light recipes. Quick appetizers, rich one-dish meals, and fruit-laden desserts make healthy eating enjoyable and stress-free.

STRAWBERRY NAPOLEONS, PAGE 331

Mocha Frappé

MAKES 3 SERVINGS
Prep: 10 min., Other: 2 hrs.

Here's a tasty way to sneak calcium into your diet. To make strong brewed coffee for the ice cubes, use 3 Tbsp. coffee grounds to 1 cup water.

1 cup strong brewed
  coffee
2 Tbsp. sugar
1 Tbsp. 2% reduced-fat
  milk

1¼ cups 2% reduced-fat
  milk
2 Tbsp. chocolate syrup
3 Tbsp. fat-free frozen
  whipped topping,
  thawed
1 tsp. dark chocolate
  shavings

1. Stir together coffee, sugar, and 1 Tbsp. milk in a small glass measuring cup. Pour into ice cube trays, and freeze at least 2 hours or until firm.

2. Process coffee ice cubes, 1¼ cups milk, and chocolate syrup in a blender until smooth. Pour into glasses. Dollop evenly with whipped topping, and sprinkle with chocolate shavings. Serve immediately.

Per serving: Calories 129 (15% from fat); Fat 2.2g (sat 1.4g, mono 0.6g, poly 0.1g); Protein 4g; Carb 23.2g; Fiber 0g; Chol 8mg; Iron 0.2mg; Sodium 66mg; Calc 131mg

From Our Kitchen

By having a glass of milk, you can improve your health and trim your waistline. The unique nutrient package of calcium, protein, phosphorous, and magnesium helps build strong bones, aids in weight loss, lowers blood pressure, and improves the overall quality of your diet.

Polenta Rounds with Black-Eyed Pea Topping

MAKES 6 APPETIZER SERVINGS
Prep: 15 min., Cook: 11 min.

*Wow your guests with these bite-size appetizers.
They're low in fat and calories and loaded with fiber and lean protein.*

½ (16-oz.) tube sun-dried tomato-flavored polenta, cut into 6 even slices (we tested with Melissa's Organic Sun-Dried Tomato Polenta)*
Vegetable cooking spray

1 (15-oz.) can black-eyed peas, rinsed and drained
½ cup finely chopped onion
¼ cup water
¼ tsp. ground red pepper
¼ tsp. salt
½ cup diced tomatoes
4 Tbsp. chopped fresh cilantro
¼ cup light sour cream

1. Cook polenta rounds in a large nonstick skillet coated with cooking spray over medium-high heat 4 minutes on each side or until lightly browned. Remove from heat, and keep warm.

2. Wipe pan with paper towel, spray with cooking spray, and cook peas and next 4 ingredients over medium heat 3 minutes or until water evaporates. Remove from heat; stir in tomatoes and 3 Tbsp. cilantro. Spoon warm black-eyed pea mixture over polenta rounds, and top evenly with sour cream. Sprinkle with remaining 1 Tbsp. cilantro.

Per serving: Calories 83 (11% from fat); Fat 1g (sat 0.6g, mono 0g, poly 0.1g); Protein 3.5g; Carb 15g; Fiber 2.6g; Chol 3mg; Iron 0.8mg; Sodium 259mg; Calc 14mg

*Find prepared polenta in the produce section of the supermarket.

Then & Now

Southern Living saluted the trend toward healthy cooking in January 1982 with its first healthy story called "Cooking Light," which has since become a magazine phenomenon itself. The early light flavors of recipes were mellow in contrast to today's high-flavor combos. Here, cilantro and sun-dried tomatoes take center stage.

Sweet Glazed Chicken Thighs

MAKES 8 SERVINGS
Prep: 15 min., Cook: 15 min.

*Serve this sweet-and-tangy dish with crisp-tender green beans, broccoli,
or sugar snap peas and chewy brown rice.*

1 cup pineapple juice
2 Tbsp. brown sugar
1 Tbsp. lite soy sauce
1 tsp. cornstarch

¾ tsp. salt
½ tsp. pepper
2 lbs. skinned and boned
    chicken thighs
3 Tbsp. all-purpose flour

1 Tbsp. butter or margarine
Vegetable cooking spray

1. Whisk together first 4 ingredients until smooth; set aside.

2. Sprinkle salt and pepper evenly over chicken. Dust evenly with flour.

3. Melt butter in a large nonstick skillet coated with cooking spray over medium-high heat. Cook chicken 5 to 6 minutes on each side. Remove chicken from pan, and keep warm. Add pineapple juice mixture to skillet, and cook, whisking constantly, 1 minute or until thickened and bubbly. Pour over chicken.

Per serving: Calories 215 (41% from fat); Fat 9.7g (sat 3.2g, mono 3.5g, poly 2g); Protein 21.6g; Carb 9g; Fiber 0.2g; Chol 79mg; Iron 1.5mg; Sodium 372mg; Calc 17mg

Chicken Cordon Bleu

MAKES 6 SERVINGS
Prep: 26 min., Cook: 40 min.

*A generous portion of ham and cheese tucked inside tender chicken breasts
makes this light meal unbelievably decadent.*

6 (6-oz.) skinned and
   boned chicken breasts
18 (¼-oz.) slices cooked
   ham (we tested with
   Oscar Mayer)
6 (⅔-oz.) slices Swiss
   cheese
2 Tbsp. chopped fresh
   parsley

½ cup seasoned dry
   breadcrumbs
¼ tsp. salt
¼ tsp. paprika
¼ tsp. pepper
⅓ cup fat-free milk
Vegetable cooking spray

1. Place each chicken breast between 2 sheets of heavy-duty plastic wrap; flatten to ¼-inch thickness, using a rolling pin or the flat side of a meat mallet. Place 3 slices of ham and 1 slice of cheese in the center of each chicken piece. Sprinkle centers with parsley. Roll up lengthwise, and secure with wooden picks.

2. Combine breadcrumbs, salt, paprika, and pepper. Dip each chicken breast into milk; roll in breadcrumb mixture. Place chicken in a 13- x 9-inch baking dish coated with cooking spray. Bake, uncovered, at 350° for 40 minutes or until chicken is done.

Per serving: Calories 328 (30% from fat); Fat 10.9g (sat 5g, mono 3.4g, poly 1.4g); Protein 46g; Carb 8.7g; Fiber 0.6g; Chol 123mg; Iron 2.1mg; Sodium 667mg; Calc 237mg

Light King Ranch Chicken Casserole

MAKES 8 SERVINGS
Prep: 20 min., Cook: 35 min.

*Your family won't believe that our rich, creamy version of
King Ranch Chicken is actually light.*

1 large onion, chopped
1 large green bell pepper, chopped
Vegetable cooking spray

2 cups chopped cooked chicken breasts
1 (10¾-oz.) can reduced-fat, reduced-sodium cream of chicken soup
1 (10¾-oz.) can reduced-fat, reduced-sodium cream of mushroom soup
1 (10-oz.) can diced tomato and green chiles
1 tsp. chili powder
½ tsp. pepper
¼ tsp. garlic powder

12 (6-inch) corn tortillas
1 (8-oz.) block reduced-fat Cheddar cheese, shredded

1. Sauté onion and bell pepper in a large skillet coated with cooking spray over medium-high heat 5 minutes or until tender.

2. Stir in chicken and next 6 ingredients; remove from heat.

3. Tear tortillas into 1-inch pieces; layer one-third tortilla pieces in a 13- x 9-inch baking dish coated with cooking spray. Top with one-third chicken mixture and one-third cheese. Repeat layers twice.

4. Bake at 350° for 30 to 35 minutes or until bubbly.

Per serving: Calories 273 (31% from fat); Fat 9.4g (sat 4.9g, mono 0.6g, poly 0.9g); Protein 21.2g; Carb 25g; Fiber 2.9g; Chol 54mg; Iron 0.8mg; Sodium 626mg; Calc 240mg

Note: Freeze casserole up to 1 month, if desired. Thaw in refrigerator overnight, and bake as directed.

Then & Now

A traditional version of King Ranch Chicken debuted in *Southern Living* in February 1994. We liked it so much that we created this light version so all could enjoy it more often guilt free.

Smoky-Hot Buffalo Chicken Pizzas

MAKES 6 APPETIZER SERVINGS
Prep: 10 min., Cook: 10 min.

Spice up your party with these fun and tasty pizzas. Blue cheese dressing beneath chipotle-bathed chicken creates a tamed heat sensation.

2 cups diced deli-roasted chicken breast
3 Tbsp. chipotle hot sauce
1 tsp. butter, melted

8 Tbsp. low-fat blue cheese dressing, divided
2 (7-inch) prebaked pizza crusts (we tested with Mama Mary's Gourmet Pizza Crusts)
½ cup (2 oz.) shredded 2% Colby-Monterey Jack cheese blend

2 green onions, thinly sliced (optional)

1. Stir together chicken, hot sauce, and butter in a microwave-safe bowl. Microwave at HIGH 45 seconds or until heated.

2. Spread 3 Tbsp. blue cheese dressing evenly over each pizza crust, leaving a 1-inch border around edges. Top evenly with chicken mixture. Sprinkle evenly with cheese.

3. Bake directly on oven rack at 450° for 8 to 10 minutes or until crusts are golden and cheese is melted. Drizzle remaining 2 Tbsp. dressing evenly over pizzas; sprinkle with green onions, if desired. Cut each pizza into 3 wedges.

Per serving: Calories 274 (27% from fat); Fat 8.3g (sat 2.7g, mono 0.7g, poly 0.4g); Protein 20.9g; Carb 26.5g; Fiber 2.4g; Chol 46mg; Iron 0.5mg; Sodium 711mg; Calc 143mg

Note: For a softer crust, bake pizza on a pizza pan or baking sheet.

Mediterranean Salmon

MAKES 4 SERVINGS
Prep: 20 min., Cook: 20 min.

*Herbed salmon fillets bake in foil packets that keep the fish moist.
If your dried tomatoes are packed in oil, be sure to drain and
pat them dry with a paper towel before using.*

4 (5-oz.) salmon fillets
¾ tsp. lemon pepper
¾ tsp. dried dillweed
¼ tsp. salt
½ cup coarsely chopped
   dried tomatoes
1 (2¼-oz.) can sliced ripe
   black olives, drained
2 oz. reduced-fat crumbled
   feta cheese with basil
   and tomatoes
¼ cup pine nuts, toasted

1. Place each salmon fillet on a 16- x 12-inch piece of heavy-duty aluminum foil. Sprinkle fillets evenly with lemon pepper, dill, and salt. Top fillets evenly with tomatoes and remaining ingredients. Fold long sides of foil over fillets; roll up short sides of foil to seal. Place foil packets, seam sides up, on a baking sheet.

2. Bake at 400° for 18 to 20 minutes or until fish flakes with a fork.

Per serving: Calories 350 (54% from fat); Fat 21g (sat 4.5g, mono 7.6g, poly 5.8g); Protein 35.4g; Carb 6.5g; Fiber 1.9g; Chol 77mg; Iron 2.2mg; Sodium 713mg; Calc 82mg

Lemon-Grilled Salmon

MAKES 4 SERVINGS
Prep: 15 min., Cook: 18 min., Other: 8 hrs.

Cedar planks impart a woody flavor and aroma.
Serve this dish with asparagus and store-bought whole wheat couscous.

2 (15- x 6-inch) cedar
    grilling planks

3 Tbsp. chopped fresh dill
3 Tbsp. chopped fresh
    parsley
2 tsp. grated lemon rind
3 Tbsp. fresh lemon juice
1 Tbsp. olive oil
1 garlic clove, pressed

4 (6-oz.) salmon fillets
½ tsp. salt
¼ tsp. pepper

1. Weigh down cedar planks with a heavier object in a large container. Add water to cover, and soak at least 8 hours.

2. Combine dill and next 5 ingredients; set aside.

3. Sprinkle fillets evenly with salt and pepper.

4. Remove cedar planks from water, and place planks on food grate on grill.

5. Grill soaked planks, covered with grill lid, over medium-high heat (350° to 400°) 2 minutes or until the planks begin to lightly smoke. Place 2 fillets on each cedar plank, and grill, covered with grill lid, 15 to 18 minutes or until fish flakes with a fork. Remove fish from planks to individual serving plates, using a spatula. (Carefully remove planks from grill using tongs.) Spoon herb mixture over fish, and serve immediately.

Per serving: Calories 308 (49% from fat); Fat 16.6g (sat 3.6g, mono 8.2g, poly 3.7g); Protein 36.4g; Carb 1.7g; Fiber 0.2g; Chol 87mg; Iron 0.8mg; Sodium 377mg; Calc 29mg

From Our Kitchen

Grilling fish on cedar planks is so easy. Not only does the wood add smoky flavor to your dish, but also the planks prevent the fish from flaking and falling through the food grate. Soak the planks in water at least eight hours before using to prevent burning. Keep a spray bottle of water handy for any flare-ups. Look for planks in the grilling section of your grocery store, home-improvement center, or specialty kitchen or garden shop.

Creamy Shrimp-and-Spinach Pasta

MAKES 6 SERVINGS
Prep: 20 min., Cook: 30 min.

Here's a one-dish meal your whole family will enjoy. Freshly grated nutmeg spices up the flavor of the cheesy white sauce that binds the ingredients.

12 oz. uncooked ziti pasta
1 (6-oz.) package fresh baby
  spinach

1 Tbsp. butter
1 (8-oz.) package sliced
  fresh baby portobello
  mushrooms
1 large white onion,
  chopped
2 tsp. minced fresh garlic

1 cup low-sodium fat-free
  chicken broth
¼ cup dry white wine*
6 oz. ⅓-less-fat cream
  cheese
½ tsp. salt
¼ tsp. plus ⅛ tsp. freshly
  grated nutmeg
¼ tsp. freshly ground black
  pepper
1 lb. peeled cooked medium
  shrimp, tails removed
  (about 41 to 50 shrimp)
⅓ cup grated Parmesan
  cheese

1. Cook pasta according to package directions, omitting salt and fat. Drain; return to pan. Stir in spinach; toss until spinach wilts. Set aside.

2. Melt 1 Tbsp. butter in a large nonstick skillet over medium-high heat. Add mushrooms, and cook, stirring occasionally, 8 minutes or until browned. Add onion, and sauté over medium heat 10 minutes or until tender. Add garlic; sauté 1 minute.

3. Stir in chicken broth and white wine. Increase heat to medium-high, and cook, stirring often, 8 minutes or until mixture thickens slightly. Reduce heat to medium. Stir in cream cheese and next 3 ingredients until smooth. Add shrimp, and cook until thoroughly heated. Pour shrimp mixture over pasta mixture; toss to combine. Sprinkle evenly with grated Parmesan cheese, and serve immediately.

Per serving: Calories 407 (25% from fat); Fat 11.2g (sat 6.4g, mono 1.1g, poly 0.9g); Protein 29.7g; Carb 46.2g; Fiber 3g; Chol 177mg; Iron 5.3mg; Sodium 697mg; Calc 152mg

*Substitute ¼ cup low-sodium fat-free chicken broth, if desired.

From Our Kitchen

Freshly grated nutmeg provides a more intense flavor than the prepackaged variety and should be used immediately. Use a nutmeg grater or the smallest blade on a regular grater to grate whole nutmeg. Whole nutmeg, stored in an airtight container, will keep for two to three years.

Beef-and-Onion Stew

MAKES 6 SERVINGS
Prep: 20 min., Cook: 1 hr.

Burgundy adds depth of flavor to this onion-adorned stew.

1 Tbsp. vegetable oil
2 lb. lean boneless sirloin,
　　cut into 1-inch cubes

3 whole cloves
1 (4-inch) stick cinnamon
1 cup Burgundy or other
　　dry red wine
¾ cup water
3 Tbsp. no-salt-added
　　tomato sauce
2 Tbsp. red wine vinegar
1 bay leaf
4 cloves garlic, minced
2 tsp. dark brown sugar
½ tsp. salt
½ tsp. ground cumin
¼ tsp. pepper

1½ lb. pearl onions

1. Heat vegetable oil in a Dutch oven. Add beef cubes, browning on all sides; drain off drippings.
2. Tie cloves and cinnamon stick in a spice bag. Add spice bag, wine, and next 9 ingredients to beef; stir well.
3. Bring to a boil; cover, reduce heat, and simmer 40 minutes. Add onions; cover and simmer 20 minutes. Discard bay leaf and spice bag.

Per serving: Calories 280 (27% from fat); Fat 8.3g (sat 2.4g, mono 3.7g, poly 0.9g); Protein 31.4g; Carb 18.9g; Fiber 0.2g; Chol 56mg; Iron 2.6mg; Sodium 283mg; Calc 56mg

Then & Now

"Today's society places a high value on being thin, and it's not all a matter of vanity. The more you weigh above your ideal body weight, the more your health risks are increased. Overweight people are more likely to have hypertension, diabetes, elevated blood cholesterol levels, and cardiovascular disease, as well as certain types of cancer. And, of course, being overweight has an adverse effect on longevity."

The words above accompanied this hearty stew when it first ran in *Southern Living* in 1987, and they're still true today. Over 25 beef stews later, this recipe remains a top pick for incorporating full flavor into a healthy lifestyle. Try it tonight, and you'll be one step closer to a leaner and healthier you.

Beef-and-Butternut Squash Chili

MAKES 8 SERVINGS
Prep: 20 min., Cook: 50 min.

Enjoy this chunky chili throughout the winter by making extra batches and freezing them. We loaded it with beef and beans for zinc and B vitamins, tomatoes and green bell peppers for vitamin C, and butternut squash for beta-carotene.

1 lb. extra-lean ground beef
1 green bell pepper, chopped
1 medium onion, chopped
2 garlic cloves, minced

2 (14½-oz.) cans Mexican-style stewed tomatoes, chopped
1 (16-oz.) can chili beans
½ small butternut squash, peeled and cubed (about 1½ cups)
1 cup low-sodium beef broth
1½ tsp. ground cumin
1½ tsp. chili powder
1 cup frozen corn kernels

1. Cook beef and next 3 ingredients in a Dutch oven over medium-high heat until meat crumbles and is no longer pink. Drain well, and return to Dutch oven.

2. Stir in tomatoes and next 5 ingredients; bring to a boil over medium-high heat. Cover, reduce heat to medium-low, and simmer, stirring occasionally, 15 minutes. Stir in corn, and cook, uncovered, 15 minutes or until squash is tender and chili is thickened.

Per serving: Calories 228 (26% from fat); Fat 6.6g (sat 2.6g, mono 2.6g, poly 0.3g); Protein 16.7g; Carb 26.2g; Fiber 6.2g; Chol 37mg; Iron 2.8mg; Sodium 601mg; Calc 54mg

From Our Kitchen

Our Test Kitchens Staff researched nature's most healthful foods and then created this recipe to help protect your body from illness. Here's some information to help you create healthy meals by stocking up on these immunity boosters.
• Beta-carotene: butternut squash, pumpkin, sweet potatoes, spinach, broccoli
• B vitamins (folate and B_{12}): spinach, legumes, peanuts, whole grains, leafy green vegetables, eggs, milk
• Vitamin C: oranges, grapefruits, strawberries, green bell peppers, cabbage
• Vitamin E: peanuts, sunflower seeds, eggs, spinach, whole grains, vegetable oils, poultry
• Zinc: fish, poultry, beef, pork, eggs, cheese, milk, peanut butter, whole grains

Corn-and-Poblano Chowder

MAKES 4 SERVINGS
Prep: 10 min., Cook: 20 min., Other: 10 min.

Frozen creamed corn and fat-free cream cheese are the base for this spicy-sweet, creamy chowder. Have a cupful for a light lunch, or serve it alongside a sandwich for a more substantial dinner.

1 large poblano chile pepper, cut in half lengthwise

1 (20-oz.) tube frozen creamed corn, thawed
1½ cups 1% low-fat or fat-free milk
¼ tsp. salt
⅛ to ¼ tsp. ground red pepper
¼ tsp. ground cumin

1½ cups reduced-sodium fat-free chicken broth
½ (8-oz.) package fat-free cream cheese, softened
Garnishes: thinly sliced jalapeño pepper strips, freshly ground black pepper

1. Broil poblano pepper halves, skin sides up, on an aluminum foil-lined baking sheet 6 inches from heat 5 to 6 minutes or until pepper looks blistered. Fold aluminum foil over pepper to seal, and let stand 10 minutes. Peel pepper; remove and discard seeds. Coarsely chop pepper; set aside.

2. Bring creamed corn and next 4 ingredients to a boil in a 3-qt. saucepan over medium-high heat, stirring mixture constantly. Reduce heat to low, and simmer, stirring often, 10 minutes.

3. Stir 1½ cups chicken broth into mixture. Whisk in softened cream cheese and chopped pepper; cook, whisking often, 5 minutes or until cream cheese melts and mixture is thoroughly heated. Garnish, if desired. Serve chowder immediately.

Per serving: Calories 222 (13% from fat); Fat 3.1g (sat 1g, mono 0.4g, poly 0.3g); Protein 11.8g; Carb 37g; Fiber 3.4g; Chol 6mg; Iron 0.6mg; Sodium 968mg; Calc 187mg

Wild Mushroom Soup

MAKES 8 SERVINGS
Prep: 25 min., Cook: 50 min., Other: 30 min.

This soup is a blend of earthy mushrooms complemented by sweet Madeira wine. Look for dried wild mushrooms in the produce section of large supermarkets. Don't substitute fresh mushrooms; they'll make the soup watery.

2 vegetable bouillon cubes
2 cups boiling water

¾ cup Madeira wine
4 cups low-sodium fat-free
   chicken broth, divided
1 (½-oz.) package dried
   porcini mushrooms,
   chopped
1 (½-oz.) package dried
   morel mushrooms,
   chopped
1 (½-oz.) package dried
   chanterelle mushrooms,
   chopped

2 Tbsp. butter or margarine
6 green onions, sliced
1 medium onion, diced

3 Tbsp. all-purpose flour
1 lb. fresh white
   mushrooms, quartered
¼ tsp. freshly ground
   pepper

Toppings: fat-free sour
   cream, chopped green
   onions
Garnish: green onions

1. Dissolve bouillon cubes in 2 cups boiling water. Set aside.

2. Bring wine, ½ cup chicken broth, and dried mushrooms to a boil in a small saucepan. Remove from heat, and let stand 30 minutes.

3. Melt butter in a Dutch oven over medium-high heat; add green onions and diced onion. Sauté until tender.

4. Stir in flour, and cook, stirring constantly, 1 minute. Gradually stir in vegetable broth mixture and remaining 3½ cups chicken broth. Stir in wild mushroom mixture, white mushrooms, and pepper. Bring to a boil, stirring occasionally; reduce heat, and simmer, stirring occasionally, 30 minutes. Cool slightly.

5. Process mixture, in batches, in a blender or food processor (or use an immersion blender) until smooth, stopping to scrape down sides. Return to Dutch oven.

6. Cook over low heat, stirring occasionally, 5 minutes or until thoroughly heated. Serve with desired toppings. Garnish, if desired.

Per serving: Calories 94 (38% from fat); Fat 4g (sat 2.1g, mono 0.9g, poly 0.2g); Protein 4.5g; Carb 10.1g; Fiber 1.5g; Chol 8mg; Iron 1.5mg; Sodium 745mg; Calc 19mg

Then & Now

Obviously, this recipe graced our magazine pages fairly recently because of the trio of unique mushrooms. In 1966, when *Southern Living* began, the only mushrooms available were canned button—if you could find them!

Creamy Hash Brown Casserole

MAKES 6 SERVINGS
Prep 10 min., Cook: 1 hr., Other: 10 min.

Even kids will like this lightened hash brown casserole. With fat-free cream of chicken soup and light sour cream, they'll never know it's not the full-fat version.

1 (32-oz.) package frozen
    hash brown potatoes
1 (10¾-oz.) can fat-free
    cream of chicken soup
1 (8-oz.) container light
    sour cream
1 small onion, chopped
1 (5-oz.) can low-fat
    evaporated milk
¼ cup light butter or
    margarine, melted
1 tsp. dried rosemary
    (optional)
½ tsp. salt
¼ tsp. pepper

Vegetable cooking spray
1 cup (4 oz.) shredded
    reduced-fat Cheddar
    cheese

1. Stir together first 9 ingredients in a large bowl.

2. Spoon mixture into an 11- x 7-inch baking dish coated with cooking spray. Sprinkle evenly with cheese.

3. Bake at 350° for 1 hour or until bubbly and golden. Remove from oven, and let stand 10 minutes.

Per serving: Calories 325 (33% from fat); Fat 11.9g (sat 7.6g, mono 0.2g, poly 0.2g); Protein 12.2g; Carb 45g; Fiber 2.5g; Chol 43mg; Iron 0.1mg; Sodium 577mg; Calc 196mg

Rosemary Green Beans

MAKES 6 SERVINGS
Prep: 20 min., Cook: 15 min.

These simple-to-prepare green beans get an extra punch of flavor from lemon rind, fresh rosemary, and toasted nuts.

1 lb. fresh green beans, trimmed
½ tsp. salt, divided

2 green onions, sliced (about ¼ cup)
2 tsp. chopped fresh rosemary
1 tsp. olive oil
¼ cup chopped pecans, toasted
2 tsp. grated lemon rind
Garnish: fresh rosemary sprigs

1. Sprinkle green beans evenly with ¼ tsp. salt, and place in a steamer basket over boiling water; cover and steam 10 minutes or until crisp-tender. Plunge green beans into ice water to stop the cooking process, and drain.

2. Sauté green onions and rosemary in hot oil in a nonstick skillet over medium-high heat 2 to 3 minutes or until softened. Add green beans, pecans, lemon rind, and remaining ¼ tsp. salt, stirring until thoroughly heated. Garnish, if desired, and serve immediately.

Per serving: Calories 64 (62% from fat); Fat 4.4g (sat 0.4g, mono 2.6g, poly 1.2g); Protein 1.8g; Carb 6g; Fiber 3g; Chol 0mg; Iron 0.9mg; Sodium 199mg; Calc 33mg

Then & Now

Green beans may have undergone more of a cooking transformation that any other popular Southern vegetable in the last couple of generations. Our grandmothers simmered them for hours, usually flavored with a ham hock, proclaiming them done only after they showed no resistance whatsoever to the fork. Today's cooks forgo the ham bone in favor of lower fat flavor alternatives, such as broth, and get them in and out of the pot as quickly as possible to maximize color, texture, and nutrients.

Frozen Chocolate Brownie Pie

MAKES 12 SERVINGS
Prep: 16 min., Cook: 15 min., Other: 8 hrs.

¼ cup butter
⅔ cup firmly packed
    brown sugar
½ cup egg substitute
¼ cup buttermilk

¼ cup all-purpose flour
⅓ cup unsweetened cocoa
¼ tsp. salt
1 tsp. vanilla extract
Vegetable cooking spray

½ gallon vanilla fat-free
    frozen yogurt,
    softened
1 qt. chocolate fat-free
    frozen yogurt, softened
12 Tbsp. chocolate syrup
Garnishes: fresh straw-
    berries, chocolate curls

1. Melt butter in a large saucepan over medium-high heat; add brown sugar, stirring with a wire whisk. Remove from heat; cool slightly. Add egg substitute and buttermilk, stirring well.

2. Combine flour, cocoa, and salt; add to buttermilk mixture, stirring until blended. Stir in vanilla. Pour into a 9-inch springform pan lightly coated with cooking spray.

3. Bake at 350° for 15 minutes. Cool completely in pan on a wire rack.

4. Spread half of vanilla yogurt over brownie; spread chocolate yogurt over vanilla yogurt, and top with remaining vanilla yogurt. Cover and freeze 8 hours or overnight. Serve with chocolate syrup. Garnish, if desired.

Per serving: Calories 352 (13% from fat); Fat 5.1g (sat 3.2g, mono 1.3g, poly 0.2g); Protein 12.6g; Carb 27.4g; Fiber 1.9g; Chol 14mg; Iron 1.7mg; Sodium 246mg; Calc 350mg

Banana Pudding

MAKES 10 SERVINGS
Prep: 33 min., Cook 25 min., Other: 30 min.

Friends and family will love this lighter rendition of iconic Southern pudding.
Fat-free sweetened condensed milk keeps it rich and creamy.

⅓ cup all-purpose flour

Dash of salt

2½ cups 1% low-fat milk

1 (14-oz.) can fat-free
     sweetened condensed
     milk

2 egg yolks

2 tsp. vanilla extract

3 cups sliced ripe banana

45 reduced-fat vanilla
     wafers

4 egg whites

¼ cup sugar

1. Combine flour and salt in a medium saucepan. Gradually stir in milks and yolks, and cook over medium heat, stirring constantly, 8 minutes or until thickened. Remove from heat; stir in vanilla.

2. Arrange 1 cup banana slices in bottom of a 2-qt. baking dish. Spoon one-third pudding mixture over bananas; top with 15 vanilla wafers. Repeat layers twice, ending with pudding; arrange remaining 15 wafers around inside edge of dish. Gently push wafers into pudding.

3. Beat egg whites at high speed with an electric mixer until foamy. Add sugar, 1 Tbsp. at a time, beating until stiff peaks form and sugar dissolves (2 to 4 minutes). Spread meringue over pudding, sealing to edge of dish.

4. Bake at 325° for 25 minutes or until golden. Cool at least 30 minutes.

Per serving: Calories 300 (9% from fat); Fat 2.9g (sat 0.8g, mono 0.6g, poly 0.2g); Protein 8.5g; Carb 59.6g; Fiber 1.3g; Chol 49mg; Iron 0.9mg; Sodium 172mg; Calc 185mg

Then & Now

In the beginning, there was porridge. Thinner, it was gruel; thicker, it was bread. When honey was found, people sweetened their porridge; they added milk when they had it and otherwise improved upon a good thing.

With experimentation, there came pudding-on-purpose: Sweetened bready mixtures, such as "plum" pudding, were boiled in a dampened, flour-rubbed cloth. With iron hearthware, it became possible to bake puddings long before ovens came into general use. Some of those baking puddings even found their way into crusts and became pies.

Today, we have many conveniences, such as sugar, refined flour, and stoves, that make puddings quicker and easier to prepare. This Southern classic pudding makes use of these conveniences so it's ready to enjoy a lot quicker than its pudding ancestors.

Blueberry-Lime Granita

MAKES 7 SERVINGS
Prep: 15 min.; Other: 8 hrs., 5 min.

*Serve this frozen concoction as a sweet-tart treat—using no-calorie sweetener
makes each serving only 25 calories!*

2 cups blueberries
½ cup sugar*
½ tsp. grated lime rind
2 tsp. fresh lime juice
3 cups diet lemon-lime soft
    drink, chilled

Garnish: lime rind twists

1. Process blueberries in a food processor or blender until smooth, stopping to scrape down sides. Add sugar, lime rind, and lime juice; process until well blended. Pour into an 11- x 7-inch baking dish. Stir in soft drink. Cover and freeze 8 hours. Remove from freezer; let stand 5 minutes.
2. Chop mixture into large chunks, and place in food processor in batches; pulse 5 to 6 times or until mixture is smooth. Serve immediately, or freeze until ready to serve. Garnish, if desired.

*Substitute ½ cup no-calorie sweetener (such as Splenda), if desired.

Per serving with sugar: Calories 80 (1% from fat); Fat 0.1g (sat 0g, mono 0g, poly 0g); Protein 0.3g; Carb 20.4g; Fiber 1g; Chol 0mg; Iron 0.1mg; Sodium 0mg; Calc 3mg

Per serving with no-calorie sweetener: Calories 25 (4% from fat); Fat 0.1g (sat 0g, mono 0g, poly 0g); Protein 0.3g; Carb 6.2g; Fiber 1g; Chol 0mg; Iron 0.1mg; Sodium 0mg; Calc 3mg

From Our Kitchen

Blueberries contain powerful antioxidants that help combat disease and fight aging.

Peach and Blueberry Parfaits

MAKES 8 SERVINGS
Prep: 30 min., Cook: 15 min., Other: 2 hrs.

*Smooth, silky vanilla sauce envelopes chunks of angel food cake,
juicy peaches, and sweet blueberries.*

2 cups 1% low-fat milk
1 large egg
⅓ cup sugar
1 Tbsp. cornstarch
1 tsp. vanilla extract

3 lb. fresh peaches, peeled
    and chopped (about
    7 cups)
1 pt. fresh blueberries
½ (14-oz.) angel food cake,
    cubed (about 6 cups)
Garnish: fresh mint sprigs

1. Whisk together first 4 ingredients in a small non-aluminum saucepan over medium-low heat, and cook, stirring constantly, 15 minutes or until slightly thickened. (Mixture should lightly coat the back of a spoon.) Remove from heat; stir in vanilla.

2. Pour mixture into a small mixing bowl, and place plastic wrap directly over surface of custard to prevent film from forming; chill 2 hours or until ready to serve.

3. Layer fruit and cake in 8 mason jars or tall glasses. Drizzle each with ¼ cup vanilla sauce. Garnish, if desired.

Per serving: Calories 215 (8% from fat); Fat 2g (sat 0.7g, mono 0.6g, poly 0.4g); Protein 5.9g; Carb 46g; Fiber 3.5g; Chol 29mg; Iron 0.8mg; Sodium 226mg; Calc 124mg

Strawberry Napoleons

MAKES 6 SERVINGS
Prep: 10 min., Cook: 4 min.

Ever thought of firing up the grill to prepare dessert? You'll be stunned by the gorgeous presentation grilled phyllo stacks make when paired with bright, sweet strawberries and honey-yogurt sauce

2 (5.3-oz.) containers plain fat-free yogurt
3 Tbsp. honey

1 (16-oz.) container fresh strawberries, sliced
2 Tbsp. sugar

4 frozen phyllo sheets, thawed
Vegetable cooking spray
1 tsp. sugar

Garnishes: fresh mint sprigs, whole strawberries

1. Stir together yogurt and honey; cover and chill yogurt sauce until ready to serve.

2. Combine strawberries and 2 Tbsp. sugar; cover and chill until ready to serve.

3. Place 1 phyllo sheet on a flat work surface. Coat with cooking spray, and sprinkle evenly with $\frac{1}{4}$ tsp. sugar. Top with 1 phyllo sheet; coat again with cooking spray, and sprinkle with $\frac{1}{4}$ tsp. sugar. Cut phyllo stack into thirds lengthwise; cut each in half, creating 6 even rectangular stacks. Repeat procedure with remaining phyllo sheets, cooking spray, and remaining $\frac{1}{2}$ tsp. sugar.

4. Grill phyllo stacks, without grill lid, over medium-low heat (300° to 350°) 1 to 2 minutes on each side or until lightly browned.

5. Place 1 grilled phyllo stack on each of 6 serving plates; top evenly with half of strawberry slices. Drizzle evenly with half of yogurt sauce. Top each with 1 grilled phyllo stack. Top evenly with remaining strawberry slices and yogurt sauce. Garnish, if desired. Serve immediately.

Per serving: Calories 141 (6% from fat); Fat 1g (sat 0.2g, mono 0.4g, poly 0.2g); Protein 4.7g; Carb 29.8g; Fiber 1.7g; Chol 2mg; Iron 0.8mg; Sodium 112mg; Calc 102mg

Fresh Fruit with Lemon-Mint Sauce

MAKES 5 SERVINGS
Prep: 20 min., Other: 2 hrs.

Serve this refreshing dish after a meal for a light dessert, enjoy it as a snack, or try it for breakfast. Its oranges, grapefruits, and lemons are packed with vitamin C, the antioxidant that helps boost the immune system, fight infection, and protect the body against influenza.

3 large oranges, peeled and sectioned
2 large red grapefruit, peeled and sectioned
2 cups seedless red grapes, halved
2 Tbsp. chopped fresh mint

1 (6-oz.) container low-fat vanilla yogurt
1 tsp. grated lemon rind
2 Tbsp. fresh lemon juice
1 tsp. honey
Garnish: fresh mint sprigs

1. Place first 4 ingredients in a medium bowl, gently tossing to combine. Cover and chill 2 hours.

2. Stir together yogurt and next 3 ingredients just before serving, and serve with fruit mixture. Garnish, if desired.

Per serving: Calories 165 (5% from fat); Fat 0.9g (sat 0.4g, mono 0.1g, poly 0.1g); Protein 3.4g; Carb 39.6g; Fiber 4.3g; Chol 2mg; Iron 0.5mg; Sodium 22mg; Calc 114mg

Kitchen Express Fresh Fruit with Lemon-Mint Sauce: Substitute 2 (24-oz.) jars refrigerated orange-and-grapefruit salad mix (we tested with Del Monte SunFresh Citrus Salad in Extra Light Syrup), drained, for oranges and grapefruits.

Key Lime Frozen Yogurt

MAKES 12 SERVINGS
Prep: 5 min., Other: 30 min.

*Press a scoop of this yogurt between graham cracker squares for
a better-for-you "ice-cream" sandwich.*

1 (32-oz.) container whole milk French vanilla yogurt (we tested with Stonyfield Farm Organic Whole Milk French Vanilla Yogurt)
1 (14-oz.) can fat-free sweetened condensed milk
½ cup Key lime juice (we tested with Joe's Famous Key West Lime Juice)

1. Whisk together all ingredients in a large mixing bowl until well blended. Pour mixture into the freezer container of a 1½-qt. electric ice-cream maker, and freeze according to manufacturer's instructions. (Instructions and times will vary.) Cover and freeze until desired firmness.

Per serving: Calories 177 (14% from fat); Fat 2.7g (sat 1.7g, mono 0g, poly 0g); Protein 5.2g; Carb 32.3g; Fiber 1g; Chol 14mg; Iron 0mg; Sodium 74mg; Calc 201mg

Holiday memories

There's a chill in the air, but warmth is in the kitchen with this selection of homestyle holiday favorites.

our best
40 years
recipes

ROASTED QUAIL WITH CRANBERRY-ORANGE-PECAN STUFFING, PAGE 350

Grapefruit Freeze

MAKES 8 CUPS
Prep: 20 min.; Other: 4 hrs., 35 min.

Almost too pretty to eat, this recipe turns a winter fruit juice into an elegant treat.

1½ cups sugar
1 cup water
½ cup fresh mint leaves, chopped
1 (64-oz.) bottle Ruby Red grapefruit juice

Garnish: fresh mint sprig

1. Bring sugar and 1 cup water to a boil in a saucepan. Add mint; cover and let stand 5 minutes. Pour through a fine wire-mesh strainer into an 8-cup container; discard mint. Add grapefruit juice.

2. Divide mixture into 2 (1-qt.) freezer containers; cover and freeze at least 4 hours. Let stand 30 minutes before serving. Scrape with a spatula or fork, or process, in batches, in a food processor. Garnish, if desired.

Raspberry-Brie Tartlets

MAKES 5 DOZEN
Prep: 1 hr., Cook: 17 min.

*All of these deliciously gooey appetizers will probably not make it to the table.
It's difficult to resist sneaking a few right off the baking sheet.*

20 white bread slices

Melted butter

1 (8-oz.) Brie wedge, cut up
1 (13-oz.) jar raspberry jam

1. Remove crusts from bread with a serrated knife. Roll and flatten each bread slice with a rolling pin. Cut 3 circles out of each bread slice with a 1¾-inch fluted or round cookie cutter.

2. Brush mini muffin pans with melted butter. Press bread circles on bottom and up sides of muffin cups; brush bread cups with melted butter.

3. Bake at 350° for 7 minutes or until lightly toasted. Reduce heat to 300°.

4. Remove bread cups from muffin pans, and place on ungreased baking sheets. Fill cups evenly with cheese pieces; top each with ¼ tsp. jam.

5. Bake at 300° for 10 minutes or until cheese is melted.

Make Ahead: Freeze toasted bread shells up to 1 month in advance. Thaw at room temperature about 30 minutes. Assemble tartlets, and bake as directed.

Cloverleaf Rolls

MAKES 2 DOZEN
Prep: 20 min.; Cook: 12 min.; Other: 1 hr., 45 min.

These tender yeast rolls deserve a prime spot on the holiday dinner table.

1 (¼-oz.) envelope active
   dry yeast
1 cup warm water
   (100° to 110°)

3 Tbsp. sugar
2 Tbsp. shortening
1 large egg
½ tsp. salt
3 to 3½ cups all-purpose
   flour

¼ cup butter or margarine,
   melted

1. Combine yeast and warm water in a 1-cup liquid measuring cup; let stand 5 minutes.

2. Combine yeast mixture, sugar, shortening, egg, salt, and half of flour in a large mixing bowl; beat at low speed with an electric mixer until smooth. Gradually stir in enough remaining flour to make a soft dough.

3. Place dough in a well-greased bowl, turning to grease top. Cover and let rise in a warm place (85°), free from drafts, 1 hour or until doubled in bulk; or cover and store in refrigerator up to 4 days. (If chilled, let dough return to room temperature before proceeding.)

4. Punch dough down; turn out onto a lightly floured surface, and knead 8 to 10 times.

5. Lightly grease muffin pans. Shape dough into 1-inch balls; place 3 balls in each muffin cup. Cover and let rise in a warm place (85°), free from drafts, 40 minutes or until doubled in bulk.

6. Bake at 400° for 10 to 12 minutes or until golden. Brush rolls with melted butter.

Citrus-Glazed Ham

MAKES 12 TO 14 SERVINGS
Prep: 10 min.; Cook: 2 hrs., 30 min.; Other: 15 min.

*This ham takes only a few steps to make. Dress it up with salad greens,
sliced oranges and apples, and ribbons of orange rind.*

1 (6- to 7-lb.) fully cooked,
    bone-in ham
30 to 32 whole cloves

1 (10-oz.) bottle orange
    juice-flavored soft drink
    (we tested with
    Orangina Sparkling
    Citrus Beverage)
1¼ cups orange marmalade
½ cup firmly packed light
    brown sugar
¼ cup Dijon mustard

Garnishes: apple slices,
    orange slices, orange
    rind, salad greens

1. Remove skin from ham, and trim fat to ¼-inch thickness. Make ¼-inch-deep cuts in a diamond pattern, and insert cloves at 1-inch intervals. Place ham in an aluminum foil-lined 13- x 9-inch pan.

2. Stir together soft drink and next 3 ingredients until smooth. Pour mixture evenly over ham.

3. Bake at 350° on lower oven rack 2½ hours, basting with pan juices every 20 minutes. Remove ham; let stand 15 minutes before serving. Garnish, if desired.

From Our Kitchen

Ham comes from the leg of the hog. You can buy ham cooked, uncooked, dry cured, or wet cured.
• A cooked ham can be served directly from the refrigerator. If you'd like to serve it hot, heat it in a 350° oven to an internal temperature of 140°. At 140°, the ham will be thoroughly warm and moist.
• An uncooked ham should be cooked to an internal temperature of 160° in a 350° oven. Depending on the size, plan to cook it 18 to 25 minutes per pound.
• Dry-cured ham is rubbed with salt, sugar, and other seasonings, and then stored until the salt penetrates the meat.
• Wet-cured ham is seasoned with a brine solution, which keeps the meat moist and produces a more tender texture.

Pork Fillets with Dark Cherry Sauce

MAKES 4 SERVINGS
Prep: 10 min., Cook: 25 min.

These tender and juicy pork fillets make an elegant yet inexpensive entrée. We tied a piece of kitchen string around extra-thick slices of pork loin to retain the round shape during cooking. Use a pair of scissors to cut the string, and then discard it before serving.

2 lb. pork loin
½ tsp. salt
½ tsp. freshly ground
    pepper

2 Tbsp. olive oil
½ cup beef broth
¼ cup bourbon

1 (17-oz.) can dark, sweet
    pitted cherries

1 Tbsp. cornstarch
2 tsp. grated lemon rind
2 Tbsp. fresh lemon juice
1½ tsp. chopped fresh
    rosemary
½ tsp. whole cloves
½ cup chopped pecans,
    toasted
Garnish: fresh watercress

1. Cut pork loin into 4 (1½-inch-thick) fillets; sprinkle evenly with salt and pepper. Securely tie a 12-inch piece of kitchen string around each fillet, if desired.
2. Cook pork fillets in hot oil in a skillet over medium-high heat 2 to 3 minutes on each side or until golden brown. Stir together beef broth and bourbon; add to skillet, stirring to loosen particles from bottom of skillet. Reduce heat to low; cover and simmer for 10 to 15 minutes or until pork is done. Remove fillets to a serving platter, reserving pan juices, and keep warm. Remove and discard kitchen string.
3. Drain cherries, reserving syrup in a small bowl.
4. Whisk together cherry syrup, cornstarch, and next 4 ingredients; add to skillet with reserved pan juices. Bring to a boil over medium heat, and cook, stirring constantly, 1 minute or until thickened. Remove from heat; remove cloves, and stir in cherries and chopped toasted pecans. Spoon mixture evenly over warm pork fillets. Garnish, if desired, and serve immediately.

From Our Kitchen

The secret to serving moist and tender pork is simple. Have the skillet or grill hot enough to sear the meat and to seal in the juices. Be careful not to overcook the meat—a little pink on the inside is fine.

Cornish Hens with Spicy Pecan-Cornbread Stuffing

MAKES 8 SERVINGS
Prep: 15 min., Cook: 55 min.

*These petite hens make a pretty presentation for any holiday gathering.
The spicy-savory blend of chili powder-crusted pecans and herbed stuffing creates a
flavor sensation guests will request year after year.*

Spicy Pecan-Cornbread
Stuffing
8 (1- to 1½-lb.) Cornish
hens
Melted butter or margarine

1. Spoon about 1 cup Spicy Pecan-Cornbread Stuffing into each hen; close opening with skewers. Place hens, breast sides up, in a roasting pan. Brush with butter.
2. Bake, covered, at 450° for 5 minutes. Reduce heat to 350°, and bake 50 more minutes or until a meat thermometer inserted in stuffing registers 165°. Remove skewers, and serve.

Taste of the South

We may not be able to agree on the official pronunciation of pecan, but we can certainly agree that few things announce the arrival of fall in the South more clearly. A simple bowlful of these freshly shelled nuts is a mouthwatering beacon for gathering friends and family.

Spicy Pecan-Cornbread Stuffing

MAKES 8 CUPS
Prep: 28 min., Cook: 40 min.

10 bacon slices

1⅓ cups yellow cornmeal
1⅓ cups all-purpose flour
2 tsp. baking powder
1 tsp. garlic powder
¾ tsp. baking soda
½ tsp. salt

½ to 2 cups chicken broth
2 large eggs
2 Tbsp. butter or margarine

1½ cups Spicy Pecans

1 large onion, diced
2 Tbsp. vegetable oil
3 celery ribs, diced
1 red bell pepper, chopped
¾ cup diced mushrooms
2 tsp. dried thyme
2 tsp. dried sage
3 to 4 large eggs, lightly
   beaten

1. Cook bacon in a 9-inch cast-iron skillet until crisp; remove bacon, and drain on paper towels, reserving 2 Tbsp. drippings in skillet. Keep skillet warm. Crumble bacon, and set aside.
2. Combine cornmeal and next 5 ingredients in a large bowl.
3. Whisk together broth, 2 eggs, and butter; add to dry ingredients, stirring just until moistened. Pour mixture into hot skillet with drippings.
4. Bake at 400° for 25 minutes or until golden around edges. Crumble cornbread onto a baking sheet; reduce heat to 350°, and bake, stirring occasionally, 15 minutes or until lightly toasted. Transfer cornbread to a large bowl, and stir in crumbled bacon and Spicy Pecans.
5. Sauté diced onion in hot oil in a large skillet over medium-high heat 5 minutes or until tender. Add diced celery, chopped bell pepper, and diced mushrooms, and cook 3 minutes; stir in thyme and sage. Stir vegetable mixture into cornbread mixture; stir in lightly beaten eggs. Stuff mixture into Cornish hens, and bake as directed.

Spicy Pecans

MAKES 1½ CUPS
Prep: 5 min., Cook: 8 min.

2 Tbsp. brown sugar
2 Tbsp. orange juice
   concentrate
1½ Tbsp. butter or
   margarine
½ tsp. salt
½ tsp. chili powder
¼ tsp. pepper
1½ cups coarsely chopped
   pecans

1. Cook first 6 ingredients in a skillet over medium-high heat, stirring until brown sugar dissolves. Remove from heat, and stir in pecans. Transfer to a lightly greased baking sheet.
2. Bake at 350° for 8 minutes or until toasted. Cool and store in an airtight container.

Sesame-Crusted Turkey Mignons

MAKES 4 SERVINGS
Prep: 20 min., Cook: 24 min.

Having company over and need dinner in a flash? Pick up some turkey mignons or tenderloins from your grocer, and you'll have an Asian-infused meal ready in no time.

½ cup sesame seeds, toasted
¼ cup olive oil
1 garlic clove, minced
1 Tbsp. chopped fresh chives
1 Tbsp. soy sauce
2 tsp. lemon juice
1 tsp. grated fresh ginger
½ tsp. sesame oil
2 (11-oz.) packages turkey mignons*

Creamy Wine Sauce
Hot cooked noodles
Garnishes: lemon slices, fresh parsley sprigs

1. Stir together first 8 ingredients; dredge turkey in sesame seed mixture. Place on a lightly greased rack in a broiler pan.
2. Broil 5½ inches from heat 12 minutes on each side or until done. Serve with Creamy Wine Sauce over hot cooked noodles. Garnish, if desired.

*Substitute 2 turkey tenderloins, cut in half, for turkey mignons, if desired.

Creamy Wine Sauce

MAKES ABOUT ¾ CUP
Prep: 5 min., Cook: 15 min.

1 cup fruity white wine (we tested with Liebfraumilch)*
2 tsp. lemon juice
¼ cup whipping cream

2 Tbsp. soy sauce
⅓ cup butter or margarine

1. Bring wine and lemon juice to a boil in a saucepan over medium-high heat. Boil 6 to 8 minutes or until mixture is reduced by half. Whisk in whipping cream. Cook 3 to 4 minutes, whisking constantly, until thickened.
2. Reduce heat to simmer, and whisk in soy sauce and butter until butter is melted.

*White grape juice may be substituted for wine.

Roasted Quail with Cranberry-Orange-Pecan Stuffing

MAKES 4 SERVINGS
Prep: 1 hr., 55 min.; Cook: 1 hr.

Treat holiday guests to a platter of roasted quail that looks as fabulous as it tastes.

1½ cups cranberry juice
1¼ cups sugar
1½ cups fresh or frozen cranberries
1½ tsp. grated orange rind

½ cup orange juice
¼ cup butter or margarine, melted

Cranberry-Orange-Pecan Stuffing
8 quail, dressed
½ tsp. salt
½ tsp. pepper

Garnish: orange rind strips

1. Cook cranberry juice and sugar in a saucepan over medium heat, stirring constantly, 25 minutes or until sugar melts and mixture thickens. Add cranberries and orange rind; cook, stirring constantly, 2 minutes or until cranberries pop. Remove cranberry glaze from heat; cool.

2. Stir together orange juice and melted butter.

3. Spoon about ¼ cup Cranberry-Orange-Pecan Stuffing into each quail, and tie legs together with string. Sprinkle with salt and pepper; place in a shallow roasting pan. Brush with orange juice mixture.

4. Bake at 325° for 1 hour, basting quail with orange juice mixture every 15 minutes. Broil 5½ inches from heat 3 to 4 minutes or until golden, if necessary. Serve with cranberry glaze. Garnish, if desired.

Cranberry-Orange-Pecan Stuffing

MAKES 2 CUPS
Prep: 30 min.

2 Tbsp. butter or margarine
½ medium onion, diced
2 celery ribs, diced
¾ cup chopped pecans,
    toasted
⅓ cup chopped orange
    sections
⅓ cup chopped cranberries
1 Tbsp. sugar

2 white bread slices, toasted
    and cut into ½-inch
    pieces
½ tsp. salt
½ tsp. dried thyme
½ tsp. rubbed sage
1 large egg, lightly beaten
2 Tbsp. orange juice

1. Melt butter in a large saucepan over medium heat; add onion and celery, and sauté until onion is tender. Stir in pecans and next 3 ingredients; remove from heat.

2. Combine bread pieces and next 3 ingredients in a bowl, and add to cranberry mixture, stirring until mixture is combined. Stir in egg and orange juice. Stuff mixture into quail, and bake as directed.

Chocolate Fudge Brownies

MAKES 32 BROWNIES
Prep: 15 min., Cook: 40 min.

Dusted with a snowy layer of powdered sugar, Chocolate Fudge Brownies nestle next to squares of Praline-Pecan Brownies and Caramel-Coconut-Pecan Brownies. A bright and shiny tart pan holds this chocolate-lover's sampler.

4 (1-oz.) unsweetened
    chocolate baking
    squares

1 cup butter, softened
2 cups sugar
4 large eggs

1 cup all-purpose flour
1 tsp. vanilla extract
1 cup semisweet chocolate
    morsels

1. Microwave chocolate squares in a microwave-safe bowl at MEDIUM (50% power) 1½ minutes, stirring at 30-second intervals until melted. Stir until smooth.

2. Beat butter and sugar at medium speed with an electric mixer until light and fluffy. Add eggs, 1 at a time, beating just until blended after each addition. Add melted chocolate, beating just until blended.

3. Add flour, beating at low speed just until blended. Stir in vanilla and chocolate morsels. Spread batter into a greased and floured 13- x 9-inch pan.

4. Bake at 350° for 35 to 40 minutes or until center is set. Cool completely on wire rack. Cut into squares.

Praline-Pecan Brownies: Prepare and bake Chocolate Fudge Brownies as directed; cool completely. Spread uncut brownies evenly with Chocolate Glaze (page 378); sprinkle evenly with 2 cups coarsely chopped Praline Pecans. Makes 32 brownies. Prep: 15 min., Cook: 40 min.

Caramel-Coconut-Pecan Brownies: Prepare batter for Chocolate Fudge Brownies as directed; spread batter into a greased and floured 13- x 9-inch pan. Sprinkle batter evenly with 2 cups sweetened flaked coconut, 1 (12-oz.) package semisweet chocolate morsels, and 1½ cups chopped pecans. Drizzle evenly with 1 (14-oz.) can sweetened condensed milk. Bake at 350° for 50 to 55 minutes or until golden brown and center is set. Makes 32 brownies. Prep: 20 min., Cook: 55 min.

From Our Kitchen

This brownie recipe offers lots of options. If you're a fan of nuts, stir 1 cup chopped, toasted pecans into the batter. After baking, sift a little powdered sugar over the top or spread with deliciously rich Chocolate Glaze (page 378). To easily remove and cut brownies, line the empty pan with greased and floured heavy-duty aluminum foil, allowing several inches to extend over sides. After baking and cooling, simply lift the block of brownies from the pan using the foil.

Praline Pecans

MAKES ABOUT 8 CUPS
Prep: 5 min., Cook: 15 min., Other: 20 min.

*Pralines are best made when the weather is dry—humidity tends to make them grainy.
Be sure to use a heavy saucepan, and work quickly when spooning the pecan
mixture onto the wax paper.*

1½ cups granulated sugar
¾ cup firmly packed
    brown sugar
½ cup butter
½ cup milk
2 Tbsp. corn syrup

5 cups toasted pecan halves

1. Stir together first 5 ingredients in a heavy 3-qt. saucepan.
Bring to a boil over medium heat, stirring constantly. Boil,
stirring constantly, 7 to 8 minutes or until a candy thermometer registers 234°.

2. Remove from heat, and vigorously stir in pecans. Spoon
pecan mixture onto wax paper, spreading in an even layer.
Let stand 20 minutes or until firm. Break praline-coated
pecans apart into pieces. Store in an airtight container at
room temperature up to 1 week. Freeze in an airtight container or zip-top freezer bag up to 1 month.

Lemon Curd Pound Cake

MAKES 10 TO 12 SERVINGS
Prep: 20 min.; Cook: 1 hr., 30 min.; Other: 15 min.

*A buttery, custard-like glaze adds the perfect amount of sweetness to
Lemon Curd Pound Cake. Prepare the Lemon Curd as the cake comes out of the oven
so it will be warm when spread over the cake.*

1 cup butter, softened
½ cup shortening
3 cups sugar
6 large eggs

3 cups all-purpose flour
½ tsp. baking powder
⅛ tsp. salt
1 cup milk
1 tsp. vanilla extract
1 tsp. lemon extract

Lemon Curd
Garnishes: fresh rosemary,
    Sugared Cranberries,
    lemon rind strips

1. Beat butter and shortening at medium speed with an electric mixer until creamy. Gradually add sugar, beating at medium speed until light and fluffy. Add eggs, 1 at a time, beating just until the yellow yolk disappears.
2. Sift together flour, baking powder, and salt; add to butter mixture alternately with milk, beginning and ending with flour mixture. Beat batter at low speed just until blended after each addition. Stir in vanilla and lemon extracts. Pour batter into a greased and floured 12-cup tube pan.
3. Bake at 325° for 1½ hours or until a long wooden pick inserted in center of cake comes out clean. Cool in pan on a wire rack 10 to 15 minutes. Remove from pan; carefully brush hot Lemon Curd over top and sides of cake. Cool completely on wire rack. Garnish, if desired.

Lemon Curd

MAKES ABOUT ¾ CUP
Prep: 10 min., Cook: 12 min.

⅔ cup sugar
1½ Tbsp. butter, melted
2 tsp. grated lemon rind
2 Tbsp. fresh lemon juice
1 large egg, lightly beaten

1. Stir together first 4 ingredients in a small, heavy saucepan; add egg, stirring until blended.
2. Cook mixture, stirring constantly, over low heat, 10 to 12 minutes or until mixture thickens slightly (a thickness similar to unwhipped whipping cream) and begins to bubble around edges. Remove from heat. (Use immediately, as mixture continues to thicken as it cools.)

Sugared Cranberries

MAKES ABOUT 1 CUP
Prep: 5 min., Cook: 5 min.

¾ cup sugar, divided
½ cup water
1 cup fresh cranberries

1. Bring ½ cup sugar, water, and cranberries to a boil in a small saucepan, stirring often, over medium-high heat. (Do not overcook; cranberries should swell and just begin to pop.)

2. Remove from heat, and drain, reserving liquid for another use. Toss cranberries with remaining ¼ cup sugar, and arrange in a single layer on wax paper. Use immediately, or let stand at room temperature, uncovered, for up to 24 hours.

Holiday Coconut Cake

MAKES 12 SERVINGS
Prep: 20 min., Cook: 25 min., Other: 10 min.

In addition to being revered by readers, Holiday Coconut Cake is special to the folks on our foods staff. For many years, in fact, this cake has been a favorite of former Senior Foods Editor Jean Wickstrom Liles—the recipe was sent in by her mother for our December 1977 issue.

⅓ cup butter or margarine, softened
⅓ cup shortening
1¾ cups sugar

3 cups sifted cake flour
1 Tbsp. plus ½ tsp. baking powder
¾ tsp. salt
1⅓ cups milk
2 tsp. vanilla extract

4 egg whites

Lemon Filling
Fluffy Frosting
Freshly grated coconut

1. Beat butter and shortening at medium speed with an electric mixer until creamy; gradually add sugar, beating well.

2. Combine flour, baking powder, and salt; add to butter mixture alternately with milk, beginning and ending with flour mixture. Mix after each addition. Stir in vanilla.

3. Beat egg whites (at room temperature) until stiff peaks form. Gently fold into batter.

4. Pour batter into 3 greased and floured 9-inch round cakepans. Bake at 350° for 22 to 25 minutes or until a wooden pick inserted in center comes out clean. Cool in pans 10 minutes; remove from pans, and cool completely on wire racks.

5. Spread Lemon Filling between layers; spread Fluffy Frosting on top and sides of cake. Sprinkle cake with coconut.

Lemon Filling

MAKES 1¾ CUPS
Prep: 5 min., Cook: 2 min.

1 cup sugar
¼ cup cornstarch
1 cup water

2 egg yolks, beaten
2 Tbsp. butter or margarine
1 Tbsp. grated lemon rind
3 Tbsp. lemon juice

1. Combine sugar and cornstarch in a heavy saucepan; add water, stirring well. Cook over medium heat, stirring constantly, until mixture thickens and boils. Boil 1 minute.

2. Gradually stir about one-fourth of hot mixture into egg yolks; add to remaining hot mixture, stirring constantly. Return to a boil; cook 1 minute or until candy thermometer registers 165°, stirring constantly. Remove from heat; stir in butter, rind, and juice. Cool filling completely before spreading.

Fluffy Frosting

MAKES 2½ CUPS
Prep: 10 min., Cook: 12 min.

1 cup granulated sugar
⅓ cup water
2 Tbsp. light corn syrup

2 egg whites
¼ cup sifted powdered
  sugar
1 tsp. vanilla extract

1. Combine first 3 ingredients in a heavy saucepan; cook over medium heat, stirring constantly, until clear. Cook, without stirring, until candy thermometer registers 236°.

2. Beat egg whites (at room temperature) until soft peaks form; continue to beat, slowly adding syrup mixture. Add powdered sugar and vanilla; continue beating until stiff peaks form and frosting is thick enough to spread.

Double Chocolate Bombe

MAKES 8 TO 10 SERVINGS
Prep: 26 min.; Cook: 20 min.; Other: 10 hrs., 10 min.

This luscious cake is a fabulous end to a holiday feast. Cutting through the rich ganache on this chocolate showstopper reveals exquisite layers of dark and white chocolate.

½ cup pecan pieces, toasted

¼ cup butter, softened
¼ cup shortening
1 cup sugar
1½ tsp. vanilla extract

3 large eggs, separated

1 cup all-purpose flour
½ tsp. baking soda
½ cup buttermilk

Chocolate Mousse

White Chocolate Mousse

Chocolate Ganache
Garnish: chocolate curls

1. Coat bottom and sides of a 15- x 10-inch jelly-roll pan with cooking spray, and line with wax paper. Coat wax paper with cooking spray; set aside.

2. Process pecans in a food processor until ground; set aside.

3. Beat butter and shortening at medium speed with an electric mixer until creamy; gradually add sugar, beating well. Add vanilla to mixture, beating until blended.

4. Add egg yolks to butter mixture, 1 at a time, beating after each addition.

5. Combine flour, baking soda, and ground pecans; add to creamed mixture alternately with buttermilk, beginning and ending with flour mixture. Mix at low speed after each addition until blended.

6. Beat egg whites at high speed until stiff peaks form; gently fold into batter. Spread batter evenly into prepared pan. Bake at 350° for 20 minutes or until a wooden pick inserted in center comes out clean. Cool in pan on a wire rack 10 minutes; remove from pan, and cool completely on wire rack.

7. Line a 3-qt. mixing bowl (8½ inches in diameter) with plastic wrap.

8. Cut cake lengthwise into 2-inch strips; line prepared bowl with cake strips; set remaining cake aside.

9. Spread Chocolate Mousse over cake in bowl; cover and chill 1 hour.

10. Pour White Chocolate Mousse into bowl over chocolate layer; cover and chill 1 more hour.

11. Cover with remaining cake strips. Press cake strips to even the base of the bombe. Cover and chill bombe at least 8 hours.

12. Invert bombe onto a large cake plate; spread Chocolate Ganache over bombe, and garnish, if desired.

Chocolate Mousse

MAKES 2½ CUPS
Prep: 8 min., Cook: 3 min., Other: 35 min.

1 cup whipping cream,
    divided
1 (8-oz.) package semisweet
    chocolate baking
    squares
¼ cup light corn syrup
¼ cup butter

2 Tbsp. powdered sugar
½ tsp. vanilla extract

1. Combine ¼ cup whipping cream and next 3 ingredients in a heavy saucepan over low heat, stirring constantly, until chocolate melts. Cool 5 min.
2. Beat remaining ¾ cup whipping cream, powdered sugar, and vanilla at high speed with an electric mixer until stiff peaks form; fold into chocolate mixture. Cover and chill at least 30 minutes.

White Chocolate Mousse

MAKES 1¼ CUPS
Prep: 5 min., Cook: 2 min., Other: 30 min.

½ cup whipping cream,
    divided
3 (1-oz.) white chocolate
    baking squares
2 Tbsp. butter

1 Tbsp. powdered sugar
¼ tsp. vanilla extract

1. Cook 2 Tbsp. whipping cream, white chocolate, and butter in a heavy saucepan, stirring constantly, over low heat until smooth. Cool.
2. Beat remaining whipping cream, powdered sugar, and vanilla at high speed with an electric mixer until stiff peaks form; fold into white chocolate mixture. Cover and chill at least 30 minutes.

Chocolate Ganache

MAKES 1 CUP
Prep: 2 min., Cook: 5 min.

1 (8-oz.) package semisweet
    chocolate baking
    squares
¼ cup whipping cream

1. Stir together chocolate and whipping cream in a heavy saucepan over low heat, stirring constantly, until chocolate melts.

Apple-Pear Pull-Up Pie

MAKES 10 TO 12 SERVINGS
Prep: 54 min., Cook: 35 min., Other: 10 min.

*This gorgeous rustic pie is not only pleasing to the eye but also to the palate.
For best results, make sure you bake this pie on a parchment paper-lined baking sheet
placed on a rack just below the center of your oven.*

6 large Granny Smith
   apples, peeled and
   quartered
   (about 2⅓ lb.)
6 large Bartlett pears,
   peeled and quartered
   (about 2½ lb.)
2 cups sugar
1 Tbsp. lemon juice

½ cup butter

1 cup whipping cream
5 Tbsp. sugar, divided
2 Tbsp. Grand Marnier

1 (15-oz.) package
   refrigerated piecrusts

1 large egg
1 Tbsp. water

1. Combine first 4 ingredients in a large bowl, tossing to coat.
2. Melt butter in a large Dutch oven. Add apple mixture; cook 20 minutes or until tender. Remove apples and pears with a slotted spoon, reserving juices in pan.
3. Meanwhile, beat whipping cream at high speed with an electric mixer until foamy; gradually add 3 Tbsp. sugar and liqueur, beating until stiff peaks form; chill.
4. Unroll piecrusts; stack on a flat surface. Roll into a 15-inch circle. Place piecrust on a parchment paper-lined baking sheet.
5. Arrange apples and pears, cut sides down, in center of pastry (this will be a large mound), leaving a 3-inch border around edges. Lift pastry edges and pull over fruit, leaving a 6-inch circle of fruit showing in center; press folds gently to secure.
6. Whisk together egg and water; brush over pastry. Sprinkle with remaining 2 Tbsp. sugar. Place lightly greased sides of a 9-inch springform pan with clasp open around pie.
7. Bake on lower rack at 425° for 30 to 35 minutes or until golden. Run a knife around edges of pie to loosen. Cool on pan on a wire rack 10 minutes; carefully remove pan sides.
8. Meanwhile, cook reserved juices over medium-high heat, stirring often, 10 to 15 minutes or until slightly thickened and caramel colored. Remove from heat; drizzle evenly over tart. Serve warm or at room temperature with sweetened whipped cream.

Brown Sugar Bread Pudding with Crème Anglaise

MAKES 9 SERVINGS
Prep: 30 min., Cook: 35 min., Other: 10 min.

We prefer using fresh French bread from the bakery to achieve the crispiest top and softest center. Save the egg yolks from the separated eggs for the Crème Anglaise.

4 egg whites
1 large egg
1¼ cups 2% reduced-fat milk
¾ cup evaporated fat-free milk
½ cup firmly packed light brown sugar
1 tsp. ground cinnamon
¼ tsp. ground nutmeg
⅛ tsp. salt
⅛ tsp. ground allspice
2 tsp. vanilla extract

1 (12-oz.) French bread loaf, cut into 1-inch cubes (about 8 cups)
4 tsp. light brown sugar
½ Tbsp. butter, cut into small pieces
¼ cup sliced almonds, toasted

Crème Anglaise
Garnish: cinnamon sticks

1. Whisk together egg whites and egg in a medium bowl until blended. Whisk in reduced-fat milk and next 7 ingredients.

2. Arrange bread cubes in an 8-inch square pan coated with cooking spray. Pour egg mixture evenly over bread. Sprinkle evenly with 4 tsp. brown sugar, butter, and almonds. Press down gently on bread cubes, and let stand 10 minutes.

3. Bake at 350° for 30 to 35 minutes or until a knife inserted in center comes out clean. Serve warm with 2 Tbsp. chilled Crème Anglaise. Garnish, if desired.

Crème Anglaise

MAKES 2 CUPS
Prep: 10 min., Cook: 8 min., Other: 4 hrs.

We prepared Crème Anglaise with milk instead of heavy cream to reduce the fat and calories. Expect a slightly thinner consistency but the same delicious flavor. Store leftover sauce in an airtight container in the refrigerator up to 1 week, and serve over fresh berries.

1¾ cups 2% reduced-fat milk

⅓ cup sugar
4 egg yolks
1 tsp. vanilla extract
2 Tbsp. bourbon

1. Heat milk in a medium saucepan over medium heat just until bubbles and steam appear (do not boil). Remove from heat.

2. Whisk together sugar and egg yolks in a medium bowl until blended. Gradually add heated milk to egg yolk mixture, whisking constantly. Return mixture to saucepan. Cover over medium heat, whisking constantly, 6 minutes or until mixture thinly coats the back of a spoon. Pour mixture into a bowl. Stir in vanilla. Place plastic wrap directly on surface of mixture, and chill at least 4 hours. (Mixture will thicken slightly as it cools.) Stir in bourbon before serving.

Our best
desserts

Chocolate dreams and ice cream screams
abound in this collection of awesome
desserts. Find cookies, cakes, pies, and
candies sure to please all.

PERFECT CHOCOLATE CAKE, PAGE 374

Chocolate Chip Supreme Cookies

MAKES 3 DOZEN
Prep: 15 min., Cook: 12 min. per batch

*Set out a plate of these cookies fresh from the oven,
and watch how fast they disappear.*

½ cup shortening
½ cup butter or margarine, softened
¾ cup firmly packed dark brown sugar
¾ cup granulated sugar
2 large eggs
1 (3.4-oz.) package vanilla instant pudding mix
1 Tbsp. vanilla extract

2¼ cups all-purpose flour
1 Tbsp. baking soda
1 tsp. ground cinnamon
½ tsp. ground nutmeg
½ tsp. salt
1 (12-oz.) package semisweet chocolate morsels
1½ cups chopped pecans
1 cup uncooked quick-cooking oats

1. Beat shortening and butter at medium speed with an electric mixer until mixture is creamy; gradually add sugars, beating well. Add eggs, beating until blended. Add pudding mix and vanilla; beat until blended.
2. Combine flour and next 4 ingredients. Gradually add to butter mixture, beating until blended. Stir in morsels, pecans, and oats.
3. Shape dough into 1½-inch balls; place on lightly greased baking sheets, and press to 1-inch thickness.
4. Bake at 375° for 10 to 12 minutes. Remove cookies to wire racks to cool.

Taste of the South

Chocolate morsels have long been the darling of bakers and chocoholics alike. These tiny morsels are irresistible, tempting us to take just one more bite of dessert or to sneak a few right out of the bag. Their smooth, intense flavor stands out in all-American chocolate chip cookies.

Peanut Butter-Chocolate Kiss Cookies

MAKES 4 DOZEN
Prep: 10 min., Cook: 10 min. per batch

These clever cookies have highlighted many a bake sale since they first graced the pages of Southern Living *20 years ago.*

½ cup shortening
½ cup peanut butter
½ cup granulated sugar
½ cup firmly packed
    brown sugar
1 large egg
2 Tbsp. milk
1 tsp. vanilla extract

1¾ cups all-purpose flour
1 tsp. baking soda
½ tsp. salt

¼ cup granulated sugar
48 milk chocolate kisses

1. Beat shortening and peanut butter at medium speed with an electric mixer until creamy; gradually add ½ cup granulated sugar and brown sugar, beating until light and fluffy. Add egg, milk, and vanilla; beat well.

2. Combine flour, soda, and salt; add to creamed mixture.

3. Roll dough into 1-inch balls; then roll in ¼ cup sugar. Place balls 2 inches apart on lightly greased baking sheets. Bake at 375° for 8 minutes. Remove from oven; press a chocolate kiss into the center of each cookie. Return to oven for 2 more minutes or until lightly browned.

Crème de Menthe Brownie Bars

MAKES 4 DOZEN
Prep: 15 min.; Cook: 30 min.; Other: 5 hrs., 20 min.

A thick layer of pretty green frosting drizzled with chocolate covers these tender brownies.

4 (1-oz.) unsweetened
  chocolate baking
  squares
1 cup butter or margarine

4 large eggs
2 cups sugar
1 cup all-purpose flour
½ tsp. salt
1 tsp. vanilla extract

Crème de Menthe Frosting

½ cup semisweet chocolate
  morsels, melted

1. Combine unsweetened chocolate and butter in a small, heavy saucepan; cook over low heat, stirring constantly, until melted. Let stand 10 minutes.

2. Beat eggs at medium speed with an electric mixer until thick and lemon colored; gradually add sugar, beating well. Add flour, salt, vanilla, and chocolate mixture; beat at low speed 1 minute.

3. Spoon mixture into a lightly greased and floured 13- x 9- inch pan. Bake at 350° for 25 to 30 minutes or until a wooden pick inserted in center comes out clean. Cool 10 minutes; spread Crème de Menthe Frosting over top. Chill at least 4 hours.

4. Drizzle melted chocolate over frosting, or pipe in desired design using metal tip No. 3 or 4. Cut into bars immediately. Remove from pan, and chill at least 1 hour. Store in an airtight container in refrigerator.

Crème de Menthe Frosting

MAKES ABOUT 6 CUPS
Prep: 5 min.

4 cups sifted powdered
  sugar
½ cup butter or margarine,
  softened
¼ cup half-and-half
¼ cup green crème de
  menthe
1 cup finely chopped
  walnuts

1. Combine first 4 ingredients in a mixing bowl; beat at high speed with an electric mixer until smooth. Stir in walnuts.

Hummingbird Cake

MAKES 12 SERVINGS
Prep: 36 min., Cook: 23 min., Other: 10 min.

3 cups all-purpose flour
1 tsp. baking soda
½ tsp. salt
2 cups sugar
1 tsp. ground cinnamon
3 large eggs, lightly beaten
¾ cup vegetable oil
1½ tsp. vanilla extract
1 (8-oz.) can crushed
  pineapple, undrained
1 cup chopped pecans
1¾ cups mashed ripe
  banana (about 4 large)

Cream Cheese Frosting

1. Combine first 5 ingredients in a large bowl; add eggs and oil, stirring just until dry ingredients are moistened. Add vanilla, pineapple, pecans, and banana, stirring just until combined.
2. Pour batter into 3 greased and floured 9-inch round cakepans.
3. Bake at 350° for 23 minutes or until a wooden pick inserted in center comes out clean. Cool in pans 10 minutes; remove from pans, and cool completely on wire racks. Spread Cream Cheese Frosting between layers and on top and sides of cake.

Cream Cheese Frosting

MAKES 3¼ CUPS
Prep: 5 min.

½ cup butter or margarine,
  softened
1 (8-oz.) package cream
  cheese, softened
1 (16-oz.) package
  powdered sugar, sifted
1 tsp. vanilla extract
½ cup chopped pecans

1. Beat butter and cream cheese at medium speed with an electric mixer until creamy. Gradually add powdered sugar, beating at low speed until blended. Beat at high speed until smooth; stir in vanilla and pecans.

Then & Now

Pineapple-laced Hummingbird Cake, with its nutty cream cheese frosting, first appeared in *Southern Living* in February 1978, and it garnered the top spot in our 25 All-Time Best Desserts story in December 1990 and the Top 25 Recipes in 25 Years in *Southern Living* Annual Recipes 2003. The cake is known to have won numerous blue ribbons at county fairs. No one knows what hummingbirds have to do with it, but the cake is so moist and delicious that no one cares!

Caramel Cake

MAKES 12 SERVINGS
Prep: 20 min., Cook: 30 min., Other: 10 min.

Caramel Frosting is tricky to make, but well worth the effort. Make sure to wash down all sugar crystals from the sides of the pan with a pastry brush when making the caramel.

1 (8-oz.) container sour cream
¼ cup milk

1 cup butter, softened
2 cups granulated sugar
4 large eggs

2¾ cups all-purpose flour
2 tsp. baking powder
½ tsp. salt
1 tsp. vanilla extract
1 tsp. rum extract

Caramel Frosting

1. Combine sour cream and milk, and set aside.
2. Beat butter and sugar at medium speed with an electric mixer until creamy. Add eggs, 1 at a time, beating until blended after each addition.
3. Combine flour, baking powder, and salt; add to butter mixture alternately with sour cream mixture, beginning and ending with flour mixture. Beat at low speed until blended after each addition. Stir in flavorings. Spread batter into 2 greased and floured wax paper-lined 9-inch round cakepans.
4. Bake at 350° for 30 minutes or until a wooden pick inserted in center comes out clean. Cool in pans on wire racks 10 minutes; remove from pans, and cool completely on wire racks.
5. Spread Caramel Frosting between layers and on top and sides of cake.

Caramel Frosting

MAKES ABOUT 4¾ CUPS
Prep: 22 min., Cook: 29 min., Other: 5 min.

3 cups sugar, divided
1 cup milk
2 Tbsp. light corn syrup

¾ cup butter, cut into chunks
1 tsp. vanilla extract

1. Combine 2½ cups sugar, milk, and corn syrup in a large saucepan. Bring to a boil over medium-high heat, stirring often. Keep warm.
2. Sprinkle remaining ½ cup sugar in a large heavy saucepan; cook over medium heat until sugar melts and is a light golden brown, swirling pan often. (This helps evenly heat and distribute the sugar to prevent it from burning.)
3. Gradually pour warm milk mixture into caramelized sugar, stirring constantly with a wooden spoon until blended and smooth; cook, without stirring, over medium heat until a candy thermometer registers 238° (soft ball stage), washing down sugar crystals on the sides of pan with a pastry brush. Add butter, stirring just until blended. Remove from heat; add vanilla. Cool 5 minutes. Beat caramel at medium speed with an electric mixer until frosting reaches spreading consistency.

White Chocolate Cake

MAKES 12 SERVINGS
Prep: 25 min., Cook: 25 min., Other: 10 min.

Originally from the 1970s, this recipe made the cut of our best for its simplicity, elegance, and white chocolaty flavor.

⅓ cup chopped white chocolate (we tested with Ghirardelli)
1 cup butter, softened
1½ cups sugar
4 large eggs, separated
1 tsp. vanilla extract

2½ cups sifted cake flour
1 tsp. baking soda
1 cup buttermilk

White Chocolate Frosting
Garnish: toasted sliced almonds

1. Microwave chocolate in a glass bowl at HIGH 45 seconds or until melted. Beat butter and sugar at medium speed with an electric mixer until creamy. Add egg yolks, 1 at a time, beating well after each addition. Add melted white chocolate and vanilla.

2. Sift flour and baking soda together; add to butter mixture alternately with buttermilk, beginning and ending with flour mixture.

3. Beat egg whites at high speed until stiff peaks form. Gently fold beaten egg whites into batter. Pour batter into 3 greased and floured 9-inch round cakepans.

4. Bake at 350° for 25 minutes or until a wooden pick inserted in center comes out clean. Cool in pans on wire racks 10 minutes; remove from pans, and cool completely on wire racks. Spread White Chocolate Frosting between layers and on top and sides of cake. Garnish, if desired.

White Chocolate Frosting

MAKES 3¼ CUPS
Prep: 8 min., Cook: 2 min., Other: 15 min.

¾ cup sugar
⅔ cup evaporated milk
6 Tbsp. butter

3 cups white chocolate morsels
2¼ tsp. vanilla extract

1. Bring sugar, milk, and butter to a full rolling boil in a heavy saucepan; boil 1 minute. Remove from heat.

2. Combine chocolate and vanilla in a medium bowl. Pour hot butter mixture over chocolate, and stir until chocolate is melted. Cool 15 minutes. Beat frosting at high speed with an electric mixer, 7 minutes, or until completely cool and spreading consistency.

Perfect Chocolate Cake

MAKES 12 SERVINGS
Prep: 23 min., Cook: 22 min., Other: 10 min.

1 cup unsweetened cocoa
2 cups boiling water

1 cup butter or margarine,
  softened
2½ cups sugar
4 large eggs

2¾ cups all-purpose flour
2 tsp. baking soda
½ tsp. baking powder
½ tsp. salt
1½ tsp. vanilla extract

Whipped Cream Filling
Perfect Chocolate Frosting

1. Combine cocoa and water; stir until smooth. Set aside.

2. Beat butter at medium speed with an electric mixer about 2 minutes or until creamy. Gradually add sugar, beating 5 to 7 minutes. Add eggs, 1 at a time, beating just until yellow disappears.

3. Combine flour and next 3 ingredients; add to butter mixture alternately with cocoa mixture, beginning and ending with flour mixture. Beat at low speed just until blended after each addition. Stir in vanilla. Do not overbeat.

4. Pour batter into 3 greased and floured 9-inch round cakepans. Bake at 350° for 22 minutes or until a wooden pick inserted in center comes out clean. Cool in pans on wire racks 10 minutes; remove from pans, and cool completely on wire racks.

5. Spread Whipped Cream Filling between layers; spread Perfect Chocolate Frosting on top and sides of cake. Chill.

Whipped Cream Filling

MAKES ABOUT 2 CUPS
Prep: 4 min.

1 cup whipping cream
1 tsp. vanilla extract
¼ cup sifted powdered
  sugar

1. Beat whipping cream and vanilla until foamy; gradually add powdered sugar, beating until soft peaks form. Cover and chill.

Perfect Chocolate Frosting

MAKES 2½ CUPS
Prep: 17 min., Cook: 5 min.

1 cup semisweet chocolate
  morsels
½ cup half-and-half
¾ cup butter or margarine
2½ cups sifted powdered
  sugar

1. Combine first 3 ingredients in a medium saucepan; cook over medium heat, stirring until chocolate melts. Remove from heat; add powdered sugar, mixing well.

2. Place saucepan in a large bowl of ice. Beat at low speed with an electric mixer until frosting holds its shape and loses its gloss. Add a few drops of half-and-half, if needed, to make a good spreading consistency.

Then & Now

Looks like Perfect Chocolate Cake is an appropriate name for the towering layers with a whipped cream filling and creamy chocolate frosting. Originally appearing in the September 1977 issue of *Southern Living*, it made an encore appearance as a winner in December 1990's All-Time Best Desserts feature, as well as in our Top 5 Chocolate Recipes from *Southern Living* Annual Recipes 2003.

Pecan Pie Cake

MAKES 12 SERVINGS
Prep: 35 min., Cook: 25 min.
(pictured on page 13)

It's no secret that we're partial to pecan pie, because the flavor essence makes an encore appearance on this spectacular dessert list in Pecan Pie Cake. Southern Living Editor John Floyd challenged Associate Foods Editor Mary Allen Perry to create a stately cake based on the South's favorite pie for our October 1998 issue, and reader mail tells us you enjoyed it as much as we did. A creamy caramel filling is sandwiched between feathery cake layers encrusted with toasted pecans. It's pretty enough for a centerpiece and worth every minute it takes to create.

3 cups finely chopped
    pecans, toasted and
    divided

½ cup butter or margarine,
    softened
½ cup shortening
2 cups sugar
5 large eggs, separated
1 Tbsp. vanilla extract

2 cups all-purpose flour
1 tsp. baking soda
1 cup buttermilk

¾ cup dark corn syrup
Pecan Pie Filling
Pastry Garnish (optional)

1. Sprinkle 2 cups pecans evenly into 3 generously buttered 9-inch round cakepans; shake to coat bottoms and sides of pans.

2. Beat butter and shortening at medium speed with an electric mixer until creamy; gradually add sugar, beating well. Add egg yolks, 1 at a time, beating just until blended after each addition; stir in vanilla.

3. Combine flour and baking soda. Add to butter mixture alternately with buttermilk, beginning and ending with flour mixture; beat at low speed just until blended after each addition. Stir in remaining 1 cup pecans.

4. Beat egg whites at medium speed until stiff peaks form; fold one-third of egg whites into batter. Gently fold in remaining beaten egg whites just until blended. (Do not overmix.) Pour into prepared pans.

5. Bake at 350° for 23 to 25 minutes or until a wooden pick inserted in center comes out clean. Cool in pans on wire racks 10 minutes. Invert layers onto wax paper-lined wire racks. Brush tops and sides of cake layers with corn syrup; cool completely.

6. Spread half of Pecan Pie Filling on 1 layer, pecan side up. Place second layer, pecan side up, on filling; spread with remaining filling. Top with remaining cake layer, pecan side up. Arrange Pastry Garnish on and around cake, if desired.

Pecan Pie Filling

MAKES ABOUT 3 CUPS
Prep: 7 min., Cook: 7 min., Other: 4 hrs.

½ cup firmly packed dark
  brown sugar
¾ cup dark corn syrup
⅓ cup cornstarch
4 egg yolks
1½ cups half-and-half
⅛ tsp. salt

3 Tbsp. butter or margarine
1 tsp. vanilla extract

1. Whisk together first 6 ingredients in a heavy 3-qt. saucepan until smooth. Bring mixture to a boil over medium heat, whisking constantly; boil 1 minute or until thickened. Remove from heat.

2. Whisk in butter and vanilla. Place a sheet of wax paper directly on surface of mixture to prevent a film from forming. Chill at least 4 hours.

Note: To chill filling quickly, pour filling into a bowl. Place bowl in a larger bowl filled with ice. Whisk constantly until cool (about 15 minutes).

Pastry Garnish

MAKES 24 PASTRY LEAVES AND 12 PECAN PASTRIES
Prep: 32 min., Cook: 18 min., Other: 10 min.

1 (15-oz.) package
  refrigerated piecrusts
1 large egg
1 Tbsp. water

24 pecan halves

1. Unroll piecrusts. Cut 12 leaves from each piecrust with a 3-inch leaf-shaped cutter. Mark leaf veins, using tip of a knife. Reserve pastry trimmings. Whisk together egg and water; brush on pastry leaves.

2. Crumple 10 to 12 small aluminum foil pieces into ½-inch balls. Coat with cooking spray, and place on a lightly greased baking sheet. Drape a pastry leaf over each ball; place remaining pastry leaves on baking sheet.

3. Bake at 425° for 6 to 8 minutes or until golden. Cool on a wire rack 10 minutes. Gently remove leaves from foil.

4. Reduce oven temperature to 350°. Pinch 12 pea-size pieces from reserved pastry trimmings. Place between pecan halves, forming sandwiches.

5. Cut remaining pastry into 2-inch pieces; wrap around pecan sandwiches, leaving jagged edges to resemble half-shelled pecans. Brush with egg mixture, and place on a lightly greased baking sheet.

6. Bake at 350° for 10 minutes or until golden. Cool on a wire rack.

Smoothest Southern Pound Cake

MAKES 12 SERVINGS
Prep: 20 min., Cook: 2 hrs., Other: 15 min.

After years of testing, our Test Kitchens have established a tried-and-true standard procedure for mixing pound cakes. But we just had to test this recipe's unusual mixing method. We worried as we watched this extremely thick batter challenge our mixers—then we shook our heads in disbelief at the spectacular baking results. Because a handheld mixer (and less adventuresome cooks) probably won't stand up to this batter, we offer our standard method as well. We're pleased with the results of both methods.

1 cup butter or margarine, softened
3 cups sugar
3 cups sifted cake flour
¼ tsp. baking soda

6 large eggs, separated
1 (8-oz.) carton sour cream
1 tsp. vanilla extract

1. Beat butter at medium speed with a heavy-duty stand mixer about 2 minutes or until creamy. Gradually add sugar, beating at medium speed 5 to 7 minutes. Combine cake flour and baking soda, and add to butter mixture 1 cup at a time. (Batter will be extremely thick.)

2. Add yolks to batter, and mix well. Stir in sour cream and vanilla.

3. Beat egg whites until stiff, and fold into batter.

4. Spoon into a greased and floured 12-cup Bundt or 10-inch tube pan. Bake at 300° for 2 hours or until a wooden pick inserted in center comes out clean. (You can also spoon batter into two 9- x 5- inch loafpans; bake at 300° for 1½ hours or until a wooden pick inserted in center comes out clean.) Cool in pan on a wire rack 10 to 15 minutes. Remove from pan; cool completely on wire rack.

Standard Mixing Method: If you're using a handheld mixer or prefer a conventional pound cake method, here's the procedure we suggest.
• Beat butter at medium speed with an electric mixer about 2 minutes or until creamy. Gradually add 3 cups sugar, beating at medium speed 5 to 7 minutes. Add eggs, 1 at a time, beating just until yellow disappears.
• Combine cake flour and baking soda; add to butter mixture alternately with sour cream, beginning and ending with flour mixture. Mix at lowest speed just until mixture is blended after each addition. Stir in vanilla. Bake as directed.

Candy Bar Cake

MAKES 12 SERVINGS
Prep: 30 min.; Cook: 1 hr., 25 min.; Other: 15 min.

A hint of candy bar in every bite of this cake satisfies any sweet tooth.

3 (2.05-oz.) chocolate-coated caramel and creamy nougat bars, chopped (we tested with Milky Way)
1 cup butter, softened and divided

2 cups sugar
4 large eggs
1 tsp. vanilla extract

3 cups all-purpose flour
½ tsp. baking soda
1 cup buttermilk
1 cup chopped pecans

1. Combine candy bars and ½ cup butter in a heavy saucepan; cook over medium heat, stirring constantly, until candy bars melt. Set aside.

2. Beat remaining ½ cup butter at medium speed with an electric mixer about 2 minutes or until creamy. Gradually add sugar, beating at medium speed 5 to 7 minutes. Add eggs, 1 at a time, beating just until yellow disappears. Stir in vanilla.

3. Combine flour and soda; add to butter mixture alternately with buttermilk, beginning and ending with flour mixture. Mix at low speed just until blended after each addition. Stir in candy bar mixture and pecans.

4. Pour batter into a greased and floured 10-inch tube pan. Bake at 325° for 1 hour and 25 minutes or until a wooden pick inserted in center of cake comes out clean. Cool in pan 15 minutes on a wire rack. Remove from pan, and cool completely on wire rack.

Chocolate Fudge Cheesecake

MAKES 12 SERVINGS
Prep: 30 min., Cook: 1 hr., Other: 8 hrs.

A chewy brownie crust forms the base of this chocolate-laden cheesecake.

2 (1-oz.) unsweetened chocolate baking squares

½ cup butter, softened
1 cup sugar
2 large eggs

½ cup all-purpose flour
1½ tsp. vanilla extract, divided
½ cup semisweet chocolate morsels

½ cup chopped pecans, toasted

2 (8-oz.) packages cream cheese, softened
¾ cup sugar
4 large eggs

Chocolate Glaze
Garnishes: fresh mint sprigs, sliced strawberries

1. Microwave chocolate squares in a microwave-safe bowl at HIGH 1 minute and 15 seconds, stirring after 45 seconds. Stir until smooth.

2. Beat butter and 1 cup sugar at medium speed with an electric mixer until light and fluffy. Add 2 eggs, 1 at a time, beating just until blended after each addition. Add melted chocolate, beating just until blended.

3. Add flour, beating at low speed just until blended. Stir in ½ tsp. vanilla and chocolate morsels.

4. Sprinkle toasted pecans evenly over bottom of a greased and floured 9-inch springform pan. Spoon batter over pecans.

5. Beat cream cheese at medium speed with an electric mixer until smooth; add ¾ cup sugar, beating until blended. Add 4 eggs, 1 at a time, beating just until blended after each addition. Stir in remaining 1 tsp. vanilla. Pour cream cheese mixture over brownie batter.

6. Bake at 325° for 1 hour or until set. Remove from oven; immediately run knife around edge of pan, releasing sides. Cool on wire racks. Spread Chocolate Glaze over top of cooled cheesecake. Cover and chill 8 hours. Remove sides of pan before serving. Garnish, if desired.

Chocolate Glaze

MAKES 1⅔ CUPS
Prep: 5 min.

1 (12-oz.) package semisweet chocolate morsels
½ cup whipping cream

1. Melt chocolate morsels and whipping cream in a 2-qt. microwave-safe bowl at HIGH 1 minute or until chocolate begins to melt. Whisk until chocolate melts and mixture is smooth.

Warm Fudge-Filled Cheesecake

MAKES 12 SERVINGS
Prep: 20 min., Cook: 1 hr., Other: 1 hr.

Dessert doesn't get much better than this cheesecake from the January 1998 issue of Southern Living. *Foods staffer Mary Allen Perry developed this recipe that reminded her of a café where she worked in the 1970s. A full 2 cups chocolate mini-morsels are sandwiched between vanilla cheesecake batter that has a crunchy pistachio crust. Serving it warm is the key to keeping the chocolate soft. The cheesecake melts in your mouth, and the pistachio crust offers a crunchy contrast.*

½ cup butter or margarine, softened
⅓ cup sugar
1 cup all-purpose flour
1 Tbsp. vanilla extract, divided
⅔ cup chopped pistachios

4 (8-oz.) packages cream cheese, softened
1½ cups sugar

4 large eggs

1 (12-oz.) package semisweet chocolate mini-morsels
Sweetened whipped cream (optional)
Garnish: chocolate shavings

1. Beat butter at medium speed with an electric mixer until creamy; add ⅓ cup sugar, beating well. Gradually add flour, beating at low speed until blended. Stir in 1 tsp. vanilla and pistachios. Press into bottom and 1½ inches up sides of a 9-inch springform pan.

2. Bake at 350° for 12 to 15 minutes or until golden. Cool on a wire rack.

3. Beat cream cheese at medium speed with an electric mixer until light and fluffy; gradually add 1½ cups sugar, beating well.

4. Add eggs, 1 at a time, beating just until yellow disappears. Stir in remaining 2 tsp. vanilla. (Do not overbeat.)

5. Pour half of batter into prepared crust; sprinkle with chocolate morsels to within ¾ inch of edge. Pour in remaining batter, starting at outer edge and working toward center. Place cheesecake on a baking sheet.

6. Bake at 350° for 1 hour or until set. Cool on a wire rack for 1 hour. If desired, serve with sweetened whipped cream and garnish.

Lemon Cheesecake Pies

MAKES 16 SERVINGS
Prep: 30 min., Cook: 42 min.

1 (15-oz.) package
    refrigerated piecrusts

2 (8-oz.) packages cream
    cheese, softened
½ cup sugar
1 large egg
Lemon Chess Pie Filling

Garnishes: whipped
    topping, crushed lemon
    candies

1. Fit each refrigerated piecrust into a 9-inch pieplate according to package directions; fold edges under, and crimp. Line pastry with aluminum foil, and fill with pie weights or dried beans.

2. Bake at 425° for 5 minutes. Remove weights and foil. Bake 2 more minutes or until light golden brown. Cool crusts completely on wire racks.

3. Beat cream cheese, sugar, and egg at low speed with an electric mixer until smooth. Spread cream cheese mixture evenly over crusts. Spoon Lemon Chess Pie Filling evenly over cream cheese mixture in crusts.

4. Bake at 350° for 35 minutes or until set, shielding edges to prevent excess browning, if needed. Cool completely on wire racks. Garnish, if desired.

Lemon Chess Pie Filling

MAKES ABOUT 3 CUPS
Prep: 10 min.

2 cups sugar
4 large eggs
¼ cup butter, melted
¼ cup milk
1 Tbsp. grated lemon
    rind
¼ cup fresh lemon juice
1 Tbsp. all-purpose flour
1 Tbsp. cornmeal
¼ tsp. salt

1. Whisk together all ingredients. Use filling immediately.

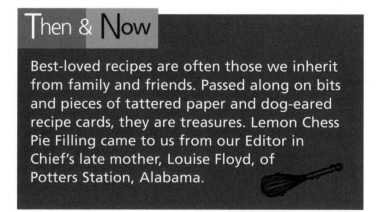

Then & Now

Best-loved recipes are often those we inherit from family and friends. Passed along on bits and pieces of tattered paper and dog-eared recipe cards, they are treasures. Lemon Chess Pie Filling came to us from our Editor in Chief's late mother, Louise Floyd, of Potters Station, Alabama.

Key Lime Pie

MAKES 8 TO 10 SERVINGS
Prep: 20 min., Cook: 28 min., Other: 8 hrs.
(pictured on cover)

*Key West locals adhere to a few universal rules when it comes to this legendary pie:
It's always made with small, round Key limes that give the creamy filling its naturally
yellow—never green—color. And any Key lime pie worth its weight—and taste—is made
with sweetened condensed milk. Our Key Lime Pie meets all these authentic criteria,
so you can prepare it with confidence.*

1¼ cups graham cracker
crumbs
¼ cup firmly packed light
brown sugar
⅓ cup butter or margarine,
melted

2 (14-oz.) cans sweetened
condensed milk
1 cup fresh Key lime juice

2 egg whites
¼ tsp. cream of tartar
2 Tbsp. granulated sugar

Garnish: lime slices

1. Combine first 3 ingredients. Press into a 9-inch pieplate.
2. Bake at 350° for 10 minutes; cool. Stir together milk and lime juice until blended. Pour into crust.
3. Beat egg whites and cream of tartar at high speed with an electric mixer just until foamy. Add sugar, 1 Tbsp. at a time, beating until soft peaks form and sugar dissolves (2 to 4 minutes).
4. Spread meringue over filling.
5. Bake at 325° for 25 to 28 minutes. Chill 8 hours. Garnish, if desired.

Taste of the South

If fresh Key limes aren't available in your area, you can opt for bottled Key lime juice. Nellie & Joe's Key lime juice is a popular brand that does not contain the preservative sulfur dioxide, which some believe gives the pie a sulfur-like aftertaste. You can order bottled juice by phone or online from Kermit's Key West Key Lime Shoppe, 1-800-376-0806, www.keylimeshop.com.

Tangerine Chess Pie

MAKES 8 TO 10 SERVINGS
Prep: 15 min., Cook: 45 min.

*With citrusy flavor from the rind and juice, this chess pie
offers sweet sunshine by the slice.*

1 (15-oz.) package
  refrigerated piecrusts

1½ cups sugar
1 Tbsp. all-purpose flour
1 Tbsp. yellow cornmeal
¼ tsp. salt
¼ cup butter or margarine,
  melted
¼ cup milk
2 tsp. grated tangerine rind
⅓ cup fresh tangerine juice
1 Tbsp. lemon juice
4 large eggs, lightly beaten

Garnishes: sweetened
  whipped cream,
  tangerine slices

1. Unroll piecrusts; stack piecrusts on a lightly floured surface. Roll into one 12-inch circle. Fit piecrust into a 9-inch pieplate according to package directions; fold edges under, and crimp.

2. Bake piecrust at 450° for 8 minutes; cool on a wire rack.

3. Whisk together sugar and next 9 ingredients until blended. Pour into piecrust.

4. Bake at 350° for 40 to 45 minutes or until center is set, shielding edges of crust with aluminum foil after 20 minutes to prevent excessive browning. Cool on a wire rack. Garnish, if desired.

Lemon-Lime Chess Pie: Substitute fresh lime juice for tangerine juice; substitute 1 teaspoon fresh lime rind and 1 teaspoon fresh lemon rind for tangerine rind. Garnish with sweetened whipped cream, lime and lemon wedges, and grated lime and lemon rind, if desired.

Orange Chess Pie: Substitute fresh orange juice and rind for tangerine juice and rind. Garnish with sweetened whipped cream, orange slices, and orange rind, if desired.

Grapefruit Chess Pie: Substitute fresh grapefruit juice and rind for tangerine juice and rind. Garnish with sweetened whipped cream, grapefruit or lime rind, and lime pieces, if desired.

Chocolate Meringue Pie

MAKES 8 SERVINGS
Prep: 20 min., Cook: 25 min.

The secret to any good chocolate pie is the meringue that crowns it.
This is one of our best versions, with just the right amount of sweetness.

1 cup sugar
3 Tbsp. cornstarch
Dash of salt

2 cups milk
3 large eggs, separated

1 (1-oz.) unsweetened
   chocolate baking square
1 Tbsp. butter or margarine
1 tsp. vanilla extract
1 baked 9-inch pastry shell

½ tsp. cream of tartar
6 Tbsp. sugar

1. Combine 1 cup sugar, cornstarch, and salt in a heavy saucepan; mix well.

2. Combine milk and egg yolks; beat with a wire whisk 1 to 2 minutes or until frothy. Gradually stir into sugar mixture, mixing well.

3. Cook over medium heat, stirring constantly, until thickened and bubbly. Remove from heat; add chocolate, butter, and vanilla, stirring until chocolate and butter melt. Spoon mixture into pastry shell; set aside.

4. Beat egg whites and cream of tartar at high speed with an electric mixer 1 minute. Gradually add 6 Tbsp. sugar, 1 Tbsp. at a time, beating until stiff peaks form and sugar dissolves (2 to 4 minutes).

5. Spread meringue over hot filling, sealing to edge of pastry. Bake at 325° for 25 minutes or until golden brown.

Chocolate-Peanut Butter Ice Cream Pie

MAKES 8 TO 10 SERVINGS
Prep: 20 min.; Other: 6 hrs., 30 min.

*The nutty, chocolaty cookie crust of this pie creates a sturdy foundation
for mounds of ice cream in a deep dish.*

21 cream-filled chocolate
sandwich cookies
½ cup unsalted dry-roasted
peanuts
¼ cup butter or margarine,
melted

3 pt. chocolate ice cream,
softened
8 (1.6-oz.) packages peanut
butter cup candies,
coarsely chopped

1 (8-oz.) jar fudge sauce
¼ cup strong brewed coffee
2 Tbsp. coffee liqueur
(optional)

1. Process cookies and peanuts in a food processor until finely crumbled. Add butter, and process until blended.
2. Press crumb mixture into a 9-inch deep-dish pieplate; freeze 15 minutes.
3. Stir together ice cream and chopped candy; spoon into piecrust. Freeze at least 6 hours. Remove from freezer, and let stand 15 minutes before serving.
4. Heat fudge sauce in a small saucepan over low heat, stirring constantly. Remove from heat; stir in coffee and, if desired, coffee liqueur. Drizzle over pie.

Double Citrus Tart

MAKES 8 TO 10 SERVINGS
Prep: 30 min., Cook: 25 min., Other: 4 hrs.

*This tart captures the bright, fresh flavors of
lemon and orange in a crisp gingersnap crust.*

1½ cups crushed
    gingersnap cookies
5 Tbsp. butter, melted
2 Tbsp. brown sugar
¼ tsp. ground cinnamon

1 (14-oz.) can sweetened
    condensed milk
⅓ cup frozen orange juice
    concentrate, thawed
¼ cup fresh lemon juice
2 large eggs, separated

1 cup heavy whipping
    cream
3 Tbsp. granulated sugar
Garnishes: fresh mint leaves,
    lemon and orange slices

1. Stir together first 4 ingredients. Press mixture evenly into a 9-inch tart pan with removable bottom; set aside.
2. Whisk together sweetened condensed milk, orange juice concentrate, lemon juice, and egg yolks until blended.
3. Beat egg whites at medium speed with an electric mixer until stiff peaks form; fold into condensed milk mixture. Pour into prepared crust.
4. Bake at 325° for 20 to 25 minutes or just until filling is set. Remove to a wire rack, and cool completely. Cover and chill at least 4 hours. Remove tart from pan, and place on a serving dish.
5. Beat whipping cream and granulated sugar at medium speed with an electric mixer until stiff peaks form. Dollop around edges of tart. Garnish, if desired.

Roasted Pecan Clusters

40 years
our best recipes

Roasted Pecan Clusters

MAKES 4 DOZEN
Prep: 12 min., Cook: 30 min., Other: 2 min.

3 Tbsp. butter or margarine
3 cups pecan pieces
6 (2-oz.) chocolate candy
    coating squares

1. Melt butter in a 15- x 10-inch jelly-roll pan while oven preheats to 300°. Spread pecans in pan, tossing to coat with butter. Bake at 300° for 30 minutes, stirring twice.

2. Melt chocolate candy coating in a heavy saucepan over low heat. Cool 2 minutes; add pecans, and stir until coated. Drop by rounded tsp. onto wax paper. Cool. Peel from wax paper; store in an airtight container.

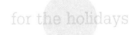

Ripple Divinity

MAKES ABOUT 3 DOZEN (ABOUT 1¾ LB.)
Prep: 15 min., Cook: 10 min.

This classic Southern candy has truly stood the test of time. First published in the late 1960s, we enjoy this divinity's texture and ripples of color as much today as we did then.

3 cups sugar
½ cup water
½ cup light corn syrup

2 large egg whites
1 tsp. vanilla extract
1 cup semisweet chocolate
    morsels

1. Combine first 3 ingredients in a 3-qt. heavy saucepan. Cook over medium-high heat, stirring constantly, until mixture comes to a boil. Wash sugar crystals from sides of pan with a small brush dipped in warm water. Insert candy thermometer, and cook without stirring until thermometer registers 260° (hard ball stage). Remove from heat.

2. Beat egg whites in a large mixing bowl at high speed with an electric mixer until stiff peaks form. Pour hot syrup in a heavy stream over beaten egg whites while beating constantly at high speed. Add vanilla, and continue beating just until mixture begins to hold its shape (3 to 4 minutes). Fold in chocolate morsels. (Chocolate morsels will not completely melt, creating a swirled effect.)

3. Working quickly, drop divinity by rounded tsp. onto wax paper; cool. Peel candy from wax paper.

Index